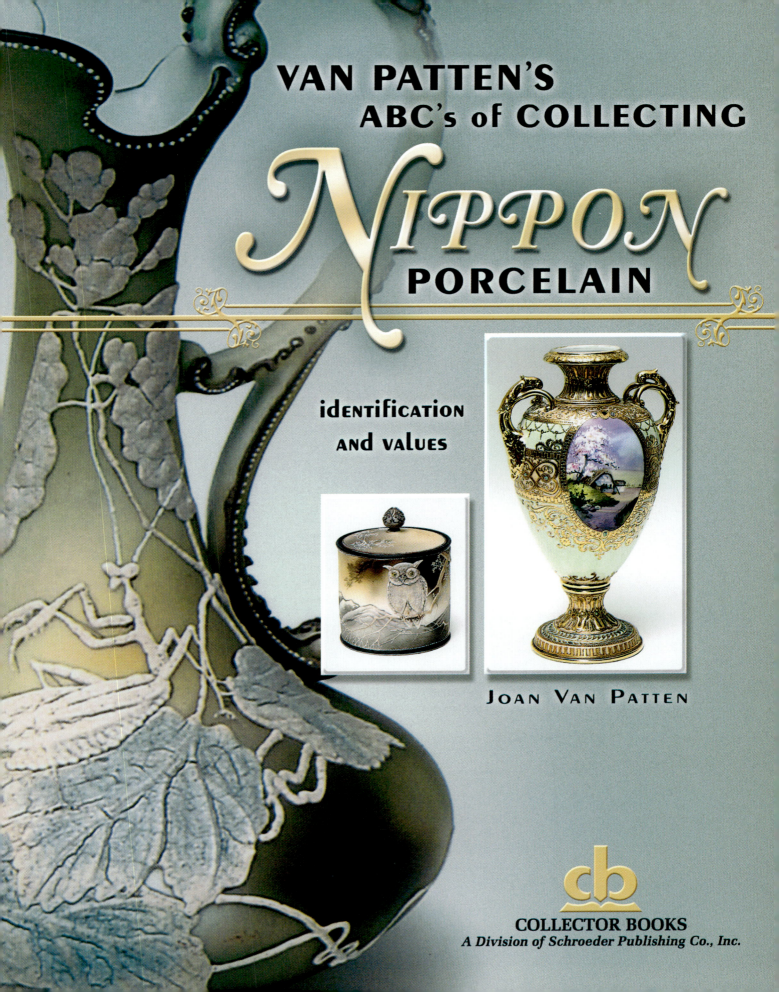

VAN PATTEN'S ABC's of COLLECTING

NIPPON PORCELAIN

identification and values

Joan Van Patten

COLLECTOR BOOKS
A Division of Schroeder Publishing Co., Inc.

Dedication

This book is dedicated to my two wonderful grandsons, Connor and Nolan. What a difference you have made in my life!

About the Author

Joan Van Patten is the author of *Collector's Encyclopedia Nippon Porcelain*, *First Through Seventh Series*, *Nippon Price Guide*, *Collector's Encyclopedia of Noritake*, *First and Second Series*, *Celluloid Treasures of the Victorian Era*, and *Nippon Dolls and Playthings*, all published by Collector Books.

She has written hundreds of trade paper and magazine articles and is a contributor to *Schroeder's Antiques Price Guide*.

Joan has been on the board of the INCC (International Nippon Collectors' Club) since its inception. As co-founder of the INCC, she also served as its first president and was a director of the club for many years. Joan edited and published the *Nippon Notebook* and the INCC Newsletter for five years. She has lectured on the subjects of Nippon, Noritake, and celluloid throughout the United States.

The research of antiques and collectibles, travel, and decorating are other major interests of the author.

Front cover: Moriage ewer, 9½" tall, blue mark #52, $1,800.00 – 2,200.00; Tapestry and moriage humidor, 6½" tall, green mark #47, $4,000.00 – 5,000.00; Urn, 16" tall, green mark #47, $4,000.00 – 4,500.00; Basket vase, 10" tall, green mark #52, $3,000.00 – 3,600.00.; Wall plaque featuring Chief Red Cloud, 10½" wide, blue mark #47, $2,000.00 – 2,400.00.

Back cover: Vase, 12¾" tall, blue mark #52, $2,200.00 – 2,600.00; Humidor, 6¾" tall, green mark #47, $2,600.00 – 3,000.00; Humidor, molded in relief, 7" tall, green mark #47, $4,000.00 – 5,000.00; Vase, 10" tall, blue mark #52, $4,000.00 – 5,000.00; Wall plaque, molded in relief, 10½" wide, green mark #47, $1,500.00 – 2,000.00.

Cover design by Beth Summers
Book design by Lonna Bradford

COLLECTOR BOOKS
P.O. Box 3009
Paducah, Kentucky 42002-3009

www.collectorbooks.com

Copyright © 2005 Joan F. Van Patten

Searching For A Publisher?

We are always looking for people knowledgeable within their fields. If you feel that there is a real need for a book on your collectible subject and have a large comprehensive collection, contact Collector Books.

Contents

Acknowledgments

Many people helped supply information and photos for this book but it all wouldn't be possible without Billy Schroeder and the staff at Collector Books. Billy came up with an idea on how we should do a new type of Nippon book and I hope that readers will be pleased with the result. I am also grateful to his father, Bill who published my first books.

Gail Ashburn, Amy Sullivan, and all the staff at Collector Books are responsible for putting together all the information and photos that I send to them. And I am always pleased how the books they edit and publish turn out. Thanks go to all of you.

Lewis Longest took over 400 photographs for me and I think his photos are quite wonderful. His sweet wife, BJ, assisted us and has my appreciation. Not only do they have a fantastic collection but also they are two of the nicest people you can ever meet. Thanks to both of you for the photos and also for your hospitality.

Many photos were also taken by Lewis at the home of Bob and Maggie Schoenherr. They have a wonderful collection and I am so happy to be able to share these items with readers of this book. Thanks to both of you.

Linda Lau sent me many photos of her collection and also provided information for two chapters. Linda and I have worked on a number of projects together and she always does a super job. Thanks Linda for all your help.

Judy Boyd also provided information for two chapters. She is always there to help me whenever I ask. I am lucky to have such a good friend. Thanks Judy.

In past books, Mark Griffin and Earl Smith submitted many wonderful photos of their collection. A number of them are shown again in this book. Mark also researched information on many different patterns, designs, decors, and scenes, and portions of his information are included again in this book. Thanks, Mark for letting me use it again and thanks to both of you for these great photos.

Jess Berry and Gary Graves are two special people in my life and continue to send me photos of their collection and some can be found in this book. Jess has also provided me with information used in past books that is being used again in this one. Thanks to both of you.

Jeff Mattison researched two different Nippon scenes, Spring and Moose in the Woods and I've included portions of what he sent to me. Thank you.

Frank and Ruth Reid sent photos even before I knew I would be doing this new book. They are always there to help me. Thanks to both of you.

Pricing the items is always so difficult. It depends on condition, rarity, different areas of the country, etc. There are also cyclical trends where one particular technique used is desirable and then a couple of years later it becomes less so. I want to thank Lewis Longest, Bob and Maggie Schoenherr, and Linda Lau for all their pricing suggestions. Most of the time we were in total agreement and when we were not I had them give me their reasons why and factored that into my decision. Thanks to all of you.

I want to thank everyone who has submitted photos and information not only for this book but all the previous ones. I couldn't do it without your help. I am blessed to have such great Nippon loving friends and I want to thank you from the bottom of my heart. You have allowed me to have a job that I love to do.

Preface

Van Patten's ABC's of Collecting Nippon Porcelain is the brain-child of Billy Schroeder and is a compilation of all the books I have written on this subject. This book has many new items included plus many of the ones previously shown in the others. For me, this is the book that I would loved to have written back in 1979 when the first *Collector's Encyclopedia of Nippon Porcelain* was published. Although I still don't know it all, I certainly know more about the subject than I did back in the seventies. I have done extensive research over the years and with the help of so many of my Nippon friends have learned so much more about the subject. I was invited to Japan by Keishi Suzuki and got to see the Noritake factory and museum in Nagoya and also the dinnerware factory in Imari. There are now seven books in the series and I was delighted to co-author a book on Nippon era dolls with Linda Lau.

Some collectors own all the Nippon books but many do not. New information was included in each volume and unless you owned them all it was difficult to have all the information available. In this book I hope to make it *the* book for collectors and dealers. Historical information is included as well as the different designs and techniques that were used. A variety of patterns, designs, decors, and various scenes are shown. A big chapter on reproductions is also included. Previously, as new patterns were located they would be shown in the newest book that was being published. Nearly 150 fake items are displayed in this new book.

The Japanese copied many different types of decorating: Gouda wares from the Netherlands, Jasperware from England, Landseer's Newfoundland dog, etc. The Japanese were both imitative as well as innovative. These items were not only sold at the local 5¢ and 10¢ store but also as souvenirs at resort areas. Both the S & H Stamp Company and the Jewel Tea Company gave Nippon items as premiums and the Manning Bowman Company made metal containers for other pieces.

Hundreds of backstamps have been located over the years and are also listed in this book for reference. It is no longer necessary for collectors to carry many books with them as a reference when they are out antiquing.

I have titled this book *The ABC's of Collecting Nippon Porcelain*. In the introduction I have included a whimsical ABC version but in the further text of this book I have put the different categories in alphabetical order for simplification in using this book. It is Billy Schroeder's intention to update this reference book with new photos and prices in the future and then that will be *the* book to have. Prices are erratic at times and the value of items needs to be updated every two years or so.

Items that sold for very little 100 years ago now often sell for hundreds and thousands and even tens of thousands today. I am sure that the Japanese companies that manufactured and the artists who decorated them could never have imagined the meteoric rise in prices. But today it is the Japanese collectors and dealers who are discovering these items that were exported to the United States and other countries. And now many of these pieces are going back to their homeland. Museum exhibits have been held in Japan featuring these wares. What used to be referred to as Japanese junk thirty or forty years ago by dealers is now looked at in a completely new way. Much of the artwork is exquisite. The Japanese artist could paint about four to six times faster than artists in other countries and worked for very a small wage. This enabled people all over the world to own beautiful pieces of art for a very small price tag. The rich could always afford beautiful items but this was the first opportunity for the middle class to have wonderful hand-painted wares in their homes.

Collecting Nippon has enabled me to decorate my home with some gorgeous pieces of porcelain. I have also learned a lot about their history and best of all I have made wonderful friends through my Nippon collecting. Thanks to Collector Books and Bill Schroeder and his son Billy Schroeder for making all this possible. Hopefully, the Nippon books have also enriched the lives of other collectors as it has mine. Happy Nipponing to all collectors, both novice and seasoned.

Introduction

Nippon **aficionados** can be found everywhere and the **allure** of their favorite collectible can make them do strange things. Some collectors **accumulate** all they can. Others hesitate and **anguish** over every purchase. Still others pretend to be **ambivalent** about the whole thing.

My **advice** is don't **accept** everything you are told. **Ask** questions. Go to as many **auctions** and **antique** shops and shows as you can. **Acquaint** yourself with the different varieties of Nippon porcelain. Some people prefer the **Azalea** pattern, some like **advertiques**. The **American** Indian is very popular, as are items employing **Art** Deco and **Art** Nouveau decoration. **Analyze** your feelings, find out what's best for you before you **acquire** too much. But beware, collecting Nippon is **addictive**!

Always **buy** what you like, forget the fads. Also, **buy** when you see the item, as it may not be there when you return.

Check out **books** on the subject at your local **bookstore** or library. **Become** familiar with the different **backstamps**. Be able to distinguish the **bas-relief** pieces (commonly referred to as **blown-outs**) from those with sprigged-on decoration. Check for missing jewels and **beading**. Get to know the **better** items and **become** familiar with the different kinds of **blanks** used.

Visit each dealer's **booth** at the shows; also check over the merchandise well **before buying**. Remember, it's **buyer beware**! But most of all enjoy what you're collecting.

Cultivate your own tastes. **Collectors** often **change** their minds and switch **categories**. **Check** out old **catalogs** to see what might be available. The more you buy, the more **contacts** you make, the more your **confidence** will build.

Some Nippon devotees **collect cloisonné** on porcelain, others **cobalt** pieces. Some like **coralene** decorated wares while there are those who prefer the **character collectibles** and **children's** items.

Those with **colossal collections** often resort to storing all the extras in **closets** or storage **containers**. **Consider** keeping your **collection** small but **choice**. Easy to say, hard to do.

No matter what it is that you **collect**, be **certain** to **check** for **cracks** and **chips**. Be **choosy**; don't **clutter** your **curio cabinets** with unworthy pieces.

You may find yourself paying **dearly** for items you want. It takes **discipline** to curb your buying and also to learn to say no if the item is priced too high. It's **difficult** to **do**, it may leave you feel-ing **depressed** and **disappointed** but it will **definitely** pay off in the long run. **Dealers** eventually lower their prices when items **don't** move off the shelf.

There are some **duplicates** found in Nippon wares but **discovering** a new **design** or **decoration** can be a real **delight**. The macabre **devil decorates** a number of pieces. Also found are moriage **dragons** and familiar **diaper** patterns. Some items may look hand painted but are merely **decorated** with **decals**. Get to know the **difference**.

Nippon **dolls** are another area of collecting that many have pursued. Collecting the related **doll** items such as children's tea sets can be a **delightful** spin-off.

Eureka, you **exclaim** when discovering an **exceptional** piece of Nippon! This is an **exciting** and **enjoyable** time. That **elusive** item can fill you with such **enthusiasm**. In fact, collecting Nippon can be down right **enchanting** at times.

Check *The Collector's Encyclopedia of Nippon Porcelain* for photos of the **English** coach and **Egyptian** Nile scenes. Also **educate** yourself by **examining** different pieces of porcelain. Learn to cut down on your **errors**. **Establishing** a rapport with a good dealer is most beneficial.

Flea markets are a **favorite** with collectors and great **finds** can often be **found** there if you have enough time to **ferret** out the items. Get **familiar** with Nippon porcelain. Get a **feeling** for it. But don't be **foolhardy** and end up with a **fake** piece. There are thousands of them **flooding** the market place. Get **familiar** with these items!

If you are **fond** of anything with a relief molded **fisherman** or even a select **fish** set, your **finances** better be in good shape. As **fascinating** as these items are, the price is usually very steep. If you **find** one **fairly** priced, you had better grab it up.

Going to **garage** sales is another **great** way to shop. You can sometimes find a **good**-looking item at one, but forget about **getting** a **guarantee** so be sure to examine items carefully before purchase.

Favorite pieces with many collectors are the **gaudy** items, also the **gold** overlay articles. The **geisha girl** pattern is collected by some, while others prefer the **Gouda** type wares. An ornate **game** set could be the crown of any collection.

A number of collectors specialize in buying only the **howo** bird pattern while others prefer the look of the **Halloween** scene.

Many of these **hand-painted** pieces are **hoarded** by Nippon-aholics. But it's not their fault, for who can resist them?

Upon **investigation**, it's almost **impossible** to find **identical items** as the hand painting naturally varies a little on each. Some pieces are even found that have the decoration **incised** on.

Don't be **indecisive**, **implement** a plan. There are some **incredible** items to be found if you just use your **intelligence**. Most are an **invitation** to **indulge** us in an **interesting** hobby and a few can even become "the **icing** on the cake."

Japan is the country of origin of these goodies and the so-called "Nippon" era spans from 1891 to 1921. After this time period the word **Japan** should appear on items rather than Nippon.

It's **jackpot** time if you find a **Jasperware** type vase reasonably priced or a **jeweled jam jar** or a hanging **jardinière**.

Many advanced collectors have become enamored with the **knights** in armor pattern and other rarer pieces, while beginning collectors usually like everything that was ever baked in the Japanese **kilns**. But the **key** to good collecting is to be **knowledgeable** in all phases of Nippon wares.

Today's extra **leisure** time gives us a chance to indulge ourselves with **lush lemonade** pitchers, **lamps,** and **luncheon** sets. Some have **lacy** designs while others are scenic, but **loyal** collectors **love** all of it. The **lure** of Nipponing is a force to be reckoned with.

Certain collectors and dealers appear to have the "**Midas** touch." Everything they buy ends up being worth its weight in gold. They seemingly are able to **make more money** than others and have a **marvelous** knack for finding the right pieces at the right price.

Reading trade **magazines** for price trends can be a big help and knowing backstamp **marks** and **meeting** with others are a **must** for all collectors and dealers. **Moriage** decorated items are evidently a **magnet** for **many** while those decorated with the **man** on the camel scene are favorites of others.

The **Morimura** Bros. Co. of Japan played a **memorable** part in Nippon history. Their superb workmanship undoubtedly has a lot to do with the **meteoric** rising prices of Nippon porcelain today.

The **Noritake** Co. Ltd. was founded in 1904, the Morimura Bros. being their predecessor. Research indicates that over 90% of all **Nippon** marked goods were made by these companies. There were of course a **number** of smaller companies that also produced these **niceties**, but **Noritake** and Morimura produced the most and usually the best.

It's **necessary** for **neophytes** to do their homework and study, study, study. **Nippon** is for **now** and tomorrow and the variety to be found is seemingly endless. Many collectors enjoy the unusual items and a **number never** say **no** to the purchase of a **novelty** piece.

These **old Oriental** gems **originate** from the East, the land of the rising sun, and **outshine** anything being made today. Their beauty has added that extra **oomph** to many a collector's life.

When checking over these **old** items it's wise to **observe** how well the **overglaze** decoration was applied. **One** will **often** discover that some pieces are superior to **others**.

Once in a while you do find a **piece** of **porcelain** that has been **poorly** executed. It's not necessary to **possess** everything so be **picky**. Don't be a **pack** rat; be **prejudiced** with your **purchases**. Remember, knowledge is **power** and buy selectively.

When finding a **prize** item, the heart may **palpitate**, but the **price** to be **paid** can often put a crimp in the **pocketbook**. Look for items in **perfect** or near **perfect** condition. Be **patient** for these **pieces** will eventually show up. **Pretty** bowls are always **popular**; also **pairs** of vases are another good find.

Some collectors have a **penchant** for dinnerware in the **phoenix** bird **pattern**. These are not too **plentiful** to find but can make for an interesting collection. **Pattern** stamped items are also desirable but difficult to locate.

Good **photographs** in books and magazines can be your **passport** to more knowledgeable collecting. **Pay** close attention to anything that **pertains** to your favorite **pastime**.

If you're in a **quandary** as to what to buy, remember **quality** is always better than **quantity**. **Question** other dealers and collectors so that you can make the best possible purchases. And speaking of buys, why not add a **queue** san baby doll to your collection. Once you've seen one you'll know why it's a must.

Again, it must be stressed, **reproductions** are everywhere. As a **result** you must learn to **recognize** them and **refuse** to purchase them. Once you **realize** what they look like you won't **repeat** the mistakes of so many others who now **regret** their lack of knowledge.

Read every **reference** book you can and take time to **re-examine** your own collection. You may make some **revealing** and **rewarding** new finds.

Some collectors **react** favorably to **relief** molded items while others are more inclined to those decorated with the **riding** scene. Both have excellent **resale** prices. **Reach** out and meet other collectors, there can often be a **rapport** found that is **rare**.

Seek and ye **shall** find, so the **saying** goes. **Scrutinize shops, search** antique **shows** and always go back for a **second** look. **Some super showpieces** might just be lurking there.

Study your **subject, subscribe** to trade newspapers and magazines, **scan** the ads; all **should** help you become more **selective. Seek** information on the Internet.

The **sophisticated** collector generally **shies** away from many of the **simple** pieces, but **some** of the **small** items **should** not be overlooked. Many of these **same** pieces were made in identical **styles** and **shapes** of the more ornate ones.

Be a **smart shopper** and watch out for the **so-called "sleepers."** Finding one of these can be a **serendipitous surprise** to both the collector with a **substantial** collection and to one whose collection is **small** in **size. Selling** and buying is the name of the game and if one is able to be a **smart shopper** it's always nice to **savor** the purchase with others.

Collectors find **silver** overlay difficult to locate, also pieces that have **sprigged-on-decoration. Sponge** tapestry decoration is rare as well as items that have **silhouettes** in their design. **Scenic** designs are usually more expensive than floral decorated pieces, and although **souvenir** items were once inexpensive that is rarely the **situation** now. **Sometsuke** (blue on white) decorated items can be the basis for an entire collection.

One of the most desirable **techniques** employed on Nippon pieces is that of **tapestry.** Some people (myself included) would **travel** many miles for one of these **treasures. Tête-à-tête tea** sets also come in the **toy** dish size and make a **terrific** addition to any collection.

Learn Nippon jargon. This can be most helpful in understanding the ads in **trade** papers, magazines, and on the Internet.

Many of the Nippon **urns** found today are **unique** and **unequaled** in beauty. The **utmost** care should be taken with these pieces as their prices continue to go **up, up, up!**

The **variety** of **vases** available can also be overwhelming. Some are found in **vivid** colors while others were manufactured in styles and designs reminiscent of the **Victorian** era. Big or small, today most are quite **valuable.**

Wow is the **word** for items decorated in the **Wedgwood** style or for Nippon **wine** or **whiskey** jugs. All are **winners.** Some **wonderful** items can also be found decorated with scenes of **windmills,** and these are **wanted** by many collectors who know their **worth.** Be **well** informed; be on the **watch** for these **wonderful** Nippon **wares.** A **word** of **warning** though, **wishing won't** get you the pieces you **want,** you have to actively seek them.

Be **eXtra** careful, don't knowingly buy damaged or repaired items. An investment in a black light which **x-rays** items is a wise move.

Yes, it's fun collecting Nippon and **yes, you** too can join the others who **yearn** for the treasures of **yesterday.**

Nippon collecting is never boring, never dull, and it sure can put some **zip, zeal,** and **zest** into your life! **Zowie,** why not start today?

Historical Information

Nippon backstamped porcelain was manufactured in Japan during the years of 1891 through 1921. Nippon is not a particular type of item but merely another name for the country of Japan. In 1890, the McKinley Tariff Act was passed by Congress, which was named for Rep. William McKinley who sponsored it. McKinley drafted this bill at the insistence of the Easterners in the United States who wanted more protection for US manufacturers. The tariff act of the Fifty-First Congress states the following:

Chapter 1244, Section 6: "That on and after the first day of March, eighteen hundred and ninety-one, all articles of foreign manufacture, such as are usually or *ordinarily marked, stamped, branded or labeled, and all packages containing such or other imported articles, shall, respectively, be plainly marked, stamped, branded or labeled in legible English words, so as to indicate the country of their origin; and unless so marked, stamped, branded or labeled they shall not be admitted to entry."*

In March of 1921, the United States government reversed its position and decided that the word Nippon was a Japanese word, the English equivalent of which is Japan. Customs agents were then instructed that as of September 1, 1921, merchandise from Japan, the marking of which is governed by this provision of law, should not be released when bearing only the Japanese word "Nippon" to indicate the country of origin. Thus the era of Nippon backstamped porcelain covered in this book was over.

In 1638, the country of Nippon was closed to all Europeans and cut off from the rest of the world. This was done to hopefully secure Japan from the Europeans and the rebellious Japanese peasants. The Japanese were forbidden to build any ship larger than a coasting boat. They could not go abroad and no foreigner could enter. The law of the land decreed a death penalty for any foreigner entering Japan and the people of Nippon lived in almost total seclusion for 214 years until Commodore Matthew Perry of the United States Navy steamed into Yedo Bay in 1853. Yedo was later renamed Tokyo, meaning eastern capitol and this period of isolation in Japan is often referred to by historians as the Yedo period.

Perry arrived with four fighting ships, two steam frigates, the *Mississippi* (the flagship), and the *Susquehanna*, and two sloops named the *Saratoga* and the *Plymouth*. He was sent to deliver President Fillmore's letter, which was written in the hope of establishing trade and friendship between the United States and Japan. The United Stated needed harbors in which to dock its ships for repairs and supplies and wanted better treatment for shipwrecked sailors. Upon arrival in Nippon, Perry sent messages to the Japanese dignitaries but received only short and unsatisfactory answers in return. The Japanese attempted to send minor officials to deal with him but he refused. At one point, Perry even threatened to land with armed forces if an answer was not soon forthcoming. Reluctantly, he withdrew his boats and troops for the winter with the promise of returning in the spring for his answer. This time, upon his arrival in February of 1854, he was met in a much friendlier fashion. This was more than likely due to the fact that he now appeared with ten ships instead of four. They were all powered by steam and mounted with many large guns. The Japanese referred to them as the "black ships," because of the clouds of black smoke they produced. These clouds could be seen all over the countryside and the Japanese were undoubtedly

impressed with this display of force. Perry proceeded to play upon their fears. This time they put up no resistance and before long trade negotiations were underway. The Kanagawa treaty, opening the small ports of Shimoda near the Bay of Yedo and Hakodate in the north was signed on March 31, 1854. Shipwrecked sailors were to receive good treatment and an American Consul was permitted to reside at Shimoda. Soon, treaties with other European countries followed. By 1865, Japan was opened to world trade and ensuing contacts with the West brought a flood of Europeans to her shores. Japan had thus been "rediscovered," her seclusion was ended and a new life began.

The Japanese have always had an eagerness to learn from others and now native painters went abroad to study and learn the ways of the new world. It has been said that the Japanese are conscious cultural borrowers, they seem to have the capacity to borrow and adapt, making it something new and quintessentially Japanese. They merely reshaped everything to suit their needs.

During this period the Japanese government also hired thousands of foreign experts to come to Japan to train their people. The Japanese artists began imitating the European styles or tried to combine both those of the Eastern and Western manner. There were no copyright laws and the Japanese copied whatever they admired. They were highly skilled and capable of quickly learning new techniques. They had previously copied the master artists from China but in order to satisfy this new Western market they now copied the arts of many other countries.

The Japanese had a famous capacity for imitation and today we find Nippon porcelain that resembled Limoges, Beleek, Royal Bayreuth, RS Prussia, the list goes on and on. All types of items were manufactured from elaborately decorated vases and punch bowl sets to plain utilitarian items such as butter tubs and reamers. One finds dolls, incense burners, and souvenir items, so varied was the market. Thus, the country of Nippon began world trade and porcelain became one of her major export items.

During this time Japan continued to be seized with a mania for anything Western. What we did not know was that it was not an underdeveloped country as we had thought but one that was highly advanced. Its development had merely followed non-Western lines. Japan now sought to catch up to the most advanced European powers. Factories had been erected, steamships built, a universal school system was established and feudalism abolished. Pottery factories were promoted and the first railway line in Japan was opened in 1872 helping to give rise to the increased trade. Within one lifetime the Meiji government increased trade, developed industries, and created an army and navy to match that of Russia's. Japan had adapted to Westernism in order to meet the West on more even terms and gain its respect.

At this time, however, Japan also found herself with a minimum of land and an over abundance of labor. There were approximately forty million people living in Japan in 1891 and by 1909 that figure had risen to fifty million. Industry kept growing and the search for overseas markets for goods became vital. Low wages were paid to almost all of the workers. The employers claimed this was necessary to enable them to compete more effectively. Japan's prices were thus kept low enabling her to sell goods all over the world.

Modern factory equipment was installed, plaster molds were introduced, and European methods of glazing were tried. Previously, the kilns had been fired by wood, now coal and oil were used. Whole villages made pottery and decorated it; in fact, children were also used to decorate some of the Nippon wares. By the time the 1900s rolled around assembly line techniques were already being employed in the making of Nippon porcelain.

It is interesting to note how much Nippon porcelain items actually sold for during this period. The 1908 Sears catalog lists vases for $.59 each, game plates were $.95 a dozen, a nine-piece tea set sold for $2.29, and a dozen cups and saucers could be purchased for as little as $1.49. They were very popular in the United States but the porcelain items being exported were not held in high esteem in the eyes of the Japanese. Old stereograph cards feature pictures of some of the workers and some of what is written is as follows: "This is one of the most famous potteries in the world; if this spectacled and wise-looking person at the wheel were allowed to follow his own inspiration in respect to form instead of catering to European and American taste, he would probably produce something thoroughly good; Japanese craftsmen have instinctive good taste and good judgment in matters aesthetic.

"The wheel revolves on a vertical axis below. The potter sets it whirling every little while with a dexterous touch of those lean hands and his manipulations of the soft grayish clay soon produce from the shapeless lump with which he started a vase of perfect symmetry and more or less elaborate design. His only tools are a few sticks of different shapes and sizes. The big bowl holds water with which to wet and soften the clay if it dries too fast to be manageable.

"The work here is all specialized. This man does modeling and nothing else, all day long. Other men are kept at work grinding and washing the crude clay to prepare it for his hands; still others prepare and apply the glazes, tend the kilns, decorate the ware with mineral paints, and add touches of gilding. Women and girls, do some of the simpler and less remunerative kinds of work, like burnishing the gilt figures and bands for final effect."

Another card takes us "into a room where a potter was at work with his wheel, shaping a vase of soft clay. Now a number of just such vases and jars are being baked in the intense heat of ovens inside these kilns. Each oven is now sealed up tightly with a mask of clay, and these men stay here to keep up the fires and make sure that the temperature is maintained at the desired degree.

"It is a matter of regret to everybody who has studied the Japanese pottery of a century or two ago that foreign influence should be so demoralizing in the matter of aesthetics. The shapes designed by Japanese workmen before the days of European and American trade were vastly better than they are now, when the Japanese producer tries to please the poorer taste of western people.

"These men work for less the wages of errand-boys in American factories, but they can live comfortably – according to their ideals – on a small fraction of the sum necessary in America. Their food is chiefly rice, tea, and fish, their clothing and bedding, cheap cotton stuff."

A third stereograph card is titled "Pretty factory girls decorating cheap pottery for the foreign market, Kyoto, Japan" and gives

the following information, "This is one of the many rooms in a porcelain factory in the eastern part of the city. All the ware you see here is cheap and intended exclusively for foreign sale. In fact, it would not sell here in Japan, for the designs in form and color, while they please the uncultivated taste of the average European or American purchaser, would never satisfy the more critical and discriminating judgment of the Japanese public!"

Beauty is definitely in the eye of the beholder. What the Western market found desirable, those in Japan found offensive. Not so today.

"Pretty factory girls…"

"Workmen watching kilns full of Awata porcelain, Kyoto, Japan."

History of Noritake Company, Ltd.

The founder of Noritake was Baron Ichizaemon Morimura, who was born in 1839 to a family of merchants who acted as purveyors to feudal lords. In 1860, when he was twenty years old, the shogunate decided that a delegation needed to be sent to the United States to return the courtesy visit of Commodore Perry. Baron Morimura was ordered to change Japanese money into American coin in the Yokohama foreign concession for the delegation to carry to the United States.

The Japanese money to be exchanged was gold coin of high purity, while the currency to be received was coin of very low quality called Mexican silver.

Baron Morimura felt that it was a great loss to the country to allow gold of such high purity to flow out of Japan and spoke about the matter to Yukichi Fukuzawa, one of the great leaders in the modernization of new Japan from the feudal shogunate governing era. Fukuzawa told Morimura that it was necessary to promote export trade so that the gold that went out of Japan would flow back into the country.

Ichizaemon Morimura and his young brother, Toyo, founded Morimura Kumi (Morimura Co.) at Ginza in Tokyo in 1876, and in the same year, Toyo formed a Japanese retail shop, Hinode Shokai (later this became Morimura Bros. Inc.), at 6th Avenue, New York City. Then the two brothers started a trade business between Tokyo and New York and exported traditional Japanese style pottery, bamboo works, and other Japanese gift items and so-called Japanese sundry goods to the United States. This business transaction was the first trade between Japan and the United States after Japan opened its door with the Western countries.

During expansion of its export business, Morimura Bros. decided to change from a retail to a wholesale business and to concentrate on ceramics. Thus Nippon Toki Kaisha (later this became the Noritake Co., Limited) was founded on January 1, 1904, at Noritake village which is the present site of the main factory. This factory's primary purpose was manufacturing and exporting high quality china mainly to the United States. Since then, the United States has been the greatest supporter and biggest customer for Noritake.

The founders were Ichizaemon Morimura, Mogobei Okkura, Saneyoshi Hirose, Yasukata Murai, Kazuchika Okura, and Kotaro Asukai. The technique to manufacture high quality dinnerware was mastered in the 1910s, and Noritake adopted a streamlined mass-production system in the twenties and thirties and enjoyed the high reputation of Noritake china all over the world.

In the course of growth during the early period, Noritake started to research the construction of the sanitary ware and insulator divisions within the company. Later, the sanitary division became independent from Noritake in 1917. It was named Toyo Toki Kaisha Ltd. (presently Toto Limited) and is known as the biggest sanitary ware and related metal fitting manufacturer in Japan. The insulator division of Noritake also became independent from Noritake in 1919, later splitting into two companies in 1936. One is known as NGK Insulator Co., Ltd., the world's largest insulator manufacturer; the other is NGK Spark Plug Co., Ltd., which is one of the top manufacturers of spark plugs in the world.

In 1939, Noritake, which had been doing extensive research on abrasive grinding wheels, decided to mass produce bonded abrasive products. The company utilized its longtime experience with its knowledge of ceramics in making this decision.

During World War II, the Noritake factory produced abrasive grinding wheels for heavy industries instead of chinaware. Although Noritake's old main office building was burned in World War II, the factory buildings suffered almost no damage. Therefore, Noritake could start the production of chinaware sooner than other factories. However, the quality of china was not up to pre-war standards because of the lack of high technology and lack of superior materials and the equipment shortages at that time. In order to maintain the reputation of Noritake China, which meant quality products, the trademark "Rose China" was adopted temporarily before a satisfactory level of quality was restored. In 1948, the trademark "Noritake" was employed again.

In November 1947, Noritake Co., Inc. of the United States was incorporated in New York City, starting a chinaware wholesale business with major department stores and specialty stores. During the course of resumption of foreign trade with the United States and other countries in and after 1948, Noritake expanded itself extensively to become the largest chinaware manufacturer in the world. The new Miyoshi dinnerware plant was completed in 1965 in the eastern end of Nagoya. Noritake also improved its porcelain formula and a new production technique for fine china, bone china, ivory china, and progression china. In 1967, Noritake Imari Porcelain Manufacturing Co. and in 1968, Noritake Kyuto Co., Ltd. were established and took charge of the production of ivory, bone, and progression china respectively.

Noritake expanded its exports to include crystal glassware, stainless steel flatware, and melamineware in the early part of the 1960s. Besides the chinaware plants, Noritake now has a stainless steel flatware factory in Tsubame, which is located in the northern part of central Japan. The Atsugi plant is located near Tokyo and manufactures high crystal glassware, and the melamineware factory in Anjo, in the eastern side of Nagoya, is the biggest manufacturer of melamineware in Japan.

In January 1970, by utilizing long experienced precision technology and also the technique of printing decals for chinaware and ceramics, Noritake decided to expand the manufacturing in the electronics field and started to manufacture electronics components and new ceramics products, such as vacuum fluorescent display tubes, thick-film printed circuit substrates, high brightness picture tubes, plasma display, ceramics for electronics components (molded parts substrates), new ceramics pipe, and dental ceramics. The electronics and new ceramics products grew

rapidly and greatly contributed to the increase of the company business. As of the end of March 1999, this division became the largest division beyond the tabletop and abrasive grinding wheel divisions.

In 1972, Noritake established Noritake Lanka Porcelain (Pvt.) Ltd. in Sri Lanka, and in 1974, established Noritake Porcelana Mfg., Inc. in the Philippines. Both factories produce porcelain ware and are now the largest chinaware suppliers among the Noritake group.

Thus, Noritake is not only a chinaware manufacturer and exporter but also abrasive grinding wheels, electronics, and new ceramics parts manufacturer and exporter.

Workers during Nippon era (1891 – 1921).

Workers at Noritake Company in Nagoya, Japan.

Old Ads for Nippon China

Imported Hand-Painted China

Chocolate Set

No. K219 GIVEN with a $3.80 purchase of Products or for $3.80 in Coupons.

Consists of 9½-in. Chocolate Pot and six Cups and Saucers. Decorated with pink flowers, green leaves and white embossed work on chocolate-color background. Gilt edges and handles. Shipping weight 8 lbs.

Condiment Set

No. 709 GIVEN with a $1.80 purchase of Products or for $1.80 in Coupons.

Set consists of Tray, 7x5 in., Mustard-Jar with Spoon, Tooth-Pick-Holder and Salt- and Pepper-Shakers. Decoration is a conventional design in burnished gold. Shipping weight 2 lbs.

Cake Set

No. 7915 GIVEN with a $3 purchase of Products or for $3 in Coupons.

A handsome Cake or Bread-and-Butter Set that matches Chocolate Set K219.

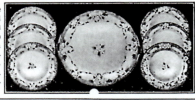

Set consists of one 10-in. Cake-Plate and six 6-in. individual Plates. Decoration is pink flowers, green leaves and white embossed work on chocolate-color background. Edges are gilt. Shipping weight 8 lbs.

Tea-Plate Set

No. 2012 GIVEN with a $2.40 purchase of Products or for $2.40 in Coupons.

Set consists of six Plates, 7½ in. in diameter. Prettily decorated with gold roses and panels of scrollwork, with pink roses and green leaves. Matches Cups and Saucers Set 714. Shipping weight 5 lbs.

Nut Set

No. 418 GIVEN with a $3.60 purchase of Products or for $3.60 in Coupons.

Set consists of one 6-in. Bowl and six 2½-in. individual Bowls. Decoration is white flowers and green leaves outlined in gold. Edges traced in gold. Shipping weight 5 lbs.

Jelly Set

No. 56010 GIVEN with a $2 purchase of Products or for $2 in Coupons.

Set consists of one handled Plate, 7¼ in. in diameter, and six individual Dishes. Conventional border design of green leaves and flowers, richly illuminated in raised gold. Edges outlined in gold. Matches Celery Set 1513. Makes an excellent butter or nut set. Shpg. wt. 2 lbs.

Cups and Saucers Set

No. 714 GIVEN with a $2.80 purchase of Products or for $2.80 in Coupons.

Six Teacups and six Saucers. Decoration consists of gold roses and panels of scroll-work, with pink roses and green leaves. Shipping weight 6 lbs.

Celery Set

No. 1513 GIVEN with a $2.60 purchase of Products or for $2.60 in Coupons.

Set consists of one Celery Tray, 12¾ x 6¼ in., and six individual Salt-Trays. Decorated in a conventional border design of green leaves and flowers, richly illuminated in raised gold. Edges outlined with gold. Shipping weight 3 lbs.

Mayonnaise Set

No. 909 GIVEN with a $1.80 purchase of Products or for $1.80 in Coupons.

Set consists of a Ladle, a 5-in. Bowl and a 6¼-in. Plate. Has a border design of light-blue and -pink flowers on a moire band in gold ribbon-effect. Shipping weight 2 lbs.

Puff-Box and Hair-Receiver Set

No. 5405 GIVEN with a $1 purchase of Products or for $1 in Coupons.

Conventional border-design of pink flowers and green leaves, richly illuminated with gold. Diameter, 3½ in. Shipping weight 2 lbs.

Jam Jar Set

No. 49010 GIVEN with a $2 purchase of Products or for $2 in Coupons.

Set consists of Jar, 3¾ in. high, Plate 6¾ in. in diameter, and Ladle. Decorated with pink, white and red roses, blended with shaded leaves. Edges are outlined in gold. Shipping weight 3 lbs.

Dresser Set

No. 717A GIVEN with a $3.50 purchase of Products or for $3.50 in Coupons.

Set consists of Brush-and-Comb-Tray, 7¾ x 10⅞ in.; Pin-Tray; Puff-Box; Hair-Receiver; Hat-Pin-Holder. Decoration is pink roses and green leaves with embossed work in gold. Shipping weight 6 lbs.

Bon Bon Dish

No. K1110 GIVEN with a $2 purchase of Products or for $2 in Coupons.

Diameter, 7 in. Inside decoration consists of a landscape with lilies in natural colors in the foreground. Has fancy gold border outside. Burnished gold edges and handles. Shipping weight 3 lbs.

Manicure Set

No. K609 GIVEN with a $1.80 purchase of Products or for $1.80 in Coupons.

Set consists of 7¾-in. Tray, oblong Powder-Box and three different size jars that can be used for cold cream, powdered pumice, cuticle-ice, etc. Decoration is pink roses and green leaves with embossed work in gold. Matches Dresser Set 717A. Shipping weight 2 lbs.

Sugar and Cream Set

No. K109 GIVEN with a $1.80 purchase of Products or for $1.80 in Coupons.

Decoration consists of combination border- and-spray design of berries and leaves in delicate tints of blue, green and red, traced in gold. Gold handles and edges. Height, 3 in. Diameter of Sugar-Bowl, 4 in.; Cream-Pitcher, 3½ in. Shipping weight 2 lbs.

All Premiums May be EARNED BY SENDING CLUB ORDERS   Read How on Pages 4 and 5

Larkin Catalog, 1916.

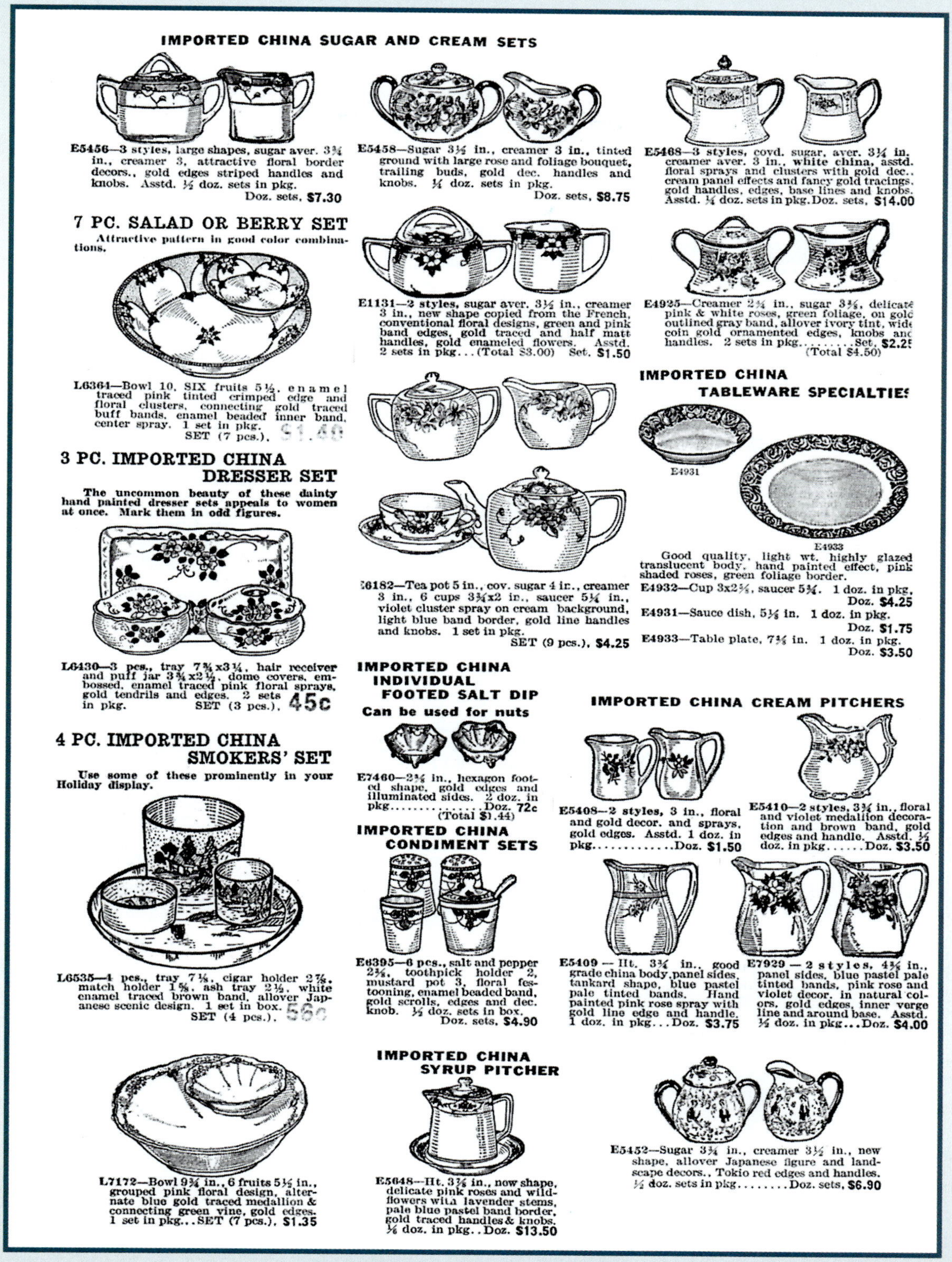

IMPORTED CHINA SUGAR AND CREAM SETS

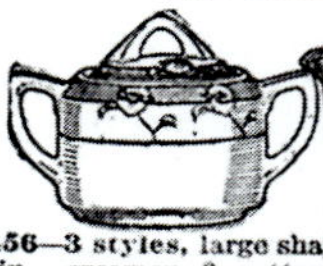

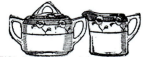

E5456—3 styles, large shapes, sugar aver. 3¾ in., creamer 3, attractive floral border decors., gold edges striped handles and knobs. Asstd. ½ doz. sets in pkg.
Doz. sets, **$7.30**

7 PC. SALAD OR BERRY SET

Attractive pattern in good color combinations.

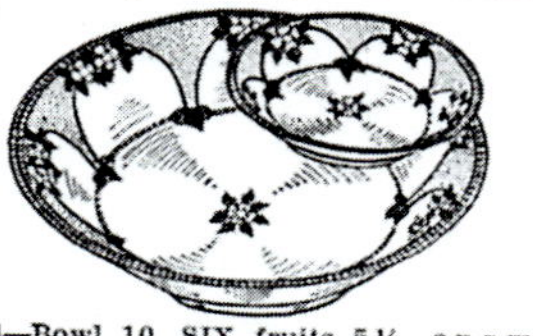

L6364—Bowl 10, SIX fruits 5½, enamel traced pink tinted crimped edge and floral clusters, connecting gold traced buff bands, enamel beaded inner band, center spray. 1 set in pkg.
SET (7 pcs.), **$1.40**

3 PC. IMPORTED CHINA DRESSER SET

The uncommon beauty of these dainty hand painted dresser sets appeals to women at once. Mark them in odd figures.

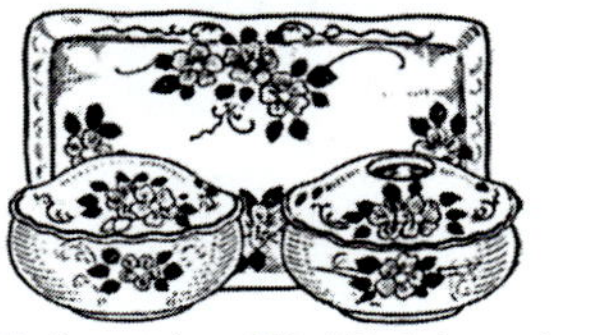

L6430—3 pcs., tray 7¾x3¼, hair receiver and puff jar 3¾x2½, dome covers, embossed, enamel traced pink floral sprays, gold tendrils and edges. 2 sets in pkg. SET (3 pcs.), **45c**

4 PC. IMPORTED CHINA SMOKERS' SET

Use some of these prominently in your Holiday display.

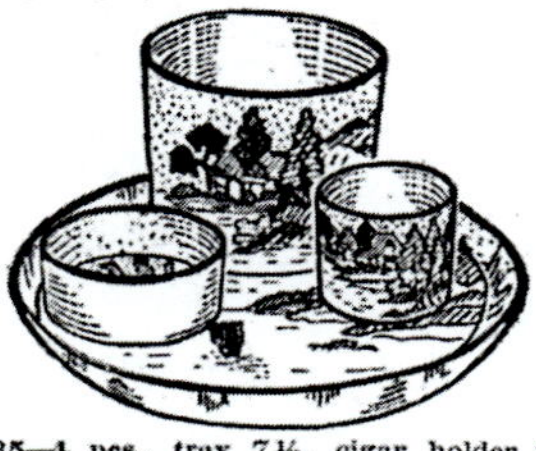

L6535—4 pcs., tray 7⅛, cigar holder 2⅞, match holder 1⅝, ash tray 2½, white enamel traced brown band, allover Japanese scenic design. 1 set in box.
SET (4 pcs.), **56c**

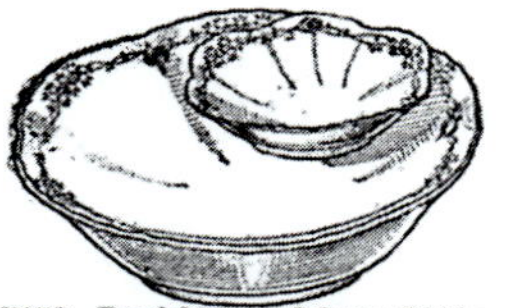

L7172—Bowl 9¾ in., 6 fruits 5½ in., grouped pink floral design, alternate blue gold traced medallion & connecting green vine, gold edges. 1 set in pkg...SET (7 pcs.), **$1.35**

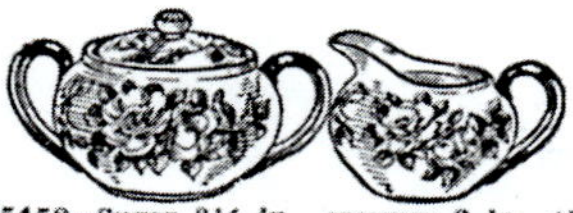

E5458—Sugar 3½ in., creamer 3 in., tinted ground with large rose and foliage bouquet, trailing buds, gold dec. handles and knobs. ¼ doz. sets in pkg.
Doz. sets, **$8.75**

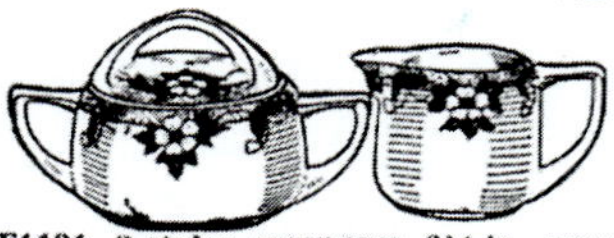

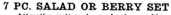

E1131—2 styles, sugar aver. 3½ in., creamer 3 in., new shape copied from the French, conventional floral designs, green and pink band edges, gold traced and half matt handles, gold enameled flowers. Asstd. 2 sets in pkg...(Total $3.00) Set, **$1.50**

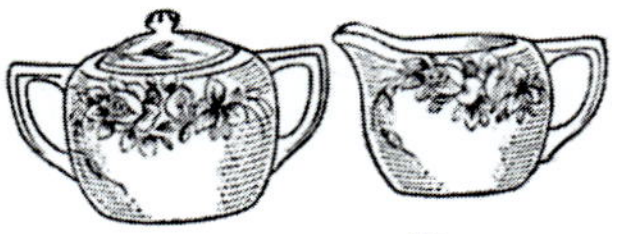

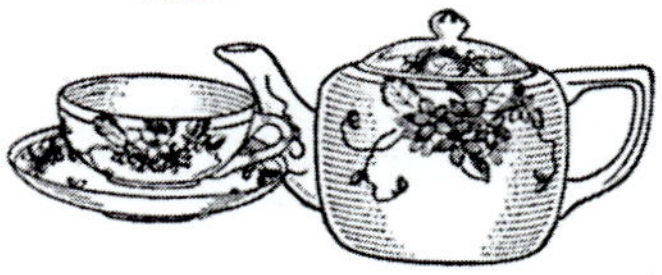

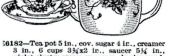

E6182—Tea pot 5 in., cov. sugar 4 in., creamer 3 in., 6 cups 3¾x2 in., saucer 5¼ in., violet cluster spray on cream background, light blue band border, gold line handles and knobs. 1 set in pkg.
SET (9 pcs.), **$4.25**

IMPORTED CHINA INDIVIDUAL FOOTED SALT DIP

Can be used for nuts

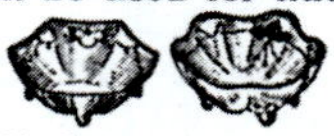

E7460—2¾ in., hexagon footed shape, gold edges and illuminated sides. 2 doz. in pkg..............Doz. **72c**
(Total $1.44)

IMPORTED CHINA CONDIMENT SETS

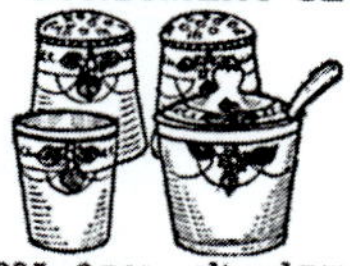

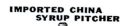

E6395—6 pcs., salt and pepper 2⅝, toothpick holder 2, mustard pot 3, floral festooning, enamel beaded band, gold scrolls, edges and dec. knob. ½ doz. sets in box.
Doz. sets, **$4.90**

IMPORTED CHINA SYRUP PITCHER

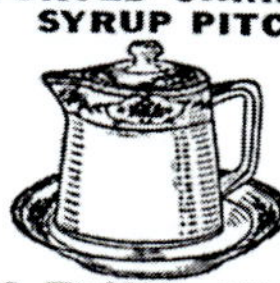

E5648—Ht. 3¾ in., new shape, delicate pink roses and wild-flowers with lavender stems, pale blue pastel band border, gold traced handles & knobs. ⅛ doz. in pkg..Doz. **$13.50**

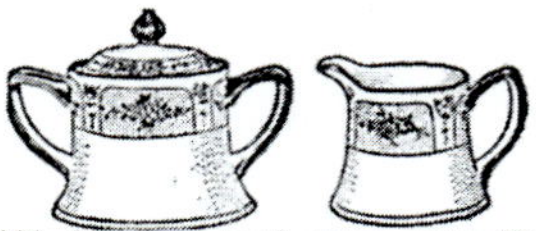

E5468—3 styles, covd. sugar, aver. 3¼ in., creamer aver. 3 in., white china, asstd. floral sprays and clusters with gold dec., cream panel effects and fancy gold tracings, gold handles, edges, base lines and knobs. Asstd. ¼ doz. sets in pkg. Doz. sets, **$14.00**

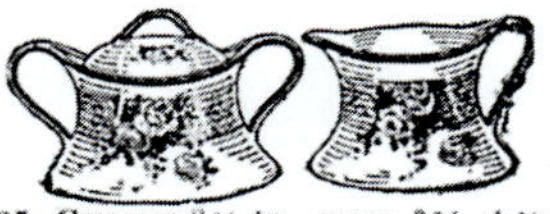

E4925—Creamer 2¾ in., sugar 3⅜, delicate pink & white roses, green foliage, on gold outlined gray band, allover ivory tint, wide coin gold ornamented edges, knobs and handles. 2 sets in pkg.........Set, **$2.25**
(Total $4.50)

IMPORTED CHINA TABLEWARE SPECIALTIES

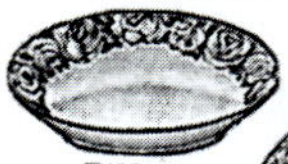

E4931

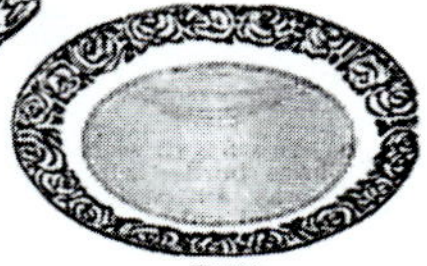

E4933

Good quality, light wt. highly glazed translucent body, hand painted effect, pink shaded roses, green foliage border.

E4932—Cup 3x2¾, saucer 5¾. 1 doz. in pkg.
Doz. **$4.25**

E4931—Sauce dish, 5¼ in. 1 doz. in pkg.
Doz. **$1.75**

E4933—Table plate, 7¾ in. 1 doz. in pkg.
Doz. **$3.50**

IMPORTED CHINA CREAM PITCHERS

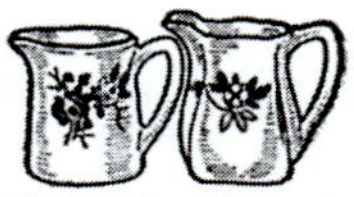

E5408—2 styles, 3 in., floral and gold decor. and sprays, gold edges. Asstd. 1 doz. in pkg..............Doz. **$1.50**

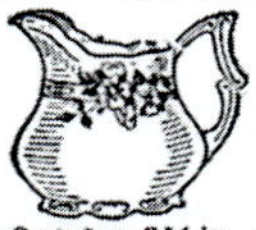

E5410—2 styles, 3¾ in., floral and violet medallion decoration and brown band, gold edges and handle. Asstd. ½ doz. in pkg......Doz. **$3.50**

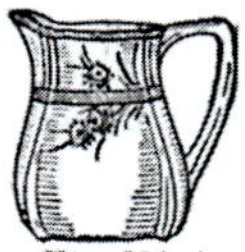

E5409 — Ht. 3¾ in., good grade china body, panel sides, tankard shape, blue pastel pale tinted bands. Hand painted pink rose spray with gold line edge and handle. 1 doz. in pkg...Doz. **$3.75**

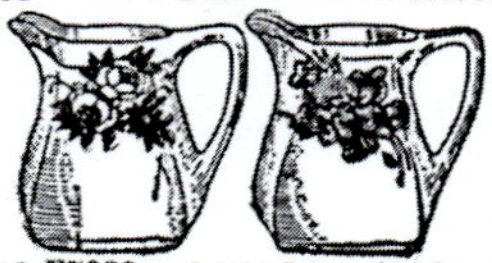

E7929 — 2 styles, 4⅜ in., panel sides, blue pastel pale tinted bands, pink rose and violet decor. in natural colors, gold edges, inner verge line and around base. Asstd. ½ doz. in pkg...Doz. **$4.00**

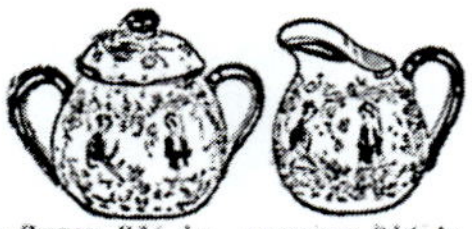

E5452—Sugar 3¾ in., creamer 3½ in., new shape, allover Japanese figure and landscape decors., Tokio red edges and handles. ½ doz. sets in pkg........Doz. sets, **$6.90**

Butler Brothers Catalog, 1919 – 1920.

L5211—Kochi Asst., **36 shapes, 2 decors.**, comprises plates, bonbon and pickle dishes, nut bowls, hair receivers and puff boxes, hatpin holders, sugar and cream sets, mayonnaise sets, rose jars, toothbrush holders, sugar shakers, cream and syrup pitchers, candlestick holders, pin and ash trays, fancy shapes, rose medallion with gold outlined old ivory scrolls, gold dec. lt. blue border; gold traced orient. medallion, gold traced lt. blue band, gold edges & dec. hdls. Asstd. 6 doz. in case, 70 lbs. Doz. **$2.25** (Total for asst. $13.50)

L5210—"Variety" Asst., **19 styles**, comprises chocolate, berry and tea sets, cups and saucers (*count as 1pc.*), plates, mustard pot, nut bowls and dishes, puff box and hair receivers, sugar shakers, salts and peppers and hatpin holders. White china enameled traced hand painted floral and Japanese landscape decorations. Retail range 10c to $1.00. Doz. **$1.08** 12 doz. in case, 120 lbs. (Total for asst. $12.96)

AWATA VASE ASSORTMENTS

L5222—9 styles, ht. 10 in., tinted and mottled bodies, floral and landscape decors. gold frames, borders, ornaments and hdls. 3 doz. in case, 174 lbs........................Doz. **$5.00**

CHINA TOOTHPICK HOLDERS

L6470—2¼ in., conventional decoration, maroon edg. 1 doz. in box......Doz. **3c**

L6471—2½ in., 2 styles and shapes, gold decorated traced conventional design, gold edge. Asstd. 1 doz. in pkg. Doz. **5c**

CHINA SPOON TRAY, PICKLE OR RELISH DISH ASSTS.

L6252—2 styles, 7¾ in., open hdls., gold traced tan border and floral inlays, gold traced roses on combination tints, beaded gold edge. Asstd. ½ doz. in pkg. Doz. **$4.00**

L1037—3 styles, aver. 7¾x4¼, white china, gold decor. floral borders with tinted outer band. gold edges. Asstd. ¼ doz. in pkg. Doz. **$4.20**

CHINA OLIVE, BONBON OR NUT DISH ASSTS.

L1031 — 3 styles, aver. 5½x4½, white china, gold ornamented floral borders. Asstd. ½ doz. in pkg................Doz. **$2.25**

L744—12 styles, aver. 5x7, white china, floral bouquets, landscape and conventional border designs. profuse gold ornamentation. Asstd. 1 doz. in pkg........Doz. **$6.00**

CHINA BISCUIT OR CRACKER JARS

L7490—4¼x6¼, pink rose and foliage sprays connecting gold scroll band, gold decor. edges, hdls. and knobs. ¼ doz. in pkg............Doz. **$9.00**

L6528—6¼x6 in., hand painted gold outlined blossom buds and leaves on long stems, shaded in vari-color, brown figured, ivory border, gold ornaments, gold lined handles. 1 in pkg....Each, **95c**

Butler Brothers Catalog, 1917 – 1918.

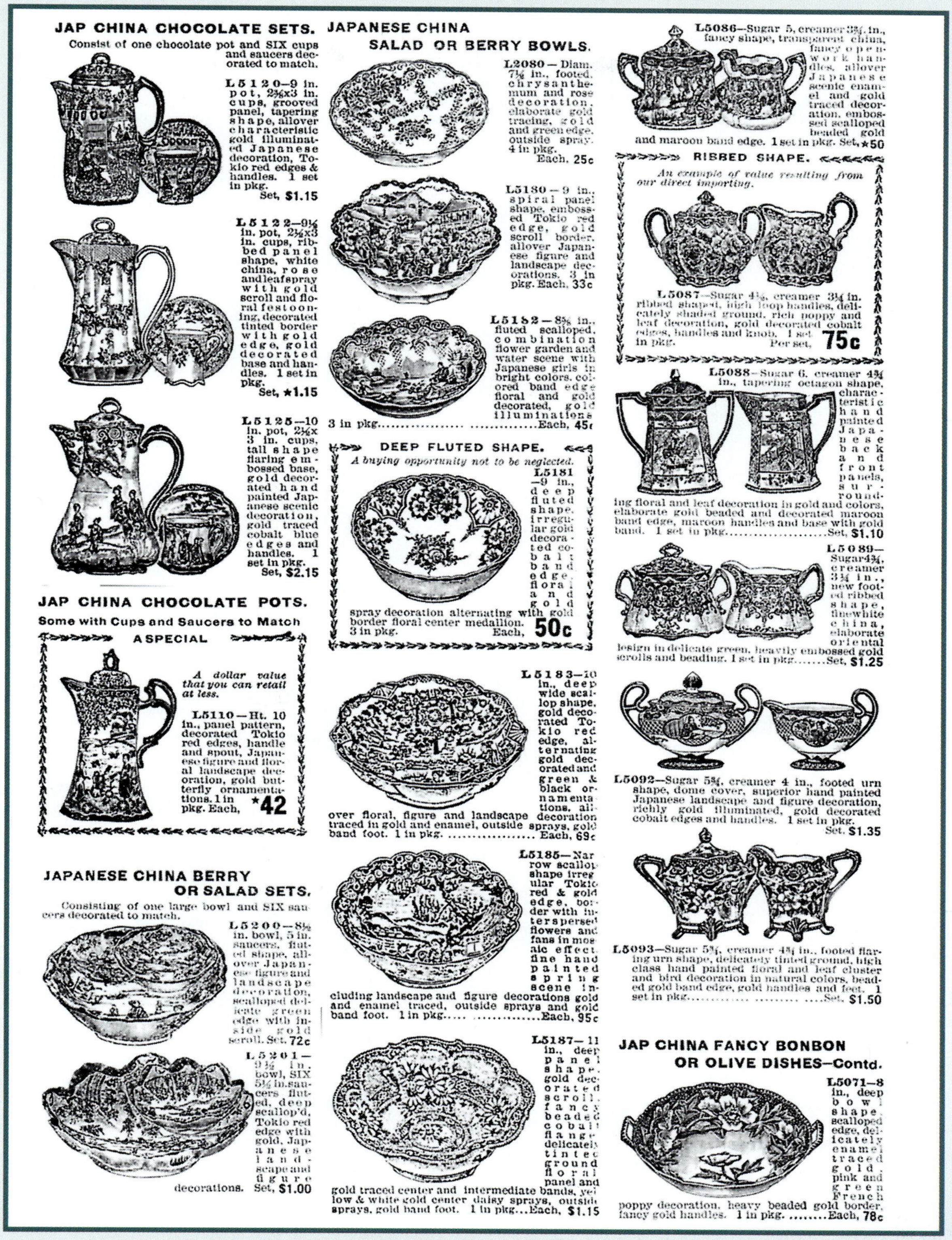

JAP CHINA CHOCOLATE SETS.

Consist of one chocolate pot and SIX cups and saucers decorated to match.

L5120—9 in. pot, 2⅜x3 in. cups, grooved panel, tapering shape, allover characteristic gold illuminated Japanese decoration, Tokio red edges & handles. 1 set in pkg. Set, $1.15

L5122—9½ in. pot, 2⅜x3 in. cups, ribbed panel shape, white china, rose and leaf spray with gold scroll and floral festooning, decorated tinted border with gold edge, gold decorated base and handles. 1 set in pkg. Set, ★1.15

L5125—10 in. pot, 2½x3 in. cups, tall shape flaring embossed base, gold decorated hand painted Japanese scenic decoration, gold traced cobalt blue edges and handles. 1 set in pkg. Set, $2.15

JAP CHINA CHOCOLATE POTS.

Some with Cups and Saucers to Match

A SPECIAL

A dollar value that you can retail at less.

L5110—Ht. 10 in., panel pattern, decorated Tokio red edges, handle and spout, Japanese figure and floral landscape decoration, gold butterfly ornamentations. 1 in pkg. Each, *42

JAPANESE CHINA BERRY OR SALAD SETS.

Consisting of one large bowl and SIX saucers decorated to match.

L5200—8½ in. bowl, 5 in. saucers, fluted shape, allover Japanese figure and landscape decoration, scalloped delicate green edge with inside gold scroll. Set, 72c

L5201—9½ in. bowl, SIX 5½ in. saucers fluted, deep scallop'd, Tokio red edge with gold, Japanese landscape and figure decorations. Set, $1.00

JAPANESE CHINA SALAD OR BERRY BOWLS.

L2080—Diam. 7½ in., footed, chrysanthemum and rose decoration, elaborate gold tracing, gold and green edge, outside spray. 4 in pkg. Each, 25c

L5180—9 in., spiral panel shape, embossed Tokio red edge, gold scroll border, allover Japanese figure and landscape decorations. 3 in pkg. Each, 33c

L5182—8¾ in., fluted scalloped, combination flower garden and water scene with Japanese girls in bright colors, colored band edge floral and gold decorated, gold illuminations 3 in pkg. .... Each, 45c

DEEP FLUTED SHAPE.

A buying opportunity not to be neglected.

L5181—9 in., deep fluted shape, irregular gold decorated cobalt band edge, floral and gold spray decoration alternating with gold border floral center medallion. 3 in pkg. Each, 50c

L5183—10 in., deep wide scallop shape, gold decorated Tokio red edge, alternating gold decorated and green & black ornamentations, allover floral, figure and landscape decoration traced in gold and enamel, outside sprays, gold band foot. 1 in pkg. .... Each, 69c

L5185—Narrow scallop shape irregular Tokio red & gold edge, border with interspersed flowers and fans in mosaic effect, fine hand painted spring scene including landscape and figure decorations gold and enamel traced, outside sprays and gold band foot. 1 in pkg.... ....Each, 95c

L5187—11 in., deep panel shape, gold decorated scroll, fancy beaded cobalt flange, delicately tinted ground floral panel and gold traced center and intermediate bands, yellow & white gold center daisy sprays, outside sprays, gold band foot. 1 in pkg...Each, $1.15

L5086—Sugar 5, creamer 3¾ in., fancy shape, transparent china, fancy openwork handles, allover Japanese scenic enamel and gold traced decoration, embossed scalloped beaded gold and maroon band edge. 1 set in pkg. Set, ★50

RIBBED SHAPE.

An example of value resulting from our direct importing.

L5087—Sugar 4½, creamer 3¼ in. ribbed shaped, high loop handles, delicately shaded ground, rich poppy and leaf decoration, gold decorated cobalt edges, handles and knob. 1 set in pkg. Per set, 75c

L5088—Sugar 6, creamer 4¾ in., tapering octagon shape, characteristic hand painted Japanese back and front panels, surrounding floral and leaf decoration in gold and colors, elaborate gold beaded and decorated maroon band edge, maroon handles and base with gold band. 1 set in pkg......................Set, $1.10

L5089—Sugar 4¾, creamer 3¼ in., new footed ribbed shape, fine white china, elaborate oriental design in delicate green, heavily embossed gold scrolls and beading. 1 set in pkg.......Set, $1.25

L5092—Sugar 5¾, creamer 4 in., footed urn shape, dome cover, superior hand painted Japanese landscape and figure decoration, richly gold illuminated, gold decorated cobalt edges and handles. 1 set in pkg. Set, $1.35

L5093—Sugar 5¾, creamer 4¾ in., footed flaring urn shape, delicately tinted ground, high class hand painted floral and leaf cluster and bird decoration in natural colors, beaded gold band edge, gold handles and feet. 1 set in pkg.............. ....Set, $1.50

JAP CHINA FANCY BONBON OR OLIVE DISHES—Contd.

L5071—8 in., deep bowl shape, scalloped edge, delicately enamel traced gold, pink and green French poppy decoration, heavy beaded gold border, fancy gold handles. 1 in pkg. ....Each, 78c

Butler Brothers Catalog, 1908.

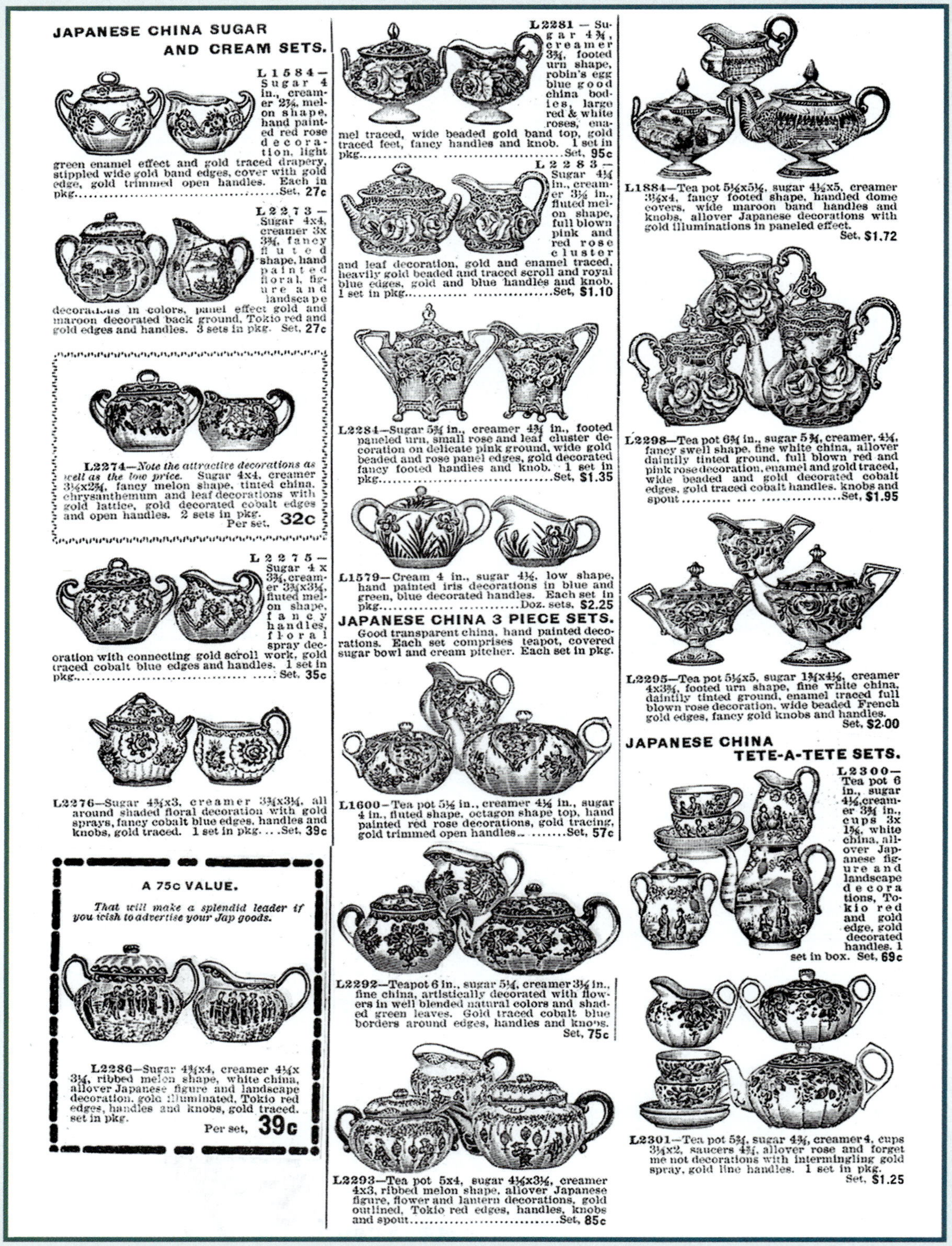

JAPANESE CHINA SUGAR AND CREAM SETS.

L1584—Sugar 4 in., creamer 2¾, melon shape, hand painted red rose decoration, light green enamel effect and gold traced drapery, stippled wide gold band edges, cover with gold edge, gold trimmed open handles. Each in pkg.........Set, 27c

L2273—Sugar 4x4, creamer 3x3¾, fancy fluted shape, hand painted floral, figure and landscape decorations in colors, panel effect gold and maroon decorated back ground, Tokio red and gold edges and handles. 3 sets in pkg. Set, 27c

L2274—*Note the attractive decorations as well as the low price.* Sugar 4x4, creamer 3½x2¾, fancy melon shape, tinted china, chrysanthemum and leaf decorations with gold lattice, gold decorated cobalt edges and open handles. 2 sets in pkg. Per set, 32c

L2275—Sugar 4x3¾, creamer 3¾x3¼, fluted melon shape, fancy handles, floral spray decoration with connecting gold scroll work, gold traced cobalt blue edges and handles. 1 set in pkg.........Set, 35c

L2276—Sugar 4¾x3, creamer 3¾x3¼, all around shaded floral decoration with gold sprays, fancy cobalt blue edges, handles and knobs, gold traced. 1 set in pkg....Set, 39c

A 75c VALUE.

That will make a splendid leader if you wish to advertise your Jap goods.

L2286—Sugar 4¾x4, creamer 4¼x3¼, ribbed melon shape, white china, allover Japanese figure and landscape decoration, gold illuminated, Tokio red edges, handles and knobs, gold traced. set in pkg. Per set, 39c

L2281—Sugar 4¾, creamer 3¾, footed urn shape, robin's egg blue good china bodies, large red & white roses, enamel traced, wide beaded gold band top, gold traced feet, fancy handles and knob. 1 set in pkg.........Set, 95c

L2283—Sugar 4¼ in., creamer 3½ in., fluted melon shape, full blown pink and red rose cluster and leaf decoration, gold and enamel traced, heavily gold beaded and traced scroll and royal blue edges, gold and blue handles and knob. 1 set in pkg.........Set, $1.10

L2284—Sugar 5¾ in., creamer 4¾ in., footed paneled urn, small rose and leaf cluster decoration on delicate pink ground, wide gold beaded and rose panel edges, gold decorated fancy footed handles and knob. 1 set in pkg.........Set, $1.35

L1579—Cream 4 in., sugar 4½, low shape, hand painted iris decorations in blue and green, blue decorated handles. Each set in pkg.........Doz. sets, $2.25

JAPANESE CHINA 3 PIECE SETS.

Good transparent china, hand painted decorations. Each set comprises teapot, covered sugar bowl and cream pitcher. Each set in pkg.

L1600—Tea pot 5½ in., creamer 4½ in., sugar 4 in., fluted shape, octagon shape top, hand painted red rose decorations, gold tracing, gold trimmed open handles.........Set, 57c

L2292—Teapot 6 in., sugar 5¼, creamer 3½ in., fine china, artistically decorated with flowers in well blended natural colors and shaded green leaves. Gold traced cobalt blue borders around edges, handles and knobs. Set, 75c

L2293—Tea pot 5x4, sugar 4½x3½, creamer 4x3, ribbed melon shape, allover Japanese figure, flower and lantern decorations, gold outlined, Tokio red edges, handles, knobs and spout.........Set, 85c

L1884—Tea pot 5½x5¼, sugar 4½x5, creamer 3½x4, fancy footed shape, handled dome covers, wide maroon band handles and knobs, allover Japanese decorations with gold illuminations in paneled effect. Set, $1.72

L2298—Tea pot 6¾ in., sugar 5¾, creamer, 4¼, fancy swell shape, fine white china, allover daintily tinted ground, full blown red and pink rose decoration, enamel and gold traced, wide beaded and gold decorated cobalt edges, gold traced cobalt handles, knobs and spout.........Set, $1.95

L2295—Tea pot 5½x5, sugar 1¾x4½, creamer 4x3¾, footed urn shape, fine white china, daintily tinted ground, enamel traced full blown rose decoration, wide beaded French gold edges, fancy gold knobs and handles. Set, $2.00

JAPANESE CHINA TETE-A-TETE SETS.

L2300—Tea pot 6 in., sugar 4½, creamer 3¾ in., cups 3x1¾, white china, allover Japanese figure and landscape decorations, Tokio red and gold edge, gold decorated handles. 1 set in box. Set, 69c

L2301—Tea pot 5¾, sugar 4¾, creamer 4, cups 3½x2, saucers 4¾, allover rose and forget me not decorations with intermingling gold spray, gold line handles. 1 set in pkg. Set, $1.25

Butler Brothers Catalog, 1907.

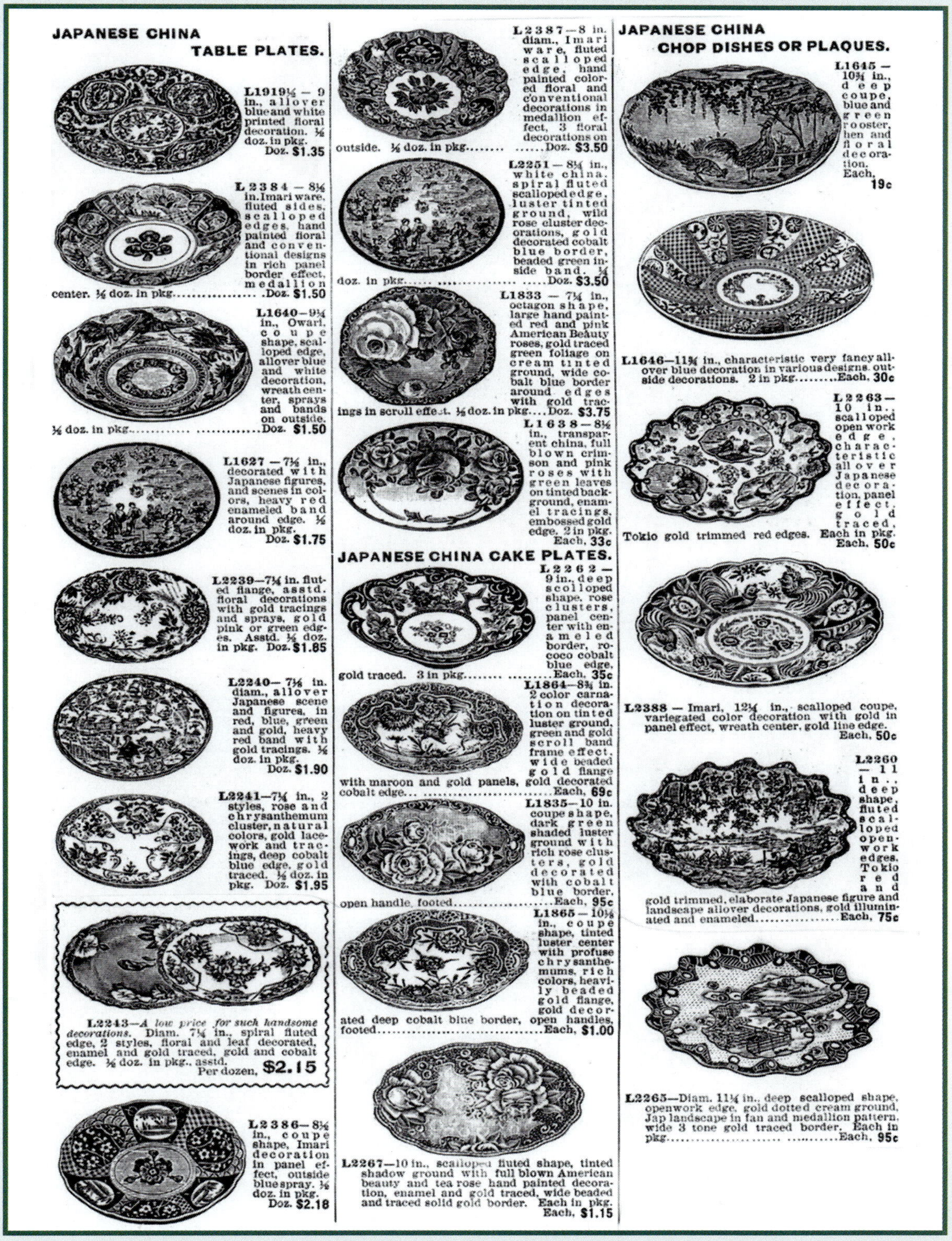

JAPANESE CHINA TABLE PLATES.

L1919½ – 9 in., allover blue and white printed floral decoration. ½ doz. in pkg. Doz. **$1.35**

L2384 – 8½ in. Imari ware, fluted sides, scalloped edges, hand painted floral and conventional designs in rich panel border effect, medallion center. ½ doz. in pkg. .... Doz. **$1.50**

L1640–9¼ in., Owari, coupe shape, scalloped edge, allover blue and white decoration, wreath center, sprays and bands on outside. ½ doz. in pkg. .... Doz. **$1.50**

L1627 – 7½ in., decorated with Japanese figures, and scenes in colors, heavy red enameled band around edge. ½ doz. in pkg. Doz. **$1.75**

L2239–7¼ in. fluted flange, asstd. floral decorations with gold tracings and sprays, gold pink or green edges. Asstd. ½ doz. in pkg. Doz. **$1.85**

L2240– 7½ in. diam., allover Japanese scene and figures, in red, blue, green and gold, heavy red band with gold tracings. ½ doz. in pkg. Doz. **$1.90**

L2241–7¼ in., 2 styles, rose and chrysanthemum cluster, natural colors, gold lacework and tracings, deep cobalt blue edge, gold traced. ½ doz. in pkg. Doz. **$1.95**

L2243–*A low price for such handsome decorations.* Diam. 7¼ in., spiral fluted edge, 2 styles, floral and leaf decorated, enamel and gold traced, gold and cobalt edge. ½ doz. in pkg., asstd. Per dozen, **$2.15**

L2386– 8½ in., coupe shape, Imari decoration in panel effect, outside blue spray. ½ doz. in pkg. Doz. **$2.18**

L2387–8 in. diam., Imari ware, fluted scalloped edge, hand painted colored floral and conventional decorations in medallion effect, 3 floral decorations on outside. ½ doz. in pkg. .... Doz. **$3.50**

L2251 – 8¼ in., white china, spiral fluted scalloped edge, luster tinted ground, wild rose cluster decorations, gold decorated cobalt blue border, beaded green inside band. ½ doz. in pkg. .... Doz. **$3.50**

L1833 – 7¼ in., octagon shape, large hand painted red and pink American Beauty roses, gold traced green foliage on cream tinted ground, wide cobalt blue border around edges with gold tracings in scroll effect. ½ doz. in pkg. .... Doz. **$3.75**

L1638–8½ in., transparent china, full blown crimson and pink roses with green leaves on tinted background, enamel tracings, embossed gold edge. 2 in pkg. Each, **33c**

JAPANESE CHINA CAKE PLATES.

L2262 – 9 in., deep scolloped shape, rose clusters, panel center with enameled border, rococo cobalt blue edge, gold traced. 3 in pkg. .... Each, **35c**

L1864–8¾ in. 2 color carnation decoration on tinted luster ground, green and gold scroll band frame effect, wide beaded gold flange with maroon and gold panels, gold decorated cobalt edge... .... Each, **69c**

L1835–10 in. coupe shape, dark green shaded luster ground with rich rose clusters, gold decorated with cobalt blue border, open handle, footed .... Each, **95c**

L1865 – 10½ in., coupe shape, tinted luster center with profuse chrysanthemums, rich colors, heavily beaded gold flange, gold decorated deep cobalt blue border, open handles, footed .... Each, **$1.00**

L2267–10 in., scalloped fluted shape, tinted shadow ground with full blown American beauty and tea rose hand painted decoration, enamel and gold traced, wide beaded and traced solid gold border. Each in pkg. Each, **$1.15**

JAPANESE CHINA CHOP DISHES OR PLAQUES.

L1645 – 10¾ in., deep coupe, blue and green rooster, hen and floral decoration. Each, **19c**

L1646–11¾ in., characteristic very fancy allover blue decoration in various designs. outside decorations. 2 in pkg. .... Each, **30c**

L2263– 10 in., scalloped open work edge, characteristic allover Japanese decoration, panel effect, gold traced, Tokio gold trimmed red edges. Each in pkg. Each, **50c**

L2388 – Imari, 12¼ in., scalloped coupe, variegated color decoration with gold in panel effect, wreath center, gold line edge. Each, **50c**

L2260 – 11 in., deep shape, fluted scalloped openwork edges, Tokio red and gold trimmed, elaborate Japanese figure and landscape allover decorations, gold illuminated and enameled .... Each, **75c**

L2265–Diam. 11¼ in., deep scalloped shape, openwork edge, gold dotted cream ground, Jap landscape in fan and medallion pattern, wide 3 tone gold traced border. Each in pkg. .... Each, **95c**

Butler Brothers Catalog, 1907.

RICH PEONY DESIGNS.

Compare prices or better order a sample lot subject to approval.

L2360 — 19 in. royal blue ground, large shaded peony decorations with enameled petals and leaves, gold decorated open handles with ring and tassel effect, gold band wave top. 1 in pkg. Each, **$2.00**

L2359   L2367

L2359 — *The new luster bronze decoration.* Ht. 16, royal blue ground, large peony and leaf decorations in shaded bronze outlined with raised gold, gold decorated green band top and base, open handles gold striped. 1 in pkg. Each, **$2.50**

L2367 — Ht. 16¼ in., fancy tapering shape, hand painted full blown American Beauty roses and leaves enclosed by heavily embossed gold scroll band, rose spray back, royal blue ground, new design, gold decorated handles. 1 in pkg.... Each, **$2.50**

L2362   L2363

L2362 — 19 in. green bronze effect, elaborate red and rose feeling decoration with leaves.

JAPANESE CHINA INDIVIDUAL BUTTER PLATES.

L1690   L1695

L1690 — Diam. 3¼ in., blue and white Sometsuke floral center with neat border. 1 doz. in box.... Doz. 18c
L1695 — Extra large round 4¼ in. diam., asstd. floral and rooster decorated center in colors. Doz. 39c

JAPANESE "AWATA" VASES.

L1795   L2351

L1795 — 7¾ in., rich red and green backgrounds with large natural colored floral decorations, heavy enamel effect, gold trimmed outlines, fancy tops, gold trimmed edges and handles. 2 in pkg. Each, 15c
L2351 — 10 in., asstd. maroon and blue grounds with embossed iris and peony decorations in natural colorings. 4 in pkg. Each, 30c

L2357   L2355

L2357 — Ht. 12½ in. royal blue ground with profuse gold and shaded bronze lotus lily and leaf decoration, green border top outlined with gold, gold decorated openwork handles. 1 in pkg. Each, **$1.00**
L2355 — Fancy tapering shape, ht. 16 in., shaded green ground, heavy gold traced iris decorations in colors, side handles. 1 in pkg. Each, **$1.35**
L2356 — Footed urn shape, ht. 16 in., deep cobalt blue, large floral and leaf decoration in natural colors with prominent gold outlines and veiling, daintily tinted raised enamel interspersed leaf scrolls, gold band top. 1 in pkg. Each, **$1.50**

L2356

L2232 — 6¼ in. all over hand painted flowers, villages, landscapes and figures, gold trimmings, gold trimmed red band around edge. ¼ doz. in pkg. Doz. **$1.25**
L1619 — 6¼ in., shaded luster surface, floral and leaf decoration interwoven with gold, asstd. Doz. **$1.35**
L2234 — 6 in., fine transparent white china, spiral fluted edge, cobalt and gold border, floral spray decoration, enamel or gold traced, 2 designs. ½ doz. in pkg. asstd. Doz. **$1.85**
L1832 — 5¾ in. octagon shape, hand painted roses on delicate tinted background, gold traced leaves, cobalt blue edge with gold lace work all around. ½ doz. in pkg. Doz. **$2.25**

JAPANESE CHINA TEA POTS.

All glazed inside.

L1772½   L1775

L1772½ — Ht. 3½, diam. 4, inside drainer, wicker handle, blue and white, floral and band decoration. 1 doz. in pkg. Doz. 96c
L1775 — Ht. 5¼ in., Banko ware, dark brown, allover brown embossed water marked design, 1 in. plain border at bottom, wicker handle, strainer attachment, straight spout. ½ doz. in box. Doz. **$1.15**

L848   L1773½

L848 — 5 in., fireproof, Kitsu ware, strainer attachment straight spout, white enameled highly glazed body, dark blue allover decorations, wicker handle. ½ doz. in pkg. Doz. **$1.45**
L1773 — Ht. 4½ in. diam. 4½, as L1772½, but porcelain handle. ½ doz. in pkg. Doz. **$1.50**
L1773½ — Ht. 4½ in., diam. 4½, as L1772½. ½ doz. in pkg. Doz. **$1.75**

L849

L849 — Ht. 6 in., fireproof, Kitsu ware, strainer attachment, straight spout, white enameled glazed body, dark blue conventional decorations, wicker handle. ¼ doz. in box. Doz. **$1.60**
L2319 — 4¼x4¾, Japanese figure decorations in panels surrounded by gold traced cobalt blue panel border, cobalt handle, knob and spout. 2 in pkg. Each, 21c

L2319

L2093 — 10 in. hexagon shape, delicately tinted ground, cream to olive, natural red poppy decoration, enamel traced, deep beaded gold cherry blossom border, gold and cobalt lip edge, outside sprays and gold band. Each, **$1.75**

L2094 — 10 in., fine china, wide panel, deep scalloped edge, tinted ground, rose cluster medallion center with maroon and gold border surrounded by rose and conventional panel decoration, heavily embossed and beaded with gold, gold decorated scroll and band edge, outside sprays, gold foot. Each, **$2.00**

L1657 — Extra deep, fluted, diam. 11 in., heavy beaded gold edge, rich shaded green luster flange and center with gold beaded and embossed lace work medallions, rich deep pink rose and gold spray decorations, rose clusters outside, gold line foot. Each, **$2.25**

Butler Brothers Catalog, 1907.

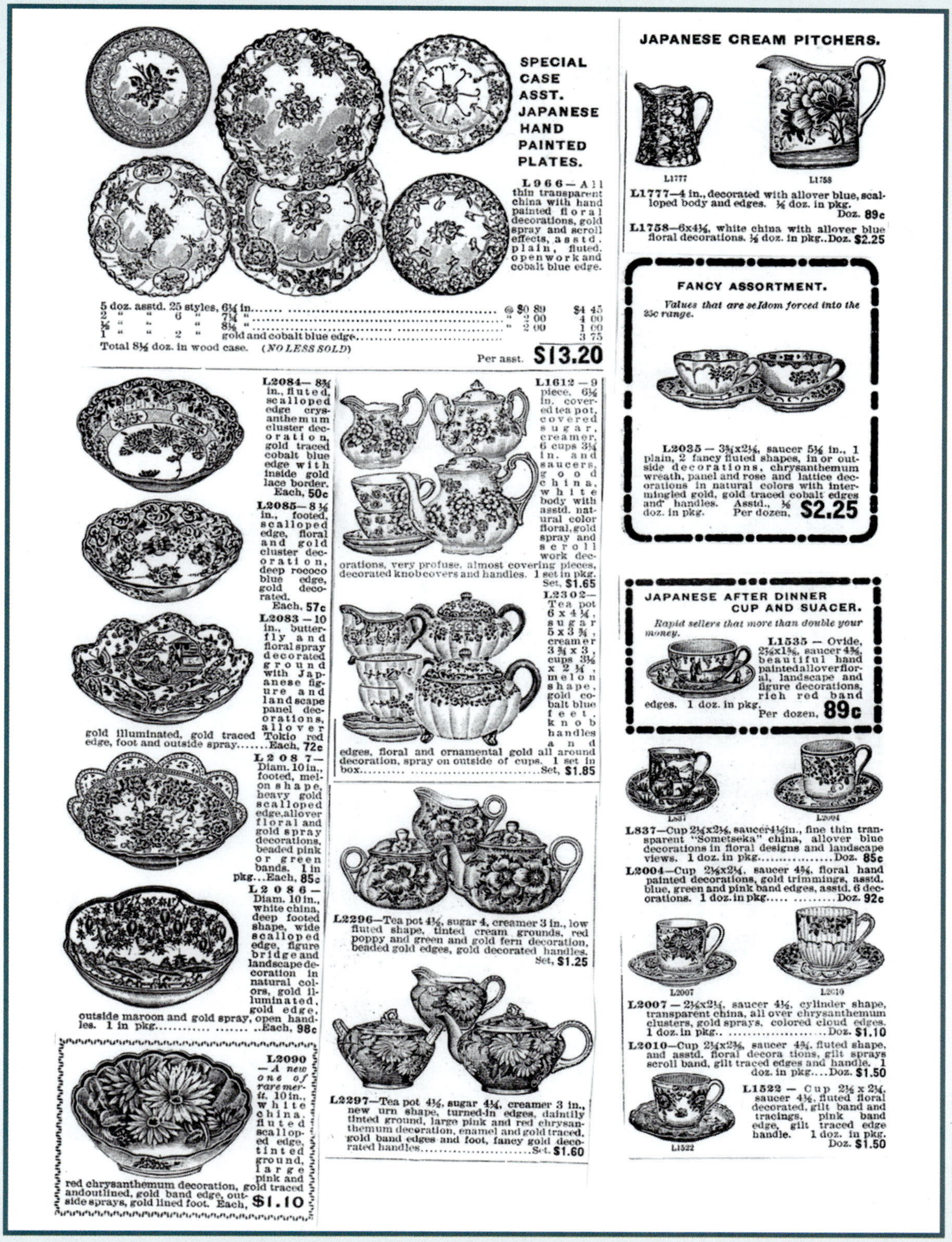

SPECIAL CASE ASST. JAPANESE HAND PAINTED PLATES.

L966—All thin transparent china with hand painted floral decorations, gold spray and scroll effects, asstd. plain, fluted, openwork and cobalt blue edge.

5 doz. asstd. 25 styles, 6¼ in.	@ $0 89	$4 45
2 " " 6 " 7¼ "	" 2 00	4 00
½ " " " 8½ "	" 2 00	1 00
1 " " 2 " gold and cobalt blue edge		3 75

Total 8½ doz. in wood case. (*NO LESS SOLD*) Per asst. **$13.20**

L2084—8¾ in., fluted, scalloped edge chrysanthemum cluster decoration, gold traced cobalt blue edge with inside gold lace border. Each, **50c**

L2085—8½ in., footed, scalloped edge, floral and gold cluster decoration, deep rococo blue edge, gold decorated. Each, **57c**

L2083—10 in., butterfly and floral spray decorated ground with Japanese figure and landscape panel decorations, allover Tokio red gold illuminated, gold traced edge, foot and outside spray.......Each, **72c**

L2087—Diam. 10 in., footed, melon shape, heavy gold scalloped edge, allover floral and gold spray decorations, beaded pink or green bands. 1 in pkg...Each, **85c**

L2086—Diam. 10 in., white china, deep footed shape, wide scalloped edge, figure bridge and landscape decoration in natural colors, gold illuminated, gold edge, outside maroon and gold spray, open handles. 1 in pkg.................Each, **98c**

L2090—*A new one of rare merit.* 10 in., white china, fluted scalloped edge, tinted ground, large pink and red chrysanthemum decoration, gold traced and outlined, gold band edge, outside sprays, gold lined foot. Each, **$1.10**

L1612—9 piece, 6½ in. covered tea pot, covered sugar, creamer, 6 cups 3¼ in. and saucers, good china, white body with asstd. natural color floral, gold spray and scroll work decorations, very profuse, almost covering pieces, decorated knob covers and handles. 1 set in pkg. Set, **$1.65**

L2302—Tea pot 6x4¼, sugar 5x3¾, creamer 3¾x3, cups 3⅜x2¼, melon shape, gold cobalt blue feet, knob handles and edges, floral and ornamental gold all around decoration, spray on outside of cups. 1 set in box.................Set, **$1.85**

L2296—Tea pot 4½, sugar 4, creamer 3 in., low fluted shape, tinted cream grounds, red poppy and green and gold fern decoration, beaded gold edges, gold decorated handles. Set, **$1.25**

L2297—Tea pot 4½, sugar 4¼, creamer 3 in., new urn shape, turned-in edges, daintily tinted ground, large pink and red chrysanthemum decoration, enamel and gold traced, gold band edges and foot, fancy gold decorated handles.......................Set. **$1.60**

JAPANESE CREAM PITCHERS.

L1777 L1758

L1777—4 in., decorated with allover blue, scalloped body and edges. ½ doz. in pkg. Doz. **89c**

L1758—6x4¼, white china with allover blue floral decorations. ½ doz. in pkg..Doz. **$2.25**

FANCY ASSORTMENT.

Values that are seldom forced into the 25c range.

L2035—3¾x2¼, saucer 5½ in., 1 plain, 2 fancy fluted shapes, in or outside decorations, chrysanthemum wreath, panel and rose and lattice decorations in natural colors with intermingled gold, gold traced cobalt edges and handles. Asstd., ½ doz. in pkg. Per dozen, **$2.25**

JAPANESE AFTER DINNER CUP AND SUACER.

Rapid sellers that more than double your money.

L1535—Ovide, 2¾x1⅝, saucer 4⅜, beautiful hand painted allover floral, landscape and figure decorations, rich red band edges. 1 doz. in pkg. Per dozen, **89c**

L837 L2004

L837—Cup 2¼x2⅜, saucer 4½ in., fine thin transparent "Sometseka" china, allover blue decorations in floral designs and landscape views. 1 doz. in pkg.................Doz. **85c**

L2004—Cup 2⅜x2¼, saucer 4⅝, floral hand painted decorations, gold trimmings, asstd. blue, green and pink band edges, asstd. 6 decorations. 1 doz. in pkg..... ....Doz. **92c**

L2007 L2010

L2007—2⅛x2¼, saucer 4½, cylinder shape, transparent china, all over chrysanthemum clusters, gold sprays, colored cloud edges. 1 doz. in pkg.. ....Doz. **$1.10**

L2010—Cup 2¼x2⅜, saucer 4¾, fluted shape, and asstd. floral decorations, gilt sprays scroll band, gilt traced edges and handle. 1 doz. in pkg....Doz. **$1.50**

L1522

L1522—Cup 2½x2¼, saucer 4½, fluted floral decorated, gilt band and tracings, pink band edge, gilt traced edge handle. 1 doz. in pkg. Doz. **$1.50**

Butler Brothers Catalog, 1907.

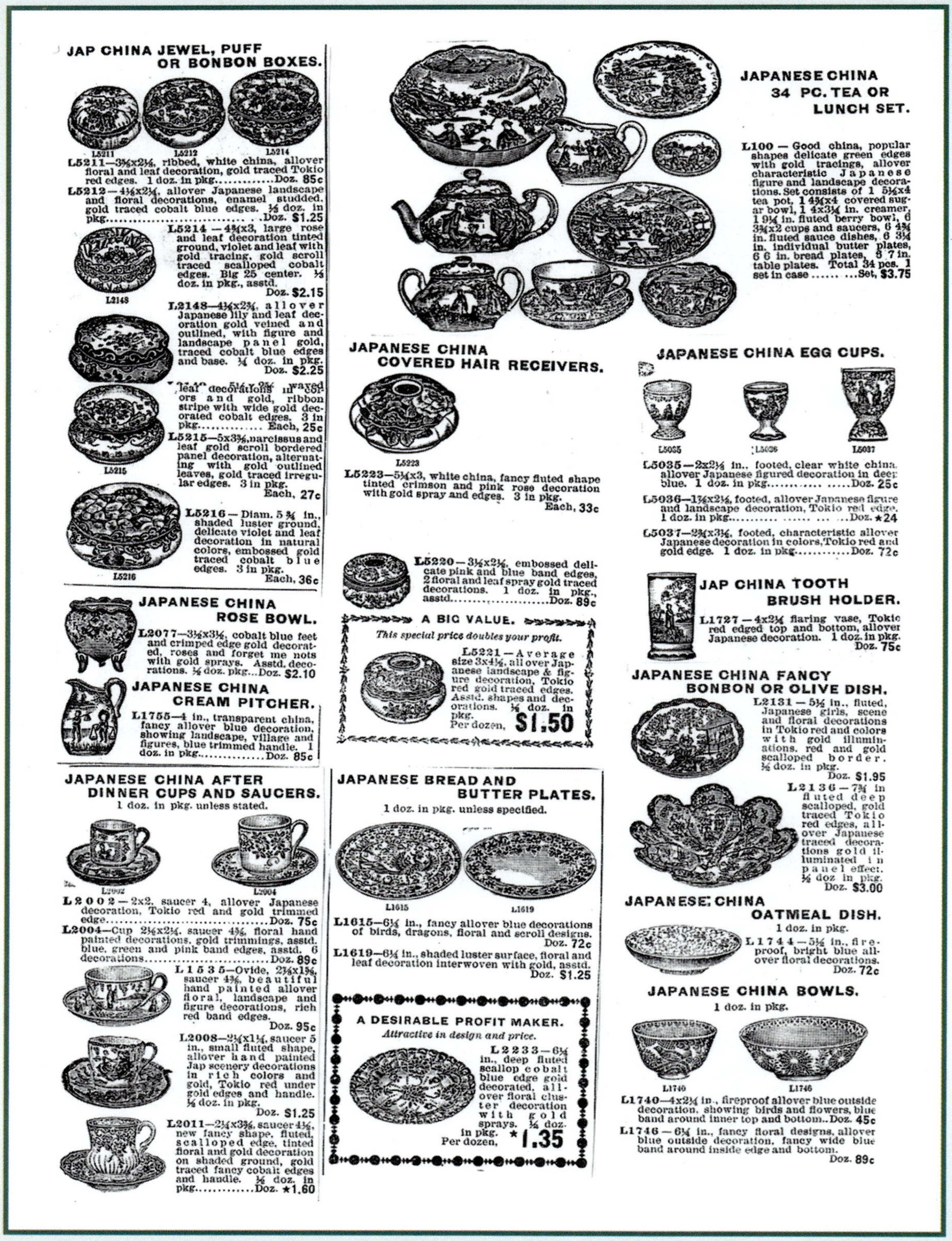

JAP CHINA JEWEL, PUFF OR BONBON BOXES.

L5211—3¼x2¼, ribbed, white china, allover floral and leaf decoration, gold traced Tokio red edges. 1 doz. in pkg.........Doz. 85c

L5212—4¼x2¼, allover Japanese landscape and floral decorations, enamel studded, gold traced cobalt blue edges. ¼ doz. in pkg................................Doz. $1.25

L5214—4¾x3, large rose and leaf decoration tinted ground, violet and leaf with gold tracing, gold scroll traced scalloped cobalt edges. Big 25 center. ½ doz. in pkg., asstd.
Doz. $2.15

L2148—4¼x2¾, allover Japanese lily and leaf decoration gold veined and outlined, with figure and landscape panel gold, traced cobalt blue edges and base. ¼ doz. in pkg.
Doz. $2.25

"leaf" decorations in natural colors and gold, ribbon stripe with wide gold decorated cobalt edges. 3 in pkg.............. Each, 25c

L5215—5x3¾, narcissus and leaf gold scroll bordered panel decoration, alternating with gold outlined leaves, gold traced irregular edges. 3 in pkg.....Each, 27c

 (L5215)

L5216—Diam. 5¾ in., shaded luster ground, delicate violet and leaf decoration in natural colors, embossed gold traced cobalt blue edges. 3 in pkg.....Each, 36c

(L5216)

JAPANESE CHINA ROSE BOWL.

L2077—3½x3¼, cobalt blue feet and crimped edge gold decorated, roses and forget me nots with gold sprays. Asstd. decorations. ⅙ doz. pkg....Doz. $2.10

JAPANESE CHINA CREAM PITCHER.

L1755—4 in., transparent china, fancy allover blue decoration, showing landscape, village and figures, blue trimmed handle. 1 doz. in pkg.................Doz. 85c

JAPANESE CHINA AFTER DINNER CUPS AND SAUCERS.

1 doz. in pkg. unless stated.

L2002—2x2, saucer 4, allover Japanese decoration, Tokio red and gold trimmed edge.....................Doz. 75c

L2004—Cup 2¼x2¼, saucer 4½, floral hand painted decorations, gold trimmings, asstd. blue, green and pink band edges, asstd. 6 decorations..................Doz. 89c

L1535—Ovide, 2¼x1¾, saucer 4⅜, beautiful hand painted allover floral, landscape and figure decorations, rich red band edges.
.................Doz. 95c

L2008—2¼x1¼, saucer 5 in., small fluted shape, allover hand painted Jap scenery decorations in rich colors and gold, Tokio red under gold edges and handle. ½ doz. in pkg......Doz. $1.25

L2011—2¼x3¾, saucer 4½, new fancy shape, fluted, scalloped, edge, tinted floral and gold decoration on shaded ground, gold traced fancy cobalt edges and handle. ½ doz. in pkg...........Doz. ★1.60

JAPANESE CHINA COVERED HAIR RECEIVERS.

L5223

L5223—5¼x3, white china, fancy fluted shape tinted crimson and pink rose decoration with gold spray and edges. 3 in pkg.
Each, 33c

L5220—3½x2½, embossed delicate pink and blue band edges, 2 floral and leaf spray gold traced decorations. 1 doz. in pkg., asstd......................Doz. 89c

A BIG VALUE.

This special price doubles your profit.

L5221—Average size 3x4½, all over Japanese landscape & figure decoration, Tokio red gold traced edges. Asstd. shapes and decorations. ½ doz. in pkg.
Per dozen, $1.50

JAPANESE BREAD AND BUTTER PLATES.

1 doz. in pkg. unless specified.

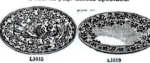

L1615   L1619

L1615—6¼ in., fancy allover blue decorations of birds, dragons, floral and scroll designs.
Doz. 72c

L1619—6¼ in., shaded luster surface, floral and leaf decoration interwoven with gold, asstd.
Doz. $1.25

A DESIRABLE PROFIT MAKER.

Attractive in design and price.

L2233—6¼ in., deep fluted scallop cobalt blue edge gold decorated, allover floral cluster decoration with gold sprays. ½ doz. in pkg.
Per dozen, ★1.35

JAPANESE CHINA 34 PC. TEA OR LUNCH SET.

L100—Good china, popular shapes delicate green edges with gold tracings, allover characteristic Japanese figure and landscape decorations. Set consists of 1 5½x4 tea pot, 1 4¾x2¼ covered sugar bowl, 1 4¼x3¼ in. creamer, 1 9¼ in. fluted berry bowl, 6 3¼x2 cups and saucers, 6 4¾ in. fluted sauce dishes, 6 3½ in. individual butter plates, 6 6 in. bread plates, 6 7 in. table plates. Total 34 pcs. 1 set in case........Set, $3.75

JAPANESE CHINA EGG CUPS.

L5035   L5036   L5037

L5035—2x2½ in., footed, clear white china, allover Japanese figured decoration in deep blue. 1 doz. in pkg.............Doz. 25c

L5036—1¾x2¼, footed, allover Japanese figure and landscape decoration, Tokio red edge. 1 doz. in pkg................Doz. ★24

L5037—2¾x3¼, footed, characteristic allover Japanese decoration in colors, Tokio red and gold edge. 1 doz. in pkg...........Doz. 72c

JAP CHINA TOOTH BRUSH HOLDER.

L1727—4x2¼ flaring vase, Tokio red edged top and bottom, allover Japanese decoration. 1 doz. in pkg.
Doz. 75c

JAPANESE CHINA FANCY BONBON OR OLIVE DISH.

L2131—5½ in., fluted, Japanese girls, scene and floral decorations in Tokio red and colors with gold illuminations. red and gold scalloped border. ½ doz. in pkg.
Doz. $1.95

L2136—7¾ in fluted deep scalloped, gold traced Tokio red edges, allover Japanese traced decorations gold illuminated in panel effect. ½ doz in pkg.
Doz. $3.00

JAPANESE CHINA OATMEAL DISH.

1 doz. in pkg.

L1744—5½ in., fireproof, bright blue allover floral decorations.
Doz. 72c

JAPANESE CHINA BOWLS.

1 doz. in pkg.

L1740   L1746

L1740—4x2¼ in., fireproof allover blue outside decoration, showing birds and flowers, blue band around inner top and bottom..Doz. 45c

L1746—6¼ in., fancy floral designs, allover blue outside decoration, fancy wide blue band around inside edge and bottom.
Doz. 89c

Butler Brothers Catalog, 1908.

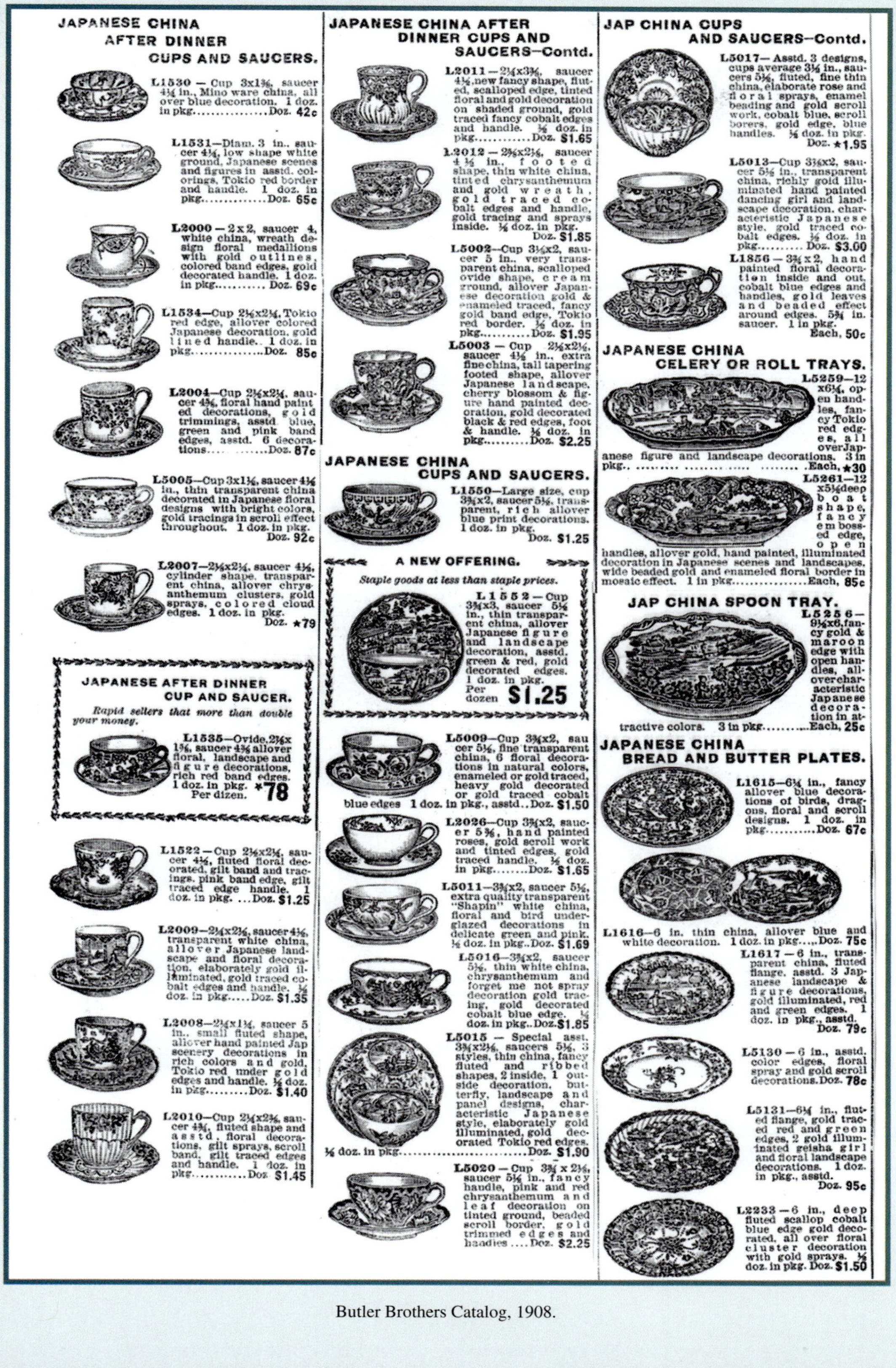

JAPANESE CHINA AFTER DINNER CUPS AND SAUCERS.

L1530 — Cup 3x1⅜, saucer 4¼ in., Mino ware china, all over blue decoration. 1 doz. in pkg...............Doz. 42c

L1531—Diam. 3 in., saucer 4¼, low shape white ground, Japanese scenes and figures in asstd. colorings, Tokio red border and handle. 1 doz. in pkg.............Doz. 65c

L2000 — 2x2, saucer 4, white china, wreath design floral medallions with gold outlines, colored band edges, gold decorated handle. 1 doz. in pkg.......... Doz. 69c

L1534—Cup 2⅛x2¼, Tokio red edge, allover colored Japanese decoration, gold lined handle. 1 doz. in pkg..............Doz. 85c

L2004—Cup 2⅛x2¼, saucer 4⅝, floral hand painted decorations, gold trimmings, asstd. blue, green and pink band edges, asstd. 6 decorations...........Doz. 87c

L5005—Cup 3x1⅜, saucer 4⅛ in., thin transparent china decorated in Japanese floral designs with bright colors, gold tracings in scroll effect throughout. 1 doz. in pkg. Doz. 92c

L2007—2⅛x2¼, saucer 4½, cylinder shape, transparent china, allover chrysanthemum clusters, gold sprays, colored cloud edges. 1 doz. in pkg. Doz. ★79

JAPANESE AFTER DINNER CUP AND SAUCER.

Rapid sellers that more than double your money.

L1535—Ovide, 2⅜x1⅝, saucer 4⅜ allover floral, landscape and figure decorations, rich red band edges. 1 doz. in pkg. Per dizen. *78

L1522—Cup 2¼x2¼, saucer 4½, fluted floral decorated, gilt band and tracings, pink band edge, gilt traced edge handle. 1 doz. in pkg. ...Doz. $1.25

L2009—2¼x2⅛, saucer 4½, transparent white china, allover Japanese landscape and floral decoration, elaborately gold illuminated, gold traced cobalt edges and handle. ½ doz. in pkg.....Doz. $1.35

L2008—2¼x1¾, saucer 5 in., small fluted shape, allover hand painted Jap scenery decorations in rich colors and gold, Tokio red under gold edges and handle. ½ doz. in pkg.........Doz. $1.40

L2010—Cup 2¼x2⅜, saucer 4¾, fluted shape and asstd. floral decorations, gilt sprays, scroll band, gilt traced edges and handle. 1 doz. in pkg...........Doz. $1.45

JAPANESE CHINA AFTER DINNER CUPS AND SAUCERS—Contd.

L2011—2¼x3⅜, saucer 4½, new fancy shape, fluted, scalloped edge, tinted floral and gold decoration on shaded ground, gold traced fancy cobalt edges and handle. ½ doz. in pkg...........Doz. $1.65

L2012 — 2⅝x2⅛, saucer 4½ in., footed shape, thin white china, tinted chrysanthemum and gold wreath, gold traced cobalt edges and handle, gold tracing and sprays inside. ½ doz. in pkg. Doz. $1.85

L5002—Cup 3½x2, saucer 5 in., very transparent china, scalloped ovide shape, cream ground, allover Japanese decoration gold & enameled traced, fancy gold band edge, Tokio red border. ½ doz. in pkg..........Doz. $1.95

L5003 — Cup 2⅛x2¼, saucer 4½ in., extra fine china, tall tapering footed shape, allover Japanese landscape, cherry blossom & figure hand painted decoration, gold decorated black & red edges, foot & handle. ½ doz. in pkg.........Doz. $2.25

JAPANESE CHINA CUPS AND SAUCERS.

L1550—Large size, cup 3¾x2, saucer 5½, transparent, rich allover blue print decorations. 1 doz. in pkg. Doz. $1.25

A NEW OFFERING.

Staple goods at less than staple prices.

L1552—Cup 3¾x3, saucer 5½ in., thin transparent china, allover Japanese figure and landscape decoration, asstd. green & red, gold decorated edges. 1 doz. in pkg. Per dozen $1.25

L5009—Cup 3¾x2, saucer 5½, fine transparent china, 6 floral decorations in natural colors, enameled or gold traced, heavy gold decorated or gold traced cobalt blue edges 1 doz. in pkg., asstd..Doz. $1.50

L2026—Cup 3¾x2, saucer 5⅜, hand painted roses, gold scroll work and tinted edges, gold traced handle. ½ doz. in pkg........Doz. $1.65

L5011—3¾x2, saucer 5½, extra quality transparent "Shapin" white china, floral and bird underglazed decorations in delicate green and pink. ½ doz. in pkg..Doz. $1.69

L5016—3¾x2, saucer 5½, thin white china, chrysanthemum and forget me not spray decoration gold tracing, gold decorated cobalt blue edge. ½ doz. in pkg..Doz.$1.85

L5015 — Special asst. 3¾x2¼, saucers 5½, 3 styles, thin china, fancy fluted and ribbed shapes, 2 inside, 1 outside decoration, butterfly, landscape and panel designs, characteristic Japanese style, elaborately gold illuminated, gold decorated Tokio red edges. ½ doz. in pkg.........................Doz. $1.90

L5020 — Cup 3¾ x 2⅛, saucer 5½ in., fancy handle, pink and red chrysanthemum and leaf decoration on tinted ground, beaded scroll border, gold trimmed edges and handles ....Doz. $2.25

JAP CHINA CUPS AND SAUCERS—Contd.

L5017— Asstd. 3 designs, cups average 3½ in., saucers 5½, fluted, fine thin china, elaborate rose and floral sprays, enamel beading and gold scroll work, cobalt blue, scroll borers, gold edge, blue handles. ½ doz. in pkg. Doz. ★1.95

L5013—Cup 3⅜x2, saucer 5½ in., transparent china, richly gold illuminated hand painted dancing girl and landscape decoration, characteristic Japanese style, gold traced cobalt edges. ½ doz. in pkg......... Doz. $3.00

L1856 — 3¾x2, hand painted floral decoration inside and out, cobalt blue edges and handles, gold leaves and beaded effect around edges. 5¾ in. saucer. 1 in pkg. Each, 50c

JAPANESE CHINA CELERY OR ROLL TRAYS.

L5259—12x6¼, open handles, fancy Tokio red edges, all overJapanese figure and landscape decorations. 3 in pkg.. .... .Each, ★30

L5261—12x5½deep boat shape, fancy embossed edge, open handles, allover gold, hand painted, illuminated decoration in Japanese scenes and landscapes, wide beaded gold and enameled floral border in mosaic effect. 1 in pkg................Each, 85c

JAP CHINA SPOON TRAY.

L5256—9½x6, fancy gold & maroon edge with open handles, allover characteristic Japanese decoration in attractive colors. 3 in pkg..........Each, 25c

JAPANESE CHINA BREAD AND BUTTER PLATES.

L1615—6¼ in., fancy allover blue decorations of birds, dragons, floral and scroll designs. 1 doz. in pkg...........Doz. 67c

L1616—6 in. thin china, allover blue and white decoration. 1 doz. in pkg....,.Doz. 75c

L1617 — 6 in., transparent china, fluted flange, asstd. 3 Japanese landscape & figure decorations, gold illuminated, red and green edges. 1 doz. in pkg., asstd. Doz. 79c

L5130 — 6 in., asstd. color edges, floral spray and gold scroll decorations.Doz. 78c

L5131—6¼ in., fluted flange, gold traced red and green edges, 2 gold illuminated geisha girl and floral landscape decorations. 1 doz. in pkg., asstd. Doz. 95c

L2233 — 6 in., deep fluted scallop cobalt blue edge gold decorated, all over floral cluster decoration with gold sprays. ½ doz. in pkg. Doz. $1.50

Butler Brothers Catalog, 1908.

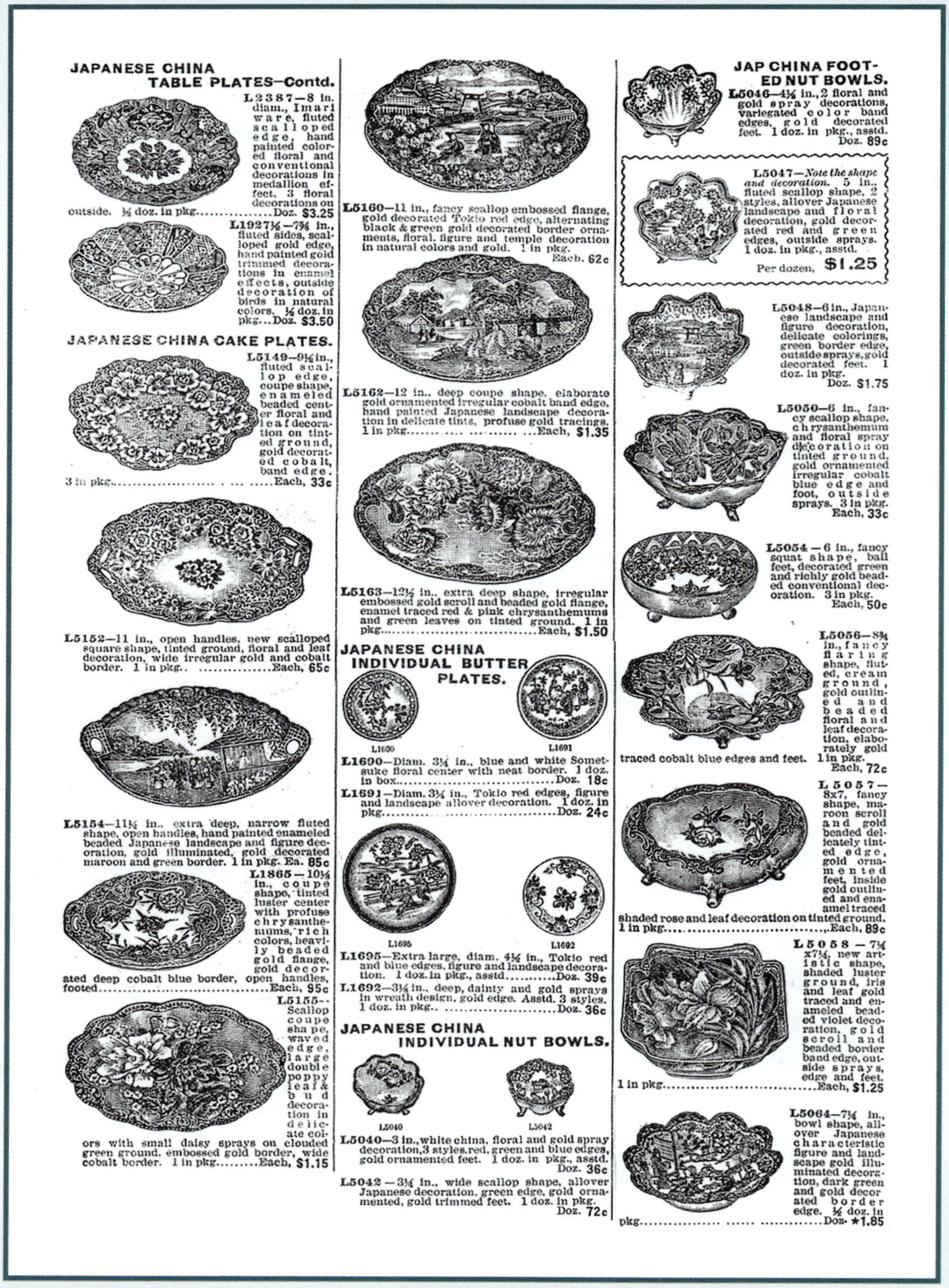
JAPANESE CHINA TABLE PLATES—Contd.

L2387—8 in. diam., Imari ware, fluted scalloped edge, hand painted colored floral and conventional decorations in medallion effect, 3 floral decorations on outside. ½ doz. in pkg..............Doz. $3.25

L1927½—7⅝ in., fluted sides, scalloped gold edge, hand painted gold trimmed decorations in enamel effects, outside decoration of birds in natural colors. ½ doz. in pkg...Doz. $3.50

JAPANESE CHINA CAKE PLATES.

L5149—9½ in., fluted scallop edge, coupe shape, enameled beaded center floral and leaf decoration on tinted ground, gold decorated cobalt, band edge. 3 in pkg....................Each, 33c

L5152—11 in., open handles, new scalloped square shape, tinted ground, floral and leaf decoration, wide irregular gold and cobalt border. 1 in pkg.. ....Each, 65c

L5154—11½ in.. extra deep, narrow fluted shape, open handles, hand painted enameled beaded Japanese landscape and figure decoration, gold illuminated, gold decorated maroon and green border. 1 in pkg. Ea. 85c

L1865—10½ in., coupe shape, tinted luster center with profuse chrysanthemums, rich colors, heavily beaded gold flange, gold decorated deep cobalt blue border, open handles, footed..................................Each, 95c

L5155—Scallop coupe shape, waved edge, large double poppy leaf & bud decoration in delicate colors with small daisy sprays on clouded green ground. embossed gold border, wide cobalt border. 1 in pkg.........Each, $1.15

L5160—11 in., fancy scallop embossed flange, gold decorated Tokio red edge, alternating black & green gold decorated border ornaments, floral. figure and temple decoration in natural colors and gold. 1 in pkg. Each. 62c

L5162—12 in.. deep coupe shape. elaborate gold ornamented irregular cobalt band edge, hand painted Japanese landscape decoration in delicate tints, profuse gold tracings. 1 in pkg..........................Each, $1.35

L5163—12½ in.. extra deep shape, irregular embossed gold scroll and beaded gold flange, enamel traced red & pink chrysanthemums and green leaves on tinted ground. 1 in pkg..............................Each, $1.50

JAPANESE CHINA INDIVIDUAL BUTTER PLATES.

L1690 L1691

L1690—Diam. 3¼ in., blue and white Sometsuke floral center with neat border. 1 doz. in box..............................Doz. 18c

L1691—Diam. 3½ in., Tokio red edges, figure and landscape allover decoration. 1 doz. in pkg..................................Doz. 24c

L1695 L1692

L1695—Extra large, diam. 4½ in., Tokio red and blue edges, figure and landscape decoration. 1 doz. in pkg., asstd..........Doz. 39c

L1692—3½ in., deep, dainty and gold sprays in wreath design, gold edge. Asstd. 3 styles. 1 doz. in pkg.. ....Doz. 36c

JAPANESE CHINA INDIVIDUAL NUT BOWLS.

L5040 L3042

L5040—3 in., white china, floral and gold spray decoration, 3 styles, red, green and blue edges, gold ornamented feet. 1 doz. in pkg., asstd. Doz. 36c

L5042—3¼ in., wide scallop shape, allover Japanese decoration, green edge, gold ornamented, gold trimmed feet. 1 doz. in pkg. Doz. 72c

JAP CHINA FOOTED NUT BOWLS.

L5046—4½ in., 2 floral and gold spray decorations, variegated color band edges, gold decorated feet. 1 doz. in pkg., asstd. Doz. 89c

L5047—*Note the shape and decoration.* 5 in., fluted scallop shape, 2 styles, allover Japanese landscape and floral decoration, gold decorated red and green edges, outside sprays. 1 doz. in pkg., asstd.

Per dozen, $1.25

L5048—6 in., Japanese landscape and figure decoration, delicate colorings, green border edge, outside sprays, gold decorated feet. 1 doz. in pkg. Doz. $1.75

L5050—6 in., fancy scallop shape, chrysanthemum and floral spray decoration on tinted ground, gold ornamented irregular cobalt blue edge and foot, outside sprays. 3 in pkg. Each, 33c

L5054—6 in., fancy squat shape, ball feet, decorated green and richly gold beaded conventional decoration. 3 in pkg. Each, 50c

L5056—8¾ in., fancy flaring shape, fluted, cream ground, gold outlined and beaded floral and leaf decoration, elaborately gold traced cobalt blue edges and feet. 1 in pkg. Each, 72c

L5057—8x7, fancy shape, maroon scroll and gold beaded delicately tinted edge, gold ornamented feet, inside gold outlined and enamel traced shaded rose and leaf decoration on tinted ground. 1 in pkg..................................Each, 89c

L5058—7¼x7¼, new artistic shape, shaded luster ground, iris and leaf gold traced and enameled beaded violet decoration, gold scroll and beaded border band edge, outside sprays, edge and feet. 1 in pkg..................................Each, $1.25

L5064—7¼ in., bowl shape, allover Japanese characteristic figure and landscape gold illuminated decoration, dark green and gold decorated border edge. ½ doz. in pkg.................. ....Doz. ★1.85

Butler Brothers Catalog, 1908.

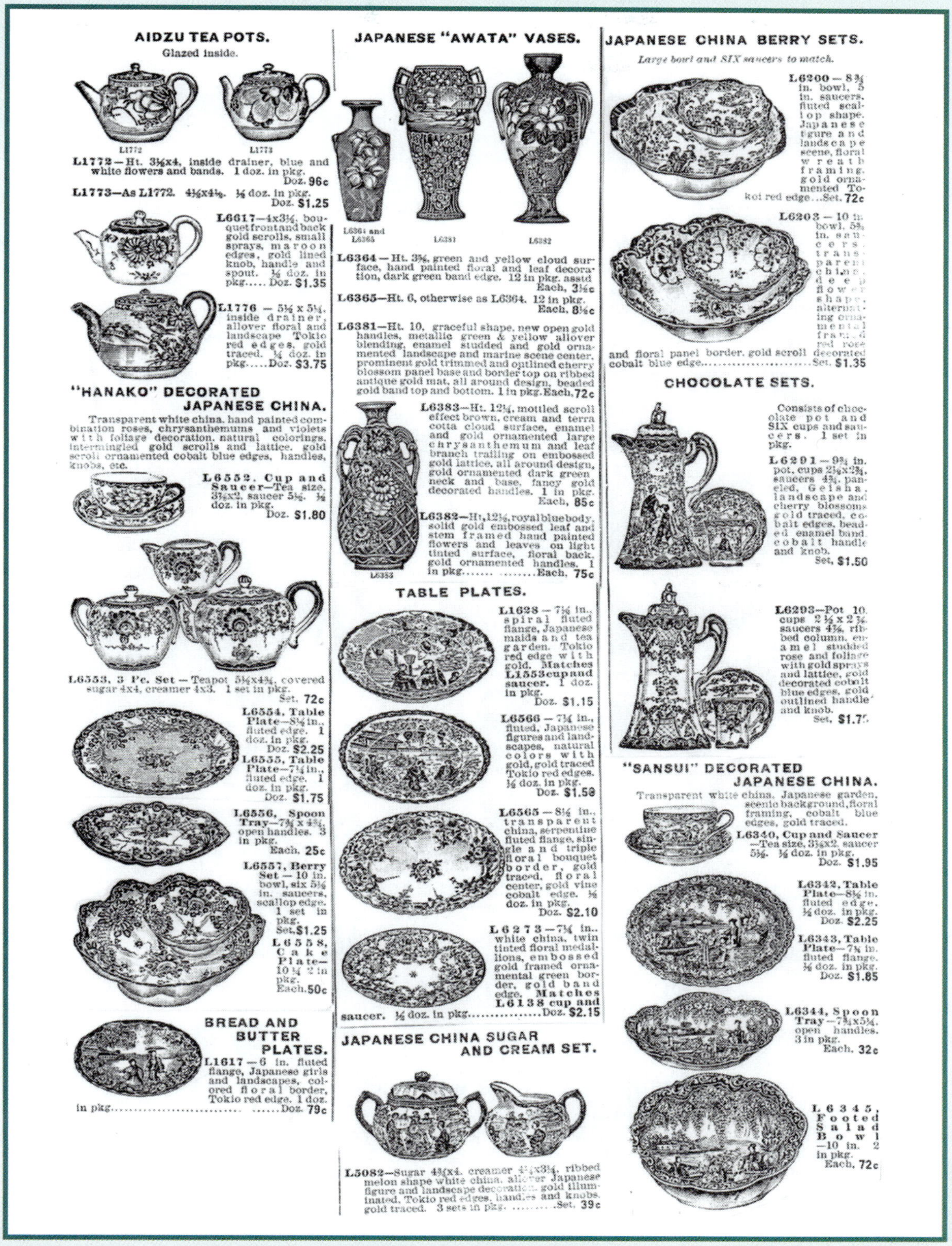

AIDZU TEA POTS.

Glazed inside.

L1772 L1773

L1772—Ht. 3⅛x4, inside drainer, blue and white flowers and bands. 1 doz. in pkg. Doz. 96c

L1773—As L1772. 4⅛x4⅛. ½ doz. in pkg. Doz. $1.25

L6617—4x3¼, bouquet front and back gold scrolls, small sprays, maroon edges, gold lined knob, handle and spout. ½ doz. in pkg..... Doz. $1.35

L1776 — 5½ x 5¼, inside drainer, allover floral and landscape Tokio red edges, gold traced. ¼ doz. in pkg.....Doz. $3.75

"HANAKO" DECORATED JAPANESE CHINA.

Transparent white china, hand painted combination roses, chrysanthemums and violets with foliage decoration, natural colorings, intermingled gold scrolls and lattice, gold scroll ornamented cobalt blue edges, handles, knobs, etc.

L6552. Cup and Saucer—Tea size, 3½x2, saucer 5½. ½ doz. in pkg. Doz. $1.80

L6553. 3 Pc. Set—Teapot 5⅛x4¾, covered sugar 4x4, creamer 4x3. 1 set in pkg. Set. 72c

L6554. Table Plate—8⅛ in., fluted edge. 1 doz. in pkg. Doz. $2.25

L6555. Table Plate—7¼ in., fluted edge. 1 doz. in pkg. Doz. $1.75

L6556. Spoon Tray—7¾ x 4¾, open handles. 3 in pkg. Each. 25c

L6557. Berry Set — 10 in. bowl, six 5⅛ in. saucers, scallop edge. 1 set in pkg. Set. $1.25

L6558. Cake Plate—10¼ 2 in pkg. Each. 50c

BREAD AND BUTTER PLATES.

L1617—6 in. fluted flange, Japanese girls and landscapes, colored floral border, Tokio red edge. 1 doz. in pkg.......Doz. 79c

JAPANESE "AWATA" VASES.

L6364 and L6365 L6381 L6382

L6364—Ht. 3¾, green and yellow cloud surface, hand painted floral and leaf decoration, dark green band edge. 12 in pkg. asstd Each, 3½c

L6365—Ht. 6, otherwise as L6364. 12 in pkg. Each, 8½c

L6381—Ht. 10, graceful shape, new open gold handles, metallic green & yellow allover blending, enamel studded and gold ornamented landscape and marine scene center, prominent gold trimmed and outlined cherry blossom panel base and border top on ribbed antique gold mat, all around design, beaded gold band top and bottom. 1 in pkg. Each, 72c

L6383—Ht. 12¼, mottled scroll effect brown, cream and terra cotta cloud surface, enamel and gold ornamented large chrysanthemum and leaf branch trailing on embossed gold lattice, all around design, gold ornamented dark green neck and base, fancy gold decorated handles. 1 in pkg. Each, 85c

L6383

L6382—Ht. 12½, royal blue body, solid gold embossed leaf and stem framed hand painted flowers and leaves on light tinted surface, floral back, gold ornamented handles. 1 in pkg..............Each, 75c

TABLE PLATES.

L1628—7½ in., spiral fluted flange, Japanese maids and tea garden. Tokio red edge with gold. Matches **L1553 cup and saucer.** 1 doz. in pkg. Doz. $1.15

L6566—7¼ in., fluted, Japanese figures and landscapes, natural colors with gold, gold traced Tokio red edges. ½ doz. in pkg. Doz. $1.50

L6565—8½ in., transparent china, serpentine fluted flange, single and triple floral bouquet border, gold traced, floral center, gold vine cobalt edge. ½ doz. in pkg. Doz. $2.10

L6273—7¼ in., white china, twin tinted floral medallions, embossed gold framed ornamental green border, gold band edge. Matches **L6138 cup and saucer.** ½ doz. in pkg................Doz. $2.15

JAPANESE CHINA SUGAR AND CREAM SET.

L5082—Sugar 4¾x4, creamer 4¼x3¼, ribbed melon shape white china, allover Japanese figure and landscape decoration, gold illuminated, Tokio red edges, handles and knobs gold traced. 3 sets in pkg. ....Set. 39c

JAPANESE CHINA BERRY SETS.

Large bowl and SIX saucers to match.

L6200—8¾ in. bowl, 5 in. saucers, fluted scallop shape, Japanese figure and landscape scene, floral wreath framing, gold ornamented Tokoi red edge...Set. 72c

L6203—10 in. bowl, 5⅝ in. saucers, transparent china, deep flower shape, alternating ornamental framed red rose and floral panel border, gold scroll decorated cobalt blue edge........................Set. $1.35

CHOCOLATE SETS.

Consists of chocolate pot and SIX cups and saucers. 1 set in pkg.

L6291—9¾ in. pot, cups 2⅛x2¾, saucers 4¾, paneled, Geisha, landscape and cherry blossoms gold traced, cobalt edges, beaded enamel band, cobalt handle and knob. Set, $1.50

L6293—Pot 10, cups 2½x2¾, saucers 4¾, ribbed column, enamel studded rose and foliage with gold sprays and lattice, gold decorated cobalt blue edges, gold outlined handle and knob. Set, $1.75

"SANSUI" DECORATED JAPANESE CHINA.

Transparent white china, Japanese garden, scenic background, floral framing, cobalt blue edges, gold traced.

L6340, Cup and Saucer—Tea size, 3⅛x2, saucer 5½. ½ doz. in pkg. Doz. $1.95

L6342, Table Plate—8⅛ in. fluted edge. ½ doz. in pkg. Doz. $2.25

L6343, Table Plate—7¼ in. fluted flange. ½ doz. in pkg. Doz. $1.85

L6344, Spoon Tray—7¾x5¼. open handles. 3 in pkg. Each. 32c

L6345, Footed Salad Bowl—10 in. 2 in pkg. Each, 72c

Butler Brothers Catalog, 1910.

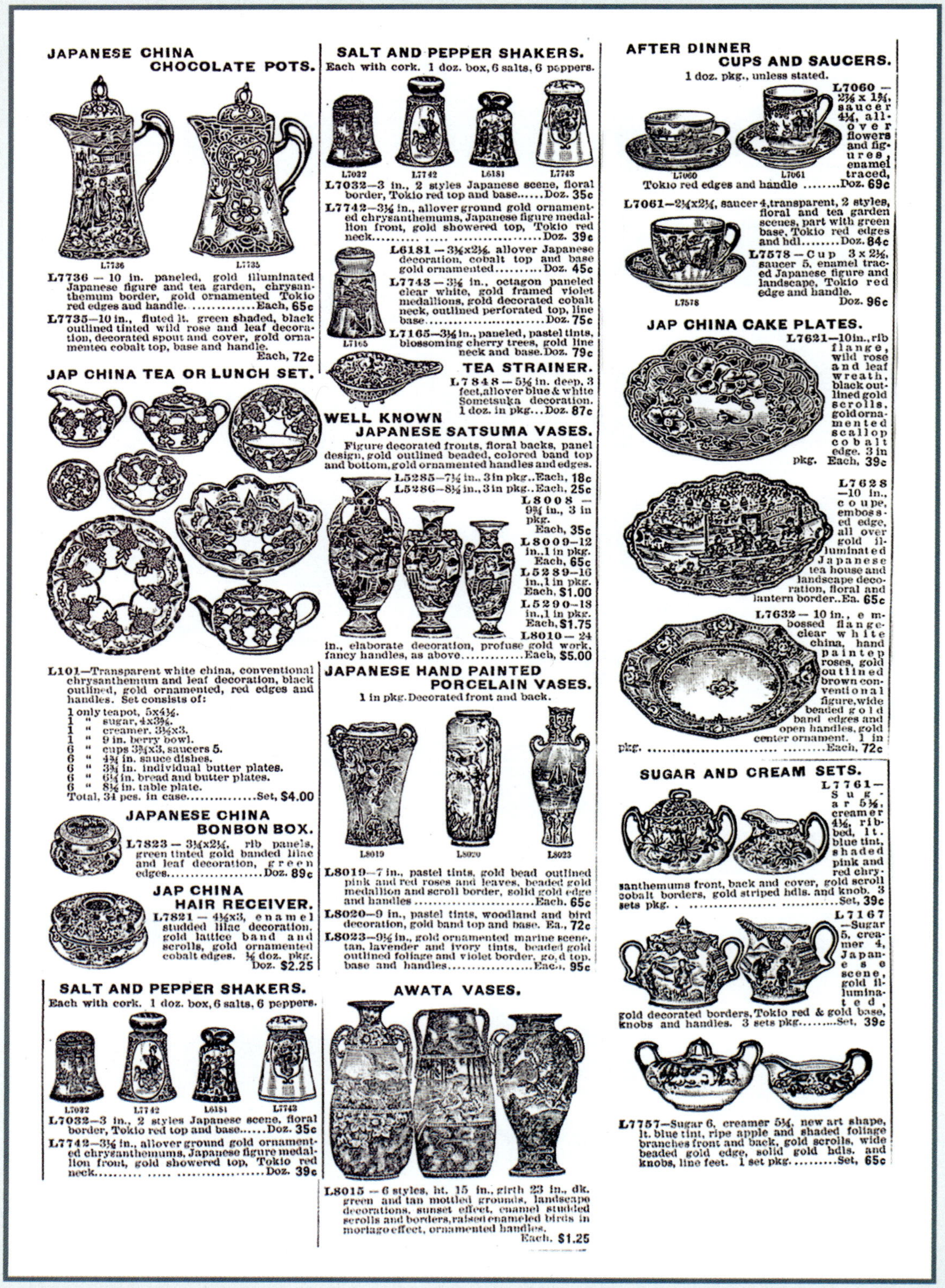

JAPANESE CHINA CHOCOLATE POTS.

L7736 L7735

L7736 — 10 in. paneled, gold illuminated Japanese figure and tea garden, chrysanthemum border, gold ornamented Tokio red edges and handle. ....Each, 65c

L7735—10 in., fluted lt. green shaded, black outlined tinted wild rose and leaf decoration, decorated spout and cover, gold ornamented cobalt top, base and handle. Each, 72c

JAP CHINA TEA OR LUNCH SET.

L101—Transparent white china, conventional chrysanthemum and leaf decoration, black outlined, gold ornamented, red edges and handles. Set consists of:

1 only teapot, 5x4½.
1 " sugar, 4x3⅝.
1 " creamer. 3⅛x3.
1 " 9 in. berry bowl.
6 " cups 3⅜x3, saucers 5.
6 " 4¾ in. sauce dishes.
6 " 3¾ in. individual butter plates.
6 " 6¼ in. bread and butter plates.
6 " 8½ in. table plate.
Total, 34 pcs. in case..............Set, $4.00

JAPANESE CHINA BONBON BOX.

L7823 — 3¼x2¼, rib panels, green tinted gold banded lilac and leaf decoration, green edges...................Doz. 89c

JAP CHINA HAIR RECEIVER.

L7821 — 4⅛x3, enamel studded lilac decoration. gold lattice band and scrolls, gold ornamented cobalt edges. ½ doz. pkg. Doz. $2.25

SALT AND PEPPER SHAKERS.
Each with cork. 1 doz. box, 6 salts, 6 peppers.

L7032 L7742 L6181 L7743

L7032—3 in., 2 styles Japanese scene, floral border, Tokio red top and base......Doz. 35c

L7742—3⅛ in., allover ground gold ornamented chrysanthemums, Japanese figure medallion front, gold showered top, Tokio red neck......... ....Doz. 39c

SALT AND PEPPER SHAKERS.

Each with cork. 1 doz. box, 6 salts, 6 peppers.

L7032 L7742 L6181 L7743

L7032—3 in., 2 styles Japanese scene, floral border, Tokio red top and base......Doz. 35c

L7742—3⅛ in., allover ground gold ornamented chrysanthemums, Japanese figure medallion front, gold showered top, Tokio red neck......... ....Doz. 39c

L6181 — 3⅛x2⅛. allover Japanese decoration, cobalt top and base gold ornamented..........Doz. 45c

L7743 — 3⅛ in., octagon paneled clear white, gold framed violet medallions, gold decorated cobalt neck, outlined perforated top, line base.......................Doz. 75c

L7165

L7165—3⅛ in., paneled, pastel tints, blossoming cherry trees, gold line neck and base. Doz. 79c

TEA STRAINER.

L7848 — 5⅛ in. deep, 3 feet, allover blue & white Sometsuka decoration. 1 doz. in pkg...Doz. 87c

WELL KNOWN JAPANESE SATSUMA VASES.

Figure decorated fronts, floral backs, panel design, gold outlined beaded, colored band top and bottom, gold ornamented handles and edges.

L5285—7½ in.. 3 in pkg..Each, 18c

L5286—8½ in., 3 in pkg..Each, 25c

L8008 — 9¾ in., 3 in pkg. Each, 35c

L8009—12 in., 1 in pkg. Each, 65c

L5289—16 in., 1 in pkg. Each, $1.00

L5290—18 in., 1 in pkg. Each, $1.75

L8010 — 24 in., elaborate decoration, profuse gold work, fancy handles, as above............Each, $5.00

JAPANESE HAND PAINTED PORCELAIN VASES.

1 in pkg. Decorated front and back.

L8019 L8020 L8023

L8019—7 in., pastel tints, gold bead outlined pink and red roses and leaves, beaded gold medallion and scroll border, solid gold edge and handles ....Each. 65c

L8020—9 in., pastel tints, woodland and bird decoration, gold band top and base. Ea., 72c

L8023—9½ in., gold ornamented marine scene, tan, lavender and ivory tints, beaded gold outlined foliage and violet border, go,d top, base and handles.................Each, 95c

AWATA VASES.

L8015 — 6 styles, ht. 15 in., girth 23 in., dk. green and tan mottled grounds, landscape decorations, sunset effect, enamel studded scrolls and borders, raised enameled birds in moriage effect, ornamented handles. Each. $1.25

AFTER DINNER CUPS AND SAUCERS.

1 doz. pkg., unless stated.

L7060 L7061

L7060 — 2⅜ x 1¾, saucer 4¼, allover flowers and figures, enamel traced, Tokio red edges and handle ....Doz. 69c

L7061—2¼x2¼, saucer 4, transparent, 2 styles, floral and tea garden scenes, part with green base, Tokio red edges and hdl........Doz. 84c

L7578

L7578 — Cup 3 x 2½, saucer 5, enamel traced Japanese figure and landscape, Tokio red edge and handle. Doz. 96c

JAP CHINA CAKE PLATES.

L7621—10 in., rib flange, wild rose and leaf wreath, black outlined gold scrolls, gold ornamented scallop cobalt edge. 3 in pkg. Each, 39c

L7628 —10 in., coupe, embossed edge, all over gold illuminated Japanese tea house and landscape decoration, floral and lantern border..Ea. 65c

L7632 — 10 in., embossed flange clear white china, hand paintep roses, gold outlined brown conventional figure, wide beaded gold band edges and open handles, gold center ornament. 1 in pkg. ....Each, 72c

SUGAR AND CREAM SETS.

L7761—Sugar 5½, creamer 4½, ribbed, lt. blue tint, shaded pink and red chrysanthemums front, back and cover, gold scroll cobalt borders, gold striped hdls. and knob. 3 sets pkg. . ...Set, 39c

L7167 —Sugar 5, creamer 4, Japanese scene, gold illuminated, gold decorated borders, Tokio red & gold base, knobs and handles. 3 sets pkg.........Set, 39c

L7757—Sugar 6, creamer 5¼, new art shape, lt. blue tint, ripe apple and shaded foliage branches front and back, gold scrolls, wide beaded gold edge, solid gold hdls. and knobs, line feet. 1 set pkg..........Set, 65c

But-
ler Brothers Catalog, 1912.

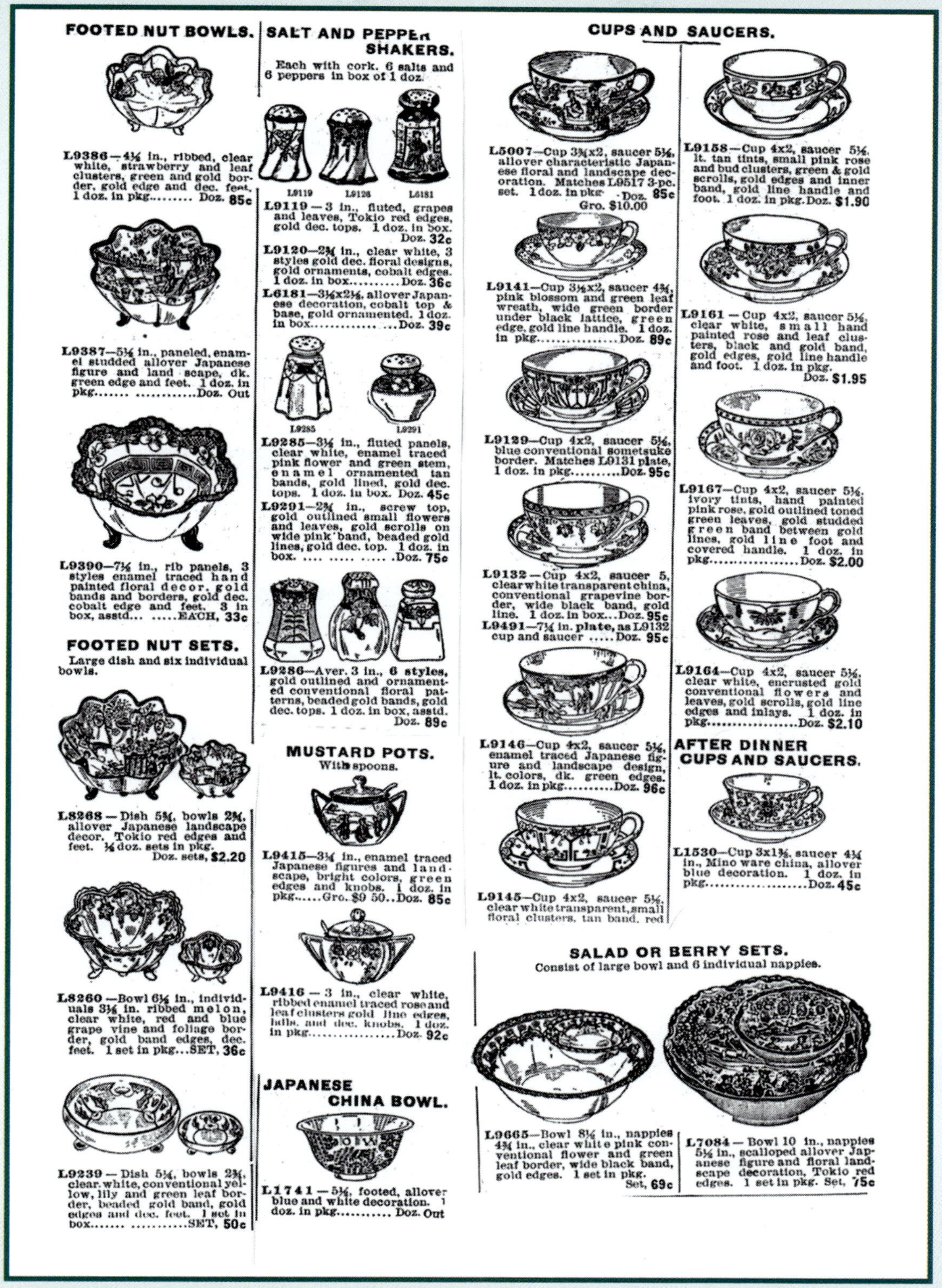

FOOTED NUT BOWLS.

L9386—4½ in., ribbed, clear white, strawberry and leaf clusters, green and gold border, gold edge and dec. feet, 1 doz. in pkg........ Doz. 85c

L9387—5½ in., paneled, enamel studded allover Japanese figure and land scape, dk. green edge and feet. 1 doz. in pkg....... ....Doz. Out

L9390—7½ in., rib panels, 3 styles enamel traced hand painted floral decor, gold bands and borders, gold dec. cobalt edge and feet. 3 in box, asstd... .....EACH, 33c

FOOTED NUT SETS.

Large dish and six individual bowls.

L8268—Dish 5¾, bowls 2¾, allover Japanese landscape decor. Tokio red edges and feet. ½ doz. sets in pkg. Doz. sets, $2.20

L8260—Bowl 6½ in., individuals 3½ in. ribbed melon, clear white, red and blue grape vine and foliage border, gold band edges, dec. feet. 1 set in pkg...SET, 36c

L9239—Dish 5¼, bowls 2¾, clear white, conventional yellow, lily and green leaf border, beaded gold band, gold edges and dec. feet. 1 set in box....... ....SET, 50c

SALT AND PEPPER SHAKERS.

Each with cork. 6 salts and 6 peppers in box of 1 doz.

L9119 L9120 L6181

L9119—3 in., fluted, grapes and leaves, Tokio red edges, gold dec. tops. 1 doz. in box. Doz. 32c

L9120—2¾ in., clear white, 3 styles gold dec. floral designs, gold ornaments, cobalt edges. 1 doz. in box..........Doz. 36c

L6181—3½x2½, allover Japanese decoration, cobalt top & base, gold ornamented. 1 doz. in box..............Doz. 39c

L9285 L9291

L9285—3½ in., fluted panels, clear white, enamel traced pink flower and green stem, enamel ornamented tan bands, gold lined, gold dec. tops. 1 doz. in box. Doz. 45c

L9291—2¾ in., screw top, gold outlined small flowers and leaves, gold scrolls on wide pink band, beaded gold lines, gold dec. top. 1 doz. in box. .... .Doz. 75c

L9286—Aver. 3 in., 6 styles, gold outlined and ornamented conventional floral patterns, beaded gold bands, gold dec. tops. 1 doz. in box, asstd. Doz. 89c

MUSTARD POTS.

With spoons.

L9415—3¾ in., enamel traced Japanese figures and landscape, bright colors, green edges and knobs. 1 doz. in pkg......Gro. $9 50..Doz. 85c

L9416—3 in., clear white, ribbed enamel traced rose and leaf clusters gold line edges, hdls. and dec. knobs. 1 doz. in pkg................Doz. 92c

JAPANESE CHINA BOWL.

L1741—5½, footed, allover blue and white decoration. 1 doz. in pkg.......... Doz. Out

CUPS AND SAUCERS.

L5007—Cup 3¾x2, saucer 5¼, allover characteristic Japanese floral and landscape decoration. Matches L9517 3-pc. set. 1 doz. in pkg Doz. 85c Gro. $10.00

L9141—Cup 3½x2, saucer 4¾, pink blossom and green leaf wreath, wide green border under black lattice, green edge, gold line handle. 1 doz. in pkg...............Doz. 89c

L9129—Cup 4x2, saucer 5½, blue conventional sometsuke border. Matches L9131 plate, 1 doz. in pkg.........Doz. 95c

L9132—Cup 4x2, saucer 5, clear white transparent china, conventional grapevine border, wide black band, gold line. 1 doz. in box...Doz. 95c

L9491—7½ in. plate, as L9132 cup and saucer .....Doz. 95c

L9146—Cup 4x2, saucer 5½, enamel traced Japanese figure and landscape design, lt. colors, dk. green edges. 1 doz. in pkg.........Doz. 96c

L9145—Cup 4x2, saucer 5½, clear white transparent, small floral clusters, tan band, red

L9158—Cup 4x2, saucer 5½, lt. tan tints, small pink rose and bud clusters, green & gold scrolls, gold edges and inner band, gold line handle and foot. 1 doz. in pkg. Doz. $1.90

L9161—Cup 4x2, saucer 5½, clear white, small hand painted rose and leaf clusters, black and gold band, gold edges, gold line handle and foot. 1 doz. in pkg. Doz. $1.95

L9167—Cup 4x2, saucer 5½, ivory tints, hand painted pink rose, gold outlined toned green leaves, gold studded green band between gold lines, gold line foot and covered handle. 1 doz. in pkg.................Doz. $2.00

L9164—Cup 4x2, saucer 5½, clear white, encrusted gold conventional flowers and leaves, gold scrolls, gold line edges and inlays. 1 doz. in pkg.................Doz. $2.10

AFTER DINNER CUPS AND SAUCERS.

L1530—Cup 3x1¾, saucer 4¾ in., Mino ware china, allover blue decoration. 1 doz. in pkg..................Doz. 45c

SALAD OR BERRY SETS.

Consist of large bowl and 6 individual nappies.

L9665—Bowl 8½ in., nappies 4¾ in., clear white pink conventional flower and green leaf border, wide black band, gold edges. 1 set in pkg. Set, 69c

L7084—Bowl 10 in., nappies 5½ in., scalloped allover Japanese figure and floral landscape decoration, Tokio red edges. 1 set in pkg. Set, 75c

Butler Brothers Catalog, 1913 – 1914.

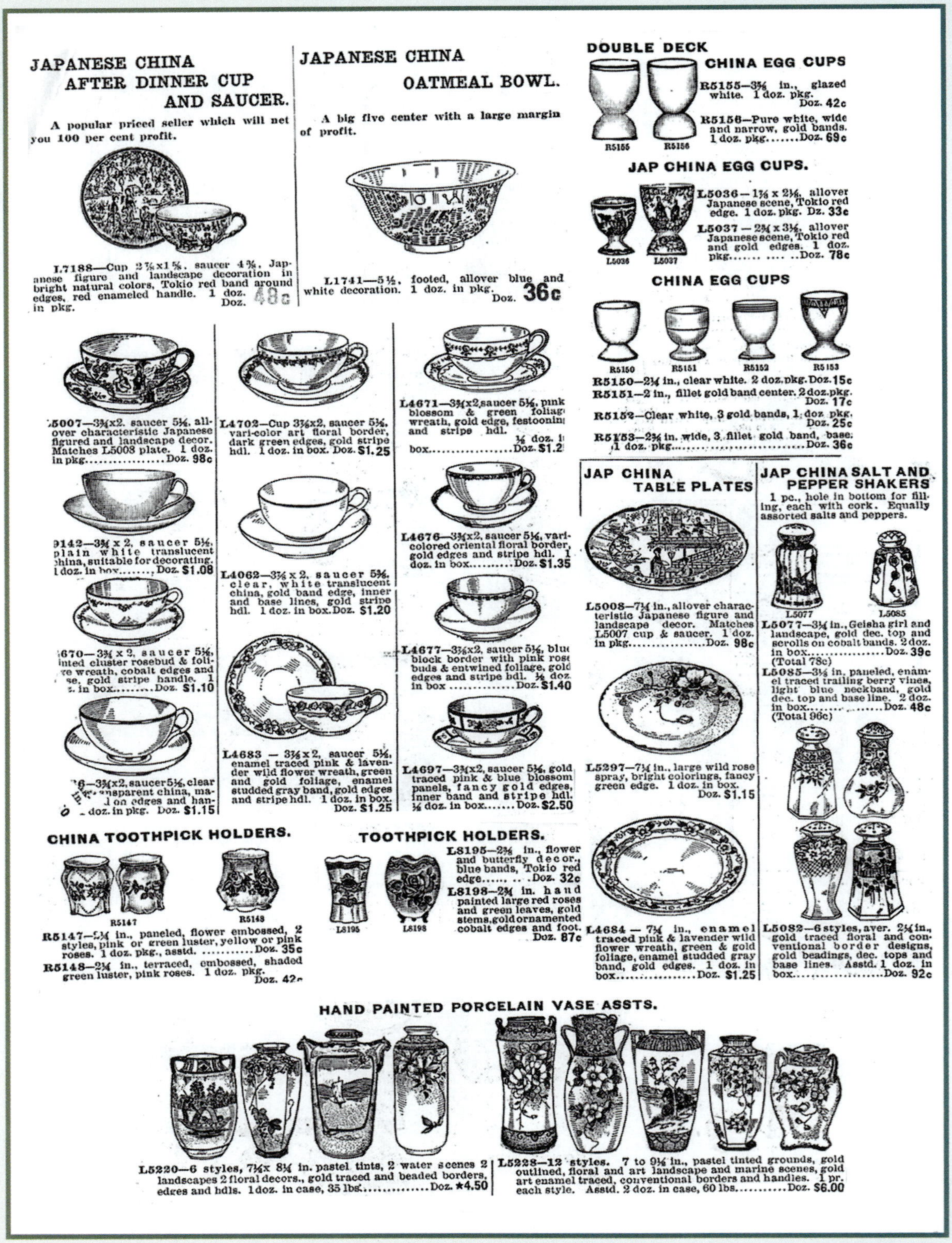

JAPANESE CHINA AFTER DINNER CUP AND SAUCER.

A popular priced seller which will net you 100 per cent profit.

L7188—Cup 2⅞x1⅝, saucer 4⅝, Japanese figure and landscape decoration in bright natural colors, Tokio red band around edges, red enameled handle. 1 doz. in pkg. Doz. 48c

JAPANESE CHINA OATMEAL BOWL.

A big five center with a large margin of profit.

L1741—5½, footed, allover blue and white decoration. 1 doz. in pkg. Doz. 36c

DOUBLE DECK CHINA EGG CUPS

R5155 R5156

R5155—3⅝ in., glazed white. 1 doz. pkg. Doz. 42c

R5156—Pure white, wide and narrow, gold bands. 1 doz. pkg.......Doz. 69c

JAP CHINA EGG CUPS.

L5036 L5037

L5036—1⅞ x 2⅛, allover Japanese scene, Tokio red edge. 1 doz. pkg. Dz. 33c

L5037—2¾ x 3½, allover Japanese scene, Tokio red and gold edges. 1 doz. pkg.......Doz. 78c

CHINA EGG CUPS

R5150 R5151 R5152 R5153

R5150—2¼ in., clear white. 2 doz. pkg. Doz. 15c

R5151—2 in., fillet gold band center. 2 doz. pkg. Doz. 17c

R5152—Clear white, 3 gold bands, 1 doz. pkg. Doz. 25c

R5153—2⅜ in. wide, 3 fillet gold band, base. 1 doz. pkg.......Doz. 36c

L5007—3¾x2, saucer 5½, allover characteristic Japanese figured and landscape decor. Matches L5008 plate. 1 doz. in pkg.......Doz. 98c

9142—3¾ x 2, saucer 5½, plain white translucent china, suitable for decorating. 1 doz. in box.......Doz. $1.08

670—3¾ x 2, saucer 5½, tinted cluster rosebud & foliage wreath, cobalt edges and base, gold stripe handle. 1 doz. in box.......Doz. $1.10

6—3¾x2, saucer 5½, clear transparent china, ... on edges and handle ... doz. in pkg. Doz. $1.15

L4702—Cup 3⅜x2, saucer 5½, vari-color art floral border, dark green edges, gold stripe hdl. 1 doz. in box. Doz. $1.25

L4062—3⅜ x 2, saucer 5⅜, clear, white translucent china, gold band edge, inner and base lines, gold stripe hdl. 1 doz. in box. Doz. $1.20

L4683—3⅜x2, saucer 5½, enamel traced pink & lavender wild flower wreath, green and gold foliage, enamel studded gray band, gold edges and stripe hdl. 1 doz. in box. Doz. $1.25

L4671—3¾x2, saucer 5½, pink blossom & green foliage wreath, gold edge, festooning and stripe hdl. ½ doz. in box.......Doz. $1.25

L4676—3¾x2, saucer 5½, vari-colored oriental floral border, gold edges and stripe hdl. 1 doz. in box.......Doz. $1.35

L4677—3⅜x2, saucer 5½, blue block border with pink rose buds & entwined foliage, gold edges and stripe hdl. ½ doz. in box.......Doz. $1.40

L4697—3¾x2, saucer 5½, gold traced pink & blue blossom panels, fancy gold edges, inner band and stripe hdl. ½ doz. in box.......Doz. $2.50

JAP CHINA TABLE PLATES

L5008—7¼ in., allover characteristic Japanese figure and landscape decor. Matches L5007 cup & saucer. 1 doz. in pkg.......Doz. 98c

L5297—7¼ in., large wild rose spray, bright colorings, fancy green edge. 1 doz. in box. Doz. $1.15

L4684—7¼ in., enamel traced pink & lavender wild flower wreath, green & gold foliage, enamel studded gray band, gold edges. 1 doz. in box.......Doz. $1.25

JAP CHINA SALT AND PEPPER SHAKERS

1 pc., hole in bottom for filling, each with cork. Equally assorted salts and peppers.

L5077 L5085

L5077—3¼ in., Geisha girl and landscape, gold dec. top and scrolls on cobalt bands. 2 doz. in box.......Doz. 39c (Total 78c)

L5085—3⅛ in. paneled, enamel traced trailing berry vines, light blue neckband, gold dec. top and base line. 2 doz. in box.......Doz. 48c (Total 96c)

L5082—6 styles, aver. 2¾ in., gold traced floral and conventional border designs, gold beadings, dec. tops and base lines. Asstd. 1 doz. in box.......Doz. 92c

CHINA TOOTHPICK HOLDERS.

R5147 R5148

R5147—2¼ in., paneled, flower embossed, 2 styles, pink or green luster, yellow or pink roses. 1 doz. pkg., asstd. ....Doz. 35c

R5148—2¼ in., terraced, embossed, shaded green luster, pink roses. 1 doz. pkg. Doz. 42c

TOOTHPICK HOLDERS.

L8195 L8198

L8195—2⅝ in., flower and butterfly decor., blue bands, Tokio red edge.......Doz. 32c

L8198—2¾ in. hand painted large red roses and green leaves, gold stems, gold ornamented cobalt edges and foot. Doz. 87c

HAND PAINTED PORCELAIN VASE ASSTS.

L5220—6 styles, 7½x 8¼ in. pastel tints, 2 water scenes 2 landscapes 2 floral decors., gold traced and beaded borders, edges and hdls. 1 doz. in case, 35 lbs.......Doz. ★4.50

L5228—12 styles. 7 to 9½ in., pastel tinted grounds, gold outlined, floral and art landscape and marine scenes, gold art enamel traced, conventional borders and handles. 1 pr. each style. Asstd. 2 doz. in case, 60 lbs.......Doz. $6.00

Butler Brothers Catalog, 1914 – 1917.

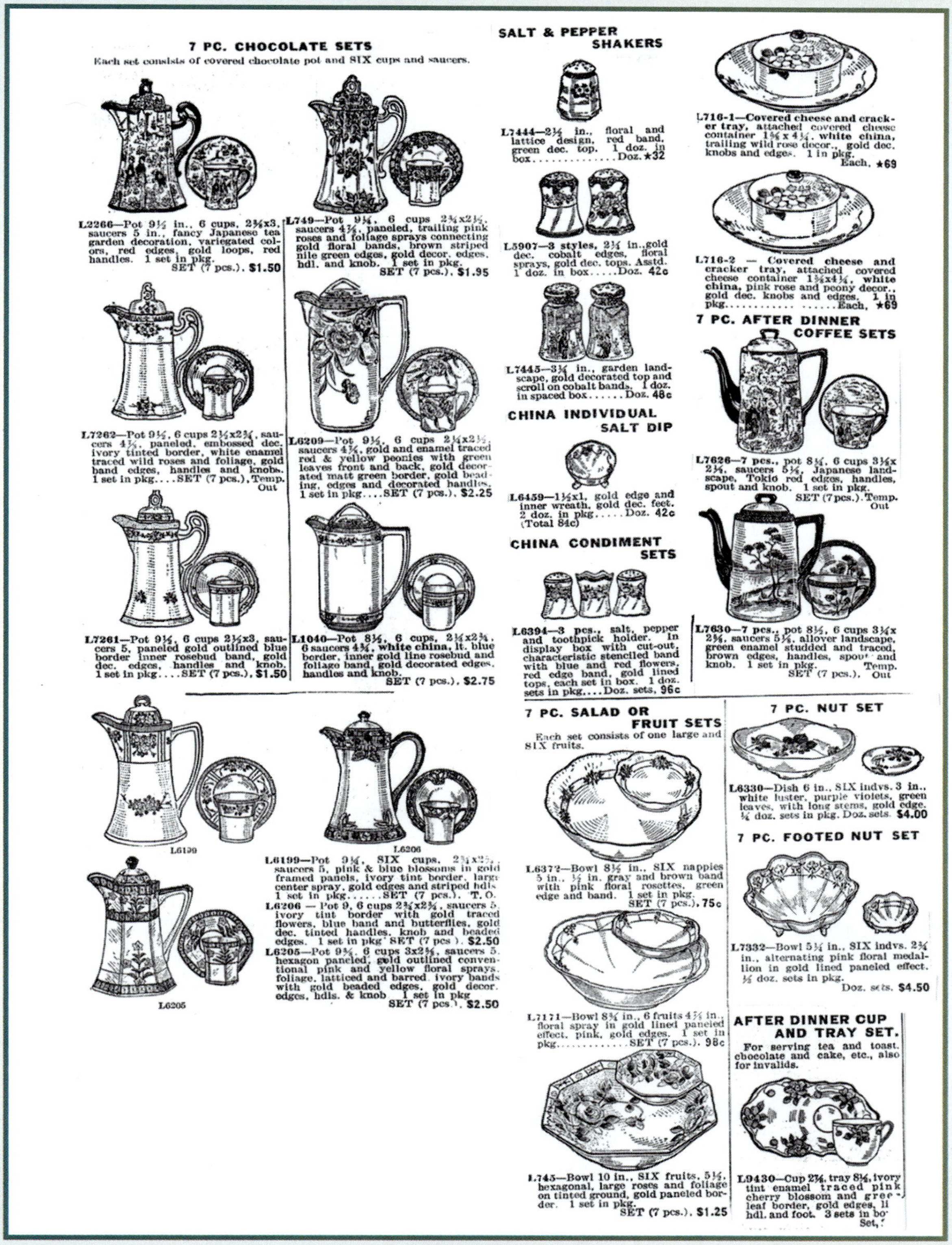

7 PC. CHOCOLATE SETS

Each set consists of covered chocolate pot and SIX cups and saucers.

L2266—Pot 9½ in., 6 cups, 2⅝x3, saucers 5 in., fancy Japanese tea garden decoration, variegated colors, red edges, gold loops, red handles. 1 set in pkg. SET (7 pcs.). **$1.50**

L749—Pot 9¼, 6 cups 2¾x2½, saucers 4¾, paneled, trailing pink roses and foliage sprays connecting gold floral bands, brown striped nile green edges, gold decor. edges, hdl. and knob. 1 set in pkg. SET (7 pcs.). **$1.95**

L7262—Pot 9½, 6 cups 2½x2¾, saucers 4⅗, paneled, embossed dec. ivory tinted border, white enamel traced wild roses and foliage, gold band edges, handles and knobs. 1 set in pkg....SET (7 pcs.), Temp. Out

L6209—Pot 9½, 6 cups 2¼x2½, saucers 4¾, gold and enamel traced red & yellow peonies with green leaves front and back, gold decorated matt green border, gold beading, edges and decorated handles. 1 set in pkg....SET (7 pcs.). **$2.25**

L7261—Pot 9½, 6 cups 2½x3, saucers 5, paneled gold outlined blue border inner rosebud band, gold dec. edges, handles and knob. 1 set in pkg....SET (7 pcs.). **$1.50**

L1040—Pot 8½, 6 cups, 2¼x2¾, 6 saucers 4¾, **white china**, lt. blue border, inner gold line rosebud and foliage band, gold decorated edges, handles and knob. SET (7 pcs.). **$2.75**

L6199

L6206

L6205

L6199—Pot 9¼, SIX cups, 2¾x2½, saucers 5, pink & blue blossoms in gold framed panels, ivory tint border, large center spray, gold edges and striped hdls. 1 set in pkg......SET (7 pcs.). T. O.

L6206 — Pot 9, 6 cups 2¾x2¾, saucers 5, ivory tint border with gold traced flowers, blue band and butterflies, gold dec. tinted handles, knob and beaded edges. 1 set in pkg SET (7 pcs.). **$2.50**

L6205—Pot 9⅝, 6 cups 3x2⅝, saucers 5, hexagon paneled, gold outlined conventional pink and yellow floral sprays, foliage, latticed and barred ivory bands with gold beaded edges, gold decor. edges, hdls. & knob. 1 set in pkg. SET (7 pcs.). **$2.50**

SALT & PEPPER SHAKERS

L7444—2½ in., floral and lattice design, red band, green dec. top. 1 doz. in box..............Doz. **★32**

L5907—3 styles, 2¼ in., gold dec. cobalt edges, floral sprays, gold dec. tops. Asstd. 1 doz. in box.....Doz. **42c**

L7445—3¼ in., garden landscape, gold decorated top and scroll on cobalt bands. 1 doz. in spaced box......Doz. **48c**

CHINA INDIVIDUAL SALT DIP

L6459—1½x1, gold edge and inner wreath, gold dec. feet. 2 doz. in pkg.....Doz. **42c** (Total 84c)

CHINA CONDIMENT SETS

L6394—3 pcs., salt, pepper and toothpick holder. In display box with cut-out, characteristic stenciled band with blue and red flowers, red edge band, gold lined tops, each set in box. 1 doz. sets in pkg....Doz. sets, **96c**

L716-1—Covered cheese and cracker tray, attached covered cheese container 1⅝x4¼, white china, trailing wild rose decor., gold dec. knobs and edges. 1 in pkg. Each, **★69**

L716-2 — Covered cheese and cracker tray, attached covered cheese container 1⅝x4¼, white china, pink rose and peony decor., gold dec. knobs and edges. 1 in pkg.................Each, **★69**

7 PC. AFTER DINNER COFFEE SETS

L7626—7 pcs., pot 8¼, 6 cups 3⅛x 2¼, saucers 5⅛, Japanese landscape, Tokio red edges, handles, spout and knob. 1 set in pkg. SET (7 pcs.). Temp. Out

L7630—7 pcs., pot 8½, 6 cups 3¼x 2⅝, saucers 5⅛, allover landscape, green enamel studded and traced, brown edges, handles, spout and knob. 1 set in pkg. SET (7 pcs.). Temp. Out

7 PC. SALAD OR FRUIT SETS

Each set consists of one large and SIX fruits.

L6372—Bowl 8½ in., SIX nappies 5 in., ½ in. gray and brown band with pink floral rosettes, green edge and band. 1 set in pkg. SET (7 pcs.), **75c**

L7171—Bowl 8¾ in., 6 fruits 4⅞ in., floral spray in gold lined paneled effect, pink, gold edges. 1 set in pkg.............SET (7 pcs.). **98c**

L745—Bowl 10 in., SIX fruits, 5½, hexagonal, large roses and foliage on tinted ground, gold paneled border. 1 set in pkg. SET (7 pcs.). **$1.25**

7 PC. NUT SET

L6330—Dish 6 in., SIX indvs. 3 in., white luster, purple violets, green leaves, with long stems, gold edge. ¼ doz. sets in pkg. Doz. sets. **$4.00**

7 PC. FOOTED NUT SET

L7332—Bowl 5¼ in., SIX indvs. 2¾ in., alternating pink floral medallion in gold lined paneled effect. ½ doz. sets in pkg. Doz. sets. **$4.50**

AFTER DINNER CUP AND TRAY SET.

For serving tea and toast, chocolate and cake, etc., also for invalids.

L9430—Cup 2¾, tray 8½, ivory tint enamel traced pink cherry blossom and gree- leaf border, gold edges, li hdl. and foot. 3 sets in bo Set,

Butler Brothers Catalog, 1918 – 1919.

Noritake Company Design Sketches and Salesman's Pages

Salesman's pages are actual paintings of items that were for sale by the Noritake Company and were shown to prospective customers. Each is hand painted and some even have penciled marks on them, indicating just what the customer had ordered. It is safe to assume that these paintings vary slightly from the finished work, as each artist would paint with different skill. A number of them are stamped "Not for Sale, Salesman Use, Made in Japan." The salesman pages have three holes on the side so that they could be placed in a three-ringed binder. There were eleven Noritake Company salesmen in the United States who would have been in possession of the salesman's pages during this time period. Most were probably thrown out much as we discard catalogs today. These pages are extremely difficult to find and when one is located, it will most likely cost considerably more than the item it portrays. Some collectors who own the salesman's pages enjoy finding the matching items and displaying the pieces together.

The wonderful design sketches used by the Noritake Company are also hand painted and are found in the bound books kept in the archives of the company. Several of these books are on display in glass cabinets at the Noritake Company Museum in Nagoya. The design sketches do not have holes on the side due to being bound in books. As far as collectors know, the museum is the only source for the design sketches.

It is believed that artists from the Noritake design studio in New York City created the majority of the Nippon era patterns and designs, and then they were sent to Japan for the ceramic artists to use as a guide when painting the various wares.

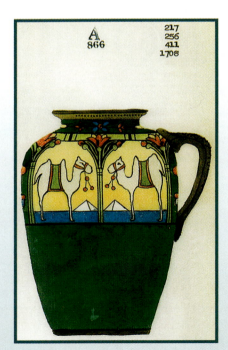

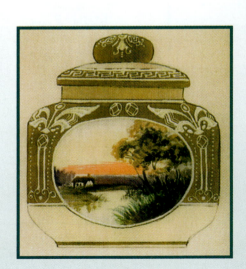

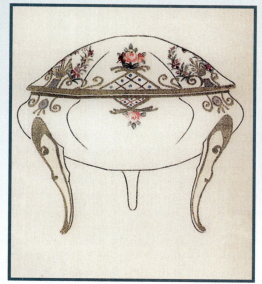

1611
2972/2
2977/12

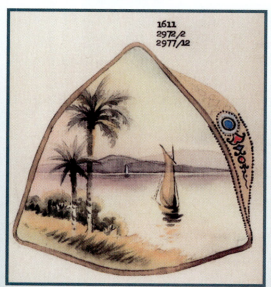

The Morimura Brothers Connection

Mr. Ikuo Fukunaga, an employee of Morimura Shoji (Morimura Brothers in English) provided the following information.

Morimura Shoji is a worldwide import-export company. They currently import various kinds of aluminum and titanium products for aircraft from the United States, bauxite from Brazil, quartz from India, magnesium from Norway, whiskey malt from the United Kingdom, and so on. They also export fine ceramic products and car parts to many countries and distribute tabular alumina produced by Moralco exclusively as the sole agent in the domestic market.

Many years ago, Morimura Brothers (Morimura Gumi in Japanese) gathered a number of potters and craftsmen to produce various ceramics under the Morimura Gumi name. For example, the Kawahara factory in Tokyo, Ishida factory in Kyoto, Saigo factory in Nagoya, and so on were all producing works for Morimura Gumi.

At that time (from the 1890s to 1920s), there were excellent designers working at Morimura Brothers in New York such as Matsutaro Waki, Toranosuke Miyanaga, Yukio Takema, Tadao Waki, and Cyril W. Leigh, an Englishman. They drew very fascinating and very fashionable designs that would appeal to American customers.

Such designs were sent to Morimura Gumi in Tokyo. The people at Morimura Gumi took these designs to the Morimura Gumi factories and gave exact instructions to the potters and craftsmen who had never been in America or Europe. They took the steps necessary to ensure that the potters and craftsmen produced Morimura "fine" china.

At the beginning of the twentieth century, Morimura Gumi decided to centralize their operation in Nagoya and moved their various craftsmen to this location. In 1904, Morimura Gumi set up their own factory, Nippon Toki (now called Noritake Company) to produce the porcelain under their own brand name, Noritake China. Noritake is the name of the place where the factory was built.

The fine china fired in this period is referred to as "old Noritake" especially the "Nippon backstamped porcelain." Morimura Gumi exported china of very high quality.

The leaders of Morimura Gumi in 1910. Back row, left to right: Kaisaku Morimura, second president of Morimura Gumi; Yasukata Murai, general manager of Morimura Bros., Inc.; Kazuchika Okura, the first president of Nippon Toki. Front row, left to right: Magobe Okura, general manager of Morimura Gumi; Ichitaro Morimura, the founder of Morimura Gumi; Saneyoshi Hirose, president of Morimura Bank.

In the middle of the eighteenth century, Ichizaemon Morimura the First arrived in Edo (now called Tokyo) from Enshu (which means a place far away from Kyoto, the old capital of Japan). Edo was the capital of Japan in the Tokugawa era and was gradually becoming a prosperous city in the eighteenth century. The Morimura family began business at a place called Kyobashi near Ginza. Their first venture was to produce saddles and harnesses for horses.

Ichizaemon Morimura the Sixth, the hero of the Morimura Gumi story, succeeded to the family business, and it was his good fortune to be in the right place at the right time. The old Japan was about to give way to a new age of opportunity. An American naval office, Commodore Perry, created this new tide. Perry commanded an American fleet, the East India Squadron. In June 1853, the Perry squadron entered Edo Bay (now called Tokyo Bay). These ships, known as "Kuro Fune" in Japanese, and black ships in English, broke more than 200 years of national isolation. Commodore Perry demanded that Japan should be opened to international trade.

With this step, the floodgates were opened, and Japan was drawn out of isolationism. In 1854, Japan concluded a treaty with America that was called The Treaty of Peace and Amity between the United States of America and the Empire of Japan. This was the first treaty Japan concluded with a foreign country. In 1859, Japan opened three ports, Yokohama, Kobe, and Nagasaki to trade.

On July 4, 1859, American Independence Day, a consulate was set up at the Honkaku Temple in Kanagawa near Yokohama. A young American by the name of Eugene Miller Van Reed was one of the legation members. He was an assistant to the consul, General Dorr. Soon after this, Van Reed opened his own company in the Yokohama foreign settlement and began to live there.

Maybe, if Ichizaemon Morimura had not met this American, Van Reed, there would not have been a Morimura Gumi or any Nippon porcelain. Ichizaemon was a man of enterprise who went to Yokohama soon after the opening of this treaty port to seek a business opportunity. In a short time Ichizaemon became a trader who bought foreign goods at Yokohama to sell them in Edo. He visited Van Reed's firm many times. He heard from Van Reed about America and the world in general. This information motivated him to think about a business venture overseas.

Eugene Van Reed was born in 1835 in Reading, Pennsylvania. The date of his birth is not recorded on his gravestone at the Oak Hill Memorial Park, San Jose, California.

The reason why Van Reed came to Japan may be due to a chance meeting in his youth. In September 1850, the Japanese cargo ship Sumiyoshi Maru was wrecked in a storm on its way from Osaka to Edo. The ship drifted in the Pacific for more than 50 days. Seventeen sailors were eventually rescued by the American merchant ship Oakland and brought to San Francisco.

Eugene Van Reed (who was fifteen years old at this time) and his father had moved from Reading to San Francisco. There, Eugene Van Reed met one of the shipwrecked sailors, Hikozo Hamada, a Japanese boy who was two years younger than himself. He learned elementary Japanese from Hikozo and took an interest in Japan, an unknown country.

Fortunately, the Japanese boy Hikozo came across what is called a long-legged uncle or a patron by the name of Thunders, a banker from Baltimore. Thunders brought this boy to his house to educate him in Baltimore in 1853. Hikozo attended a mission school and was baptized as a Catholic. After this, he became known as Joseph Heco and was the first Japanese to be naturalized as an American citizen, in 1858.

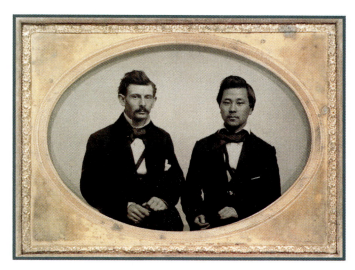

Left: Eugene Miller Van Reed (1835 – 1873).
Right: Hikozo Hamada/Joseph Heco (1837 – 1897).

In June 1858, Joseph Heco visited Reading to see Eugene Van Reed. Joseph Heco wrote in his autobiography *The Narrative of a Japanese*, "I was given a heart-warming welcome in Reading." It was a trip to say goodbye to Van Reed. In July, soon after this, Joseph left Baltimore and on September 26, 1858, set sail for Japan from San Francisco on board a surveying schooner, the *Fenimore Cooper*.

After Joseph Heco left America, Van Reed felt an even greater desire to see Japan for himself. Van Reed asked his friend, Jacob Knabb, who was the chief editor of *Berks and Schuylkill Journal*, a Reading newspaper, to appoint him as a correspondent for the newspaper. After getting Knabb's approval, Van Reed hurried back to San Francisco.

On February 2, 1859, he took passage on a clipper called the *Sea Serpent* from San Francisco. Margaret, Van Reed's younger sister, said in her later years, "My brother started for Japan being urged by the spirit of adventure." On April 6, Van Reed arrived in Hong Kong, where he wrote "California to Japan." This article appeared in the newspaper, *Berks and Schuylkill Journal* on June 25.

Ichizaemon Morimura, who learned various things about the foreign world, such as the state of affairs in America from Van Reed, persuaded his younger brother, Toyo, to enter the Keio Gijyuku University with the idea of making him proficient in English. Ichizaemon thought that English would be necessary if they were to begin a foreign trade venture.

Two years later in 1878, this partnership was dissolved and Toyo became independent. Hinode Shokai was reorganized and became Morimura Brothers. Morimura Gumi in Tokyo collected various Japanese goods, such as antiques, china, bronze, fans, dolls, and so on, and forwarded them to Hinode Shokai and Morimura Bros. These Japanese goods sold very well for good prices. Morimura Brothers in New York City began to get prosperous, and this situation continued until World War II.

The fine china line, a new business of Morimura Gumi and Morimura Brothers began in about 1887. Japan had a long tradition of producing fine quality china, and Morimura Gumi enlisted the services of many factories and craftsmen around the country.

Van Reed riding his horse on the grounds of his house at No. 33 in the foreign settlement.

In the spring of 1876, Ichizaemon and his younger brother, Toyo, established a small company, Morimura Gumi at their family store, Ginza, Tokyo. On March 10, Toyo went on board an American liner, the *Oceanic*, with four colleagues, who wished to learn American business under the supervision of Momotaro Sato, who had stayed many years in America. He had learned business at commercial schools and had already set up his own company on Front Street in Manhattan.

On April 10, 1876, the *Oceanic* group arrived in New York. After finishing a short course at the Eastman Business College in Poughkeepsie, New York, Toyo Morimura established a retail store named Hinode Shokai meaning "Rising Sun Firm" at 258 Sixth Street, New York City, in a partnership with Momotaro Sato, and another colleague, each of whom invested $3,000.00.

Noritake dinnerware of a pure white color produced by Nippon Toki was introduced in 1914, after a ten year trial-and-error period, with great success. From this point on Nippon Toki began to produce less and less hand-painted fine china.

By coincidence, this was the year that saw the outbreak of war in Europe. This prevented American merchants from importing bisque dolls from Europe, that were mainly produced in France and Germany. The American market ran short of stock, and this created a favorable situation for Morimura Gumi to establish a factory for producing bisque dolls in Nagoya.

As a first step, Morimura Gumi set up a ceramic research laboratory for the production of ceramic toys on the site of the Nippon Toki factory in March 1916. In 1917, Morimura Gumi established

Nippon Gangu (Japan Toy) Co. with a capital of 200,000 yen and constructed a factory for making Morimura bisque dolls at Sanbon Aze 1,616, Sakou-cho, Nishiku, Nagoya. Hirose Jikko was made president and Yamachi Torataro, general manager.

On this project, Morimura Gumi worked in concert with Frobel House, a playthings shop in Kanda, Tokyo, which still exists at Kanda Ogawa-cho 3-1, Chou-ku, Tokyo. Frobel House provided technical assistance and dispatched some personnel to Nippon Gangu. Morimura Brothers distributed the so-called Morimura bisque dolls in the American market.

However, World War I drew to a close in 1918, and the European producers returned to the American market. Although the quality of Morimura bisque dolls was on a par with that of European products, Morimura Brothers were forced to withdraw from the American market as they were unable to compete on price with the devaluation of European currencies. Nippon Gangu closed its door in 1921.

Morimura Brothers Store, New York City, 1879.

The business activities of Morimura Brothers in the United States continued for 65 years until 1941, the beginning of World War II.

Dinner celebration in honor of the 40th anniversary of Morimura Brothers and the opening of their new building at No. 53-55-57 W. 23rd St., New York, February 9, 1917.

U.S. Companies Giving Nippon Porcelain as Premiums

Several companies in the United States gave Nippon Porcelain as premiums. Three well-known ones are…
The Manning Bowman Company, S&H Stamps, and the Jewel Tea Company.

ᐧ *The Manning Bowman Connection* ᐧ

Some Nippon pieces were designed to be placed in metal holders of either polished copper or nickel plate. All are engraved with the words Manning Bowman Quality, Meriden, Connecticut, along with their catalog number.

The Manning Bowman Company was founded in Middletown, Connecticut, in 1832 and moved to Meriden, Connecticut, in 1872. They specialized in manufacturing pots, pans, ladles, and funnels, which were peddled throughout nearby towns by horse and wagon.

To date, all the Nippon china found with these metal containers has been backstamped with the magenta M in wreath mark, which means that the porcelain was manufactured and decorated by the Noritake Company. Some pieces have also been found with the initials MB in gold. The Nippon porcelain items found with these copper and nickel plated wares are referred to as imported hand-decorated china in the old Manning Bowman catalogs. It's easy to imagine that some of these holders have disappeared over the years and that pieces we now own may have originally been sold as a set from Manning Bowman.

Some of the Nippon items sold by Manning Bowman were bon-bon dishes, mayonnaise or whipped cream bowls, dessert sets, almond sets, fruit bowls, salad bowls, tea ball tea pots, coffee sets, bouillon cups, sherbet cups, olive dishes, serving trays, cake trays, comports, and berry sets.

Demitasse cups and holders, 2" tall,
Manning Bowman, magenta mark #47, $60.00 – 85.00.

Bouillon cups and holders, Manning Bowman,
holders are 6¼" wide including handles,
magenta mark #47, $70.00 – 90.00 each.

Sherbet cup, #2202, 4¹/₄" tall, magenta mark #47, each holds
6 oz., $70.00 – 90.00 each.

Sherbet close-up.

⌒ *S&H Stamps* ⌒

Remember those little green stamps? Years ago, we got them when we made a purchase at the local gas station or grocery market. They were pasted in the booklets provided by S&H and when the required amount had been saved they could be redeemed at the local Sperry & Hutchinson redemption center for an array of goodies. What fun! Something for free!

So what does this have to do with Nippon era (1891 – 1921) porcelain? Recently when I was on one of my shopping expeditions, I found a large, heavily enameled, jeweled vase that had a paper sticker affixed to the bottom. A large 18" vase is always exciting to locate, but one bearing a sticker with "This premium given in exchange for three books filled with the Sperry and Hutchinson green trading stamps" printed on it was really a find. The vase has a blue maple leaf backstamp that indicates manufacture between 1891 – 1911 by the Morimuras/Noritake Co. in Nagoya, Japan. It's about 100 years old, and the sticker never got washed off during this entire time period!

S&H began issuing trading stamps (small pieces of gummed paper) in 1896. The first redemption center opened in 1897 so that dates this particular vase between 1897 and 1911. S&H sold its stamps to retailers for use as customer incentives. The retailers gave the stamps to consumers, typically at a rate of one for each ten cents worth of purchases as a bonus for their patronage. Consumers would then paste the stamps in books of 1,200 and exchange the books for "gifts" at S&H redemption centers.

Although S&H stamps are no longer being given out nationwide as in the past, the Sperry and Hutchinson Co. is still in business. And yes, people still are pasting green stamps in books. But the company has also gone high tech. You can now use a small card about the size of a credit card when you make your purchase. It's swiped on a machine and the number of the stamps you earned is automatically tallied and recorded for future redemption. No more Saturday afternoons spent pasting stamps in those little books!

The Sperry and Hutchinson Company presently has an office in New York City, and in their lobby one can view an old Rolodex that was once used at a redemption center during the early years. They have no old catalogs from the Nippon era in their files, but the cards used in the Rolodex are large, approximately 7¹/₂" x 13¹/₂" in size, and featured all types of items from paintings to pickle casters, and yes, there were Japanese items. Although the Rolodex is locked in a plastic case, one of the employees was kind enough to go through the cards and photocopy those featuring Nippon items.

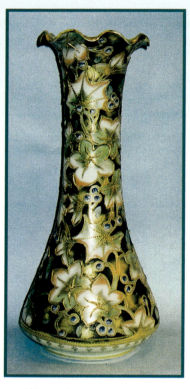

18" vase that has S&H sticker on bottom (shown below), blue mark #52, $4,000.00 – 5,000.00.

The first cards of the Rolodex have printed: "Just look at the premiums on the next page — don't you wish you had one? It's easy! They cost you nothing." "Collect S&H Green Stamps. Delay is waste. Begin earning a valuable premium today by collecting 'S&H' Green Stamps." Only two cards had Nippon era items featured, but what a treat it was to see the premiums given years ago.

It's been known that Nippon items were given as premiums for both the Larkin and Jewel Tea Company, but now S&H can be added to this list.

From the Sperry and Hutchinson Company archives is a news article featured in *The Daily Chronicle* in 1897. It shows a photo of the first S&H redemption center that was opened in February of that year. The article goes on to say:

> *"Sensational new notion of Sperry Hutchinson is really catching on! They call them green stamps, and they're going through the roof.*
>
> *"It's a brand new idea in marketing and it's catching on like crazy. Some industry bigs predict it could transform the whole business if its success rate keeps up this pace.*
>
> *"S&H Green Stamps is what the new company calls its concept. It is so simple and yet so effective that the main question being asked is why didn't anybody think of it before?*
>
> *"Picture this. You're about to leave the store after buying your usual weekly groceries and the clerk hands you some little green stamps. The more groceries you buy, the more stamps you get. When you get home, you paste them into a booklet provided by the S&H people.*
>
> *"When you have enough stamps, you take your books to a special shop and redeem them for a gift. A real nice gift, too, if the S&H catalogue is anything to go by.*
>
> *"Sperry and Hutchinson, the clever new corporation that thought up the notion told me that the catalogue will be regularly updated with some of the finest brand names in the country gracing its pages.*
>
> *"How does it work? Amazingly simple. The benefits to the retailer are just as great as those to the average Joe like you and me. The terrific giveaways so attract clientele that market owners are posting record sales. And all because of the little stamps."*

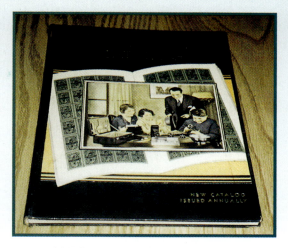

Right: Close-up of Rolodex.

S&H Green Stamp Merchants Redemption
Catalog from early 1920s.

Left: Old Rolodex in lobby of S&H
Company in New York City.

✑ *The Jewel Tea Company* ✑

Nippon era items were both inexpensive and plentiful. They could be found in the five and dimes, department stores, and souvenir shops, anywhere and everywhere. And recently, I discovered that they were also given as premiums by the Jewel Tea Company.

As a little girl, I can remember seeing the Jewel Tea man drive up and down our rural highway and, of course, he stopped every two weeks or so at my grandmother's house. She bought vanilla and other baking supplies from him as well as obtaining pieces of the Autumn Leaf Hall china. For years I thought that was the only premium the Jewel Tea Company offered. But, lo and behold, much to my surprise and delight, I discovered that Nippon items were offered as premiums during the early years. One glance at the old ads in the booklet "Jewel Ways" and collectors will immediately recognize the chocolate sets, vases, lemonade sets, berry sets, sweetmeat sets — the lists goes on and on. Three special ladies helped me in my hunt — Gwynneth Harrison, Harriet Kurshadt, and Catherine Otto. Gwynn got me started and led me to the others.

Catherine wrote to me telling of the "special" vase she had passed down to her. Her grandmother resided in South Baltimore, Maryland, in the early 1900s, and from the time Catherine was a little girl, she knew the story of the vase. Her grandmother had received it as a premium for buying Jewel Tea products. She, too, can remember the Jewel Tea man coming every two weeks or so in a truck marked with the Jewel Tea logo.

Her grandmother and mother would buy vanilla, tea, assorted spices, and other food items. When her grandmother died in the early 1940s, her mother inherited the vase. When Catherine's mother died, it became hers. She says it means the world to her because it has remained in the family for so many years.

Because Catherine remembers the circumstances so vividly, we now know for certain that this particular piece is one of the premiums of the Jewel Tea Company and bore the backstamp shown below.

Gwynn has located two lemonade cups that look like those featured in one of the old ads. The mark is our China E-Oh backstamp. She wonders if it could be a logo for the Jewel Tea Company. The letters JT were incorporated in some of their other backstamps, so perhaps she's right. Maybe further research will give us the answer.

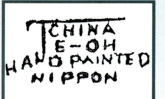

Front view.

Back view.

Most items bearing the China E-Oh backstamp are not of the same fine quality as our Noritake Company wares, but that is probably to be expected since they were premiums given by the Jewel Tea Company. The sweetmeat set shown below is typical of these premiums. The case is 12" across and each crescent dish measures 5$^{1}/_{2}$" across. Only the center dish is backstamped.

From *Sharing*, a publication for the
People of Jewel Companies, Inc.

JEWEL WAYS
9

Place These Articles of Specified Merchandise in Every Home

No. 1225. Price..$2.50.

The attractive Oriental decorations make these Chocolate Sets highly desirable for Jewel customers. White body and gold border.

No. 617. Price...$2.50.

A Chocolate Set is always in demand and this one in particular. It is decorated with Oriental figures in native costumes on a white background

No. 761. Price...$2.50.

The floral design on a white body is much sought after by admirers of hand painted china. We have a limited number of these Coffee Sets.

No. 1850. Price...$2.50.

Here is the ever wanted Pansy design on the popular white body of the Coffee Set. The pretty shape of the cups is also attractive.

No. 7221. Price...$2.50.

Because the artists painted Violets and other flowers in profusion, some salesmen have placed dozens of these Coffee Sets among their customers.

No. 1852. Price...$2.25.

Once more are red and pink roses used with telling effect on these popular Chocolate Sets. The border is Blue and Gold.

1916 – 1917 "Jewel Ways."

10
JEWEL WAYS

Advance Your Customers THIS IMPORTED Hand-Painted China

No. 1730. Price..$2.50.

At this time of the year, our salesmen place thousands of these beautiful Berry Sets. This one shows hand painted water-lilies on a white background, with tracings of gold.

No. 1852. Price..$2.00.

Our stock of Berry Sets as pictured above is now at its best. But red and pink roses of such dainty appearance are popular.

No. 2160. Sweet Meat Sets.
Red Case — Landscape Design.
No. 2161. Green case—Bird and flower design. Price.........$3.00
Sweet Meat Sets are always desirable as presents.

No. 1206. Price..$2.00.

This Berry Set is also used for Ice Cream. It has an artistic floral design on a white body. The border is of gold. Only a few remaining.

No. 1225. Price..$2.50.

For those who desire a genuine Oriental pattern on a Berry Set, the above is recommended. The body is white with tracings of gold.

1916 – 1917 "Jewel Ways."

No. 357.
Price.......$2.50

This 16-inch hand painted vase with pink rose design on greenish-tan background makes a very attractive ornament for the living room.

No. 433.
Price.......$2.50

This is a handsome 16-inch hand-painted vase with richly colored Japanese figures, that ought to be very popular with all who have a taste for the oriental.

1916 – 1917 "Jewel Ways."

JEWEL WAYS

Advance Your Customers THIS IMPORTED Hand-Painted China

No. 1730. Price..$2.50.
At this time of the year, our salesmen place thousands of these beautiful Berry Sets. This one shows hand painted water-lilies on a white background, with tracings of gold.

No. 1852. Price..$2.00.
Our stock of Berry Sets as pictured above is now at its best. But red and pink roses of such dainty appearance are popular.

No. 2160. Sweet Meat Sets.
Red Case — Landscape Design.
No. 2161. Green case—Bird and flower design. **Price.........$3.00**
Sweet Meat Sets are always desirable as presents.

No. 1206. Price..$2.00. **No. 1225. Price..$2.50.**

1916 – 1917 "Jewel Ways."

No. 1730 — Price $2.75
Water lillies in profusion decorate this Popular Lemonade Set of 7 Pieces.

THOUSANDS of pieces of imported china have been distributed throughout the entire Jewel System during the past three weeks.

Customers are only too eager to have these handsome articles of specified merchandise presented to them, many never before having had the opportunity to acquire such longed-for things.

Tell your patrons how fortunate you are in being able to deliver these articles inasmuch as very few stores in the country are able to obtain them at any price. Assure them that it is all genuine, hand painted china, imported especially for this company.

JEWEL TEA CO., Inc.

1916 – 1917 "Jewel Ways."

JAPANESE CHINA

We carry a complete line of Fancy Japanese China, including the following items: Vases, Chocolate Sets, Lemonade Sets, Dresser Sets, Cake Sets, Berry Sets, Coffee Sets, Table Sets, Cups and Saucers, Sugars, Creamer and Tea Pot Sets, Cracker Sets, Fancy Plates, Salads, Bon Bon Dishes, Chop Plates, Fern Dishes, Tankards and Sweet Meat Sets.

1917 Merchandise Price List.

Manners, Culture, and Dress in the Nippon Era

The time period that items were backstamped with the word Nippon spanned from 1891 to 1921, the Gay Nineties to the Roaring Twenties. The porcelain reflected what was happening during that era not only with the various designs found but also with the numerous types of items that were manufactured.

The Victorian period historically ended in 1901, but its influence lasted until the outbreak of World War I in 1914. During this time, there was a compulsion to purchase, accumulate, and display possessions. Clutter was in and there was bric-a-brac everywhere.

In the Edwardian age, there was great ostentation and extravagance. Beginning in 1908 you could even purchase a home from Sears Roebuck. You just had to wait for the boxcar to arrive. It was possible to order a two-room cottage to a twelve-room residence.

Catalogs doubled as school aids. Children would practice their arithmetic by adding up orders, they could study geography from postal zone maps and all contained poetry and household tips. The Butler Brothers Company was a mail-order wholesaler to mainly country merchants and provided a wide range of items through their catalogs. Montgomery Ward and Sears Roebuck sold Nippon wares in their stores and through their catalogs.

In 1905, Sears began the Iowaization scheme. They sent two dozen catalogs to each Iowa customer and asked them to give the catalogs to friends and relatives. Then the customers were instructed to send in these names, which were monitored by Sears. Premiums were sent to those who got new customers for the company.

The Jewel Tea Company, Sperry and Hutchinson (S&H), and the Larkin Co. also gave premiums of Nippon wares to their customers. Nippon marked items were found everywhere.

In 1900, unskilled workers made an average of $8.37 a week and a girl of 12 – 13 tending a textile loom got $2.00 a week. By 1918, a woman working in a factory, six days a week made $1.50 a day. The average workweek in 1914 was 55 hours. Rent was $9.00 – 12.00 a month for the working class and food for a couple was $3.00 – 4.00 a week. In that same year, five cents could purchase three rolls or donuts or an order of coffee and hotcakes or a quarter of a pie! However, when America entered World War I labor got a boost and so did wages.

In 1915 many rural families and city dwellers still had no running water. The kitchen usually held an icebox, as refrigerators only became available around the late 1910s. Coal stoves heated most homes and records show that over 7,000 models had been patented by 1919. But this required an hour a day just to shuttle the coal, tend the fire, and sift the ashes. Cleaning house took enormous time and effort. There usually was no electricity and no indoor plumbing. Dishwater, cooking slops, and chamber pots had to be taken outside. It's been estimated that the average housewife spent 27 hours a week cleaning her home.

Victorians took dining very seriously. In the grandest homes, elaborate dinners were served entirely by servants and the wealthy were helpless without their staff. In middle-class households, however, the residents had to do more work.

Dining etiquette required that conversation must be kept going but it was unheard of to chatter across the table. At the beginning of the meal, the hostess began conversing with the gentleman on her right, and the other ladies opened discussion with the gentlemen on their right. They talked through the first course and then, as the next course was served, the hostess began talking to the man on her left. All the other ladies followed suit. This was called "turning the table." At the end of the meal, the hostess put her napkin on the table, gathered up her gloves, looked at the other ladies, and stood up. The gentlemen stood as well and pulled back the chairs as the ladies filed from the table. The ladies clustered together in the ornate, feminine parlor while the men remained in the dining room. The tablecloth was removed, and decanters of wine and brandy were circulated — always clockwise as counterclockwise was considered bad luck. Dining in the Victorian era was never considered just eating. It was taken very seriously and many people suffered a great deal of anxiety about the manners required.

Dining etiquette manuals were published to instill a more aristocratic style of behavior, and etiquette has never strayed very far from its original intent: to protect rulers from contact with "lesser persons." (See illustrations on next page.)

Calling cards were part of proper etiquette during this time period. They were also called name cards or visiting cards and visitors were expected to furnish themselves with these cards. Though the ritual of paying calls was time consuming, it provided a system for forming and maintaining friendships. Women had what was called a "visiting list." And it was necessary to call on everyone at least twice a year. Of course, calls were made more often between closer friends, and it was always necessary to make calls in cases of illness, bereavement, or after being entertained by someone. These calls had to be returned, for a lack of reciprocity meant a resolution to discontinue the friendship!

On the visiting card, the address was usually placed under the name, towards the bottom of the card, and in smaller letters. Mourning cards were surmounted with a broad black margin about a ¼" in size, whereas half mourning only required a small black edge.

Calling cards were once the size of playing cards, but by the middle of the nineteenth century, the cards had shrunk to the dimensions of today's business cards.

In an old album of collected calling cards were the words "a left corner fold indicates that it's family, a right corner fold means a Mr. and Mrs., and no fold indicates that it is a single person."

before a return visit was made. People in this way gave you notice whether they wished to see you often or seldom.

Gentlemen could simply put their calling cards into their pockets, but ladies usually carried them in a small elegant portfolio, called a card-case.

The telephone gradually replaced calling cards and today, calling card trays from the Nippon era are difficult to locate. (Photos on next page.)

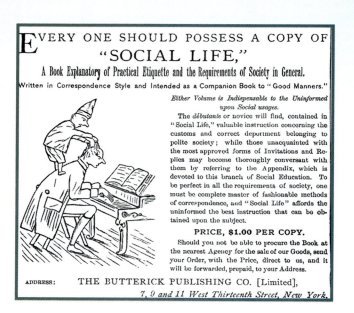

The "call" consisted of a ceremonial visit lasting ten to fifteen minutes in length. The visiting lady did not even remove her hat or gloves; she merely perched on the edge of a chair with her purse on her lap. Both ladies made small talk and then the visitor would leave her card on the way out. There would be an appropriate receptacle for cards on the front hall table.

There were special rules for visiting as well. Visits of ceremony must be necessarily short. They were not to be made before the hour, nor yet during the time of luncheon. One should ascertain what the family hour for luncheon was and act accordingly. Evening visits were paid only to close friends, and morning visits should always be extremely brief.

One must always keep an account of one's visits and ladies were instructed to remember the intervals at which the visit was returned for it was necessary to let a similar interval elapse

Tea goes back so far that its true beginning has been lost in time. Chinese legend has it that in 2737 BCE, Emperor Shen Nung watched some small, dry leaves flutter into a pot of boiling water that hung in his garden. He smelled the liquid, and decided that he liked it. He called it "cha" and from then on the beverage became part of his daily diet.

For years, the brewing of tea was unknown outside of China, but once the Far East could be reached by sea, traders discovered this beverage. Soon tea drinking became the rage all over Europe. There are three different types of tea — black, green, and oolong. They all come from the same tea bush, but it's what happens in the factory that makes them different.

Many people considered tea time in the Victorian era as a formal occasion complete with elegant silver, china, and dainty sandwiches. During this time, teabags did not exist and loose tea was used when preparing a cup of tea. To avoid getting tea leaves in the cup, a tea strainer was placed over the cup and the tea was poured through it. The loose tea was caught in the strainer, and then the strainer was put back on the base to drip.

Calling card tray.

Tea strainer.

Victorian-era calling cards.

Collectors should always look for tea strainers that have both the strainer and the drip-bowl. Old ads for Nippon wares indicate that they were sold in this manner.

There were also special rules for home etiquette in the Victorian era, and many books were published on this subject. A lady's dressing room had to be furnished with a low dressing-bureau, a washstand, an easy chair placed in front of the dressing bureau, one or two other chairs, a sofa or couch if there is sufficient room, and a large wardrobe if there are not sufficient closet conveniences.

The dressing-bureau should contain the lady's dressing case, her jewel box, pincushion, ring stand, and hair pin cushion. There should also be a tray with various kinds of combs, frizettes, bottles of perfumes, etc.

The following description was found in a book on manners written in 1891, "Tea and coffee should never be poured into a saucer. If a person wishes to be served with more tea or coffee, he should place his spoon in the saucer. If he has had sufficient, let it remain in the cup." So it seems that teacups were not the only things used for drinking tea, saucers were used as well!

A Ceramic Art Company catalog, circa 1900, listed many different types of "in the white" blanks for sale and among the items featured were tea strainers. An article entitled "Over the Teacups" told readers, "Have you poured tea? Then you know the sense of utter helplessness that comes when the cup is full and you have no place for the dripping strainer. We have met this difficulty by providing a drip-bowl large enough for every use, with a base so broad that it cannot tip over, and in such excellent proportion to the strainer that both together form a dainty table ornament. Besides its utility and beauty of design, this little article, indispensable on a well-equipped tea-table, has much in the quality of its fabric to recommend it to the amateur."

HOME ETIQUETTE.

Picture from home etiquette book.

Wash stand pictured in *Godey's Lady's Book*.

Hair wreath in shadow box.

Hair receiver (above) and how it looks opened (below).

CHINA 6 PIECE TRINKET, BUREAU OR BOUDOIR SETS.

Each set in pkg.

K4910—11½x8 deep tray, 3¼ in. covered puff box, two 1⅞ in. pomade jars, 5⅜x3⅜ in. pin tray, 2x3⅜ in. ring branch, embossed borders, gold showered edges, handles and ring branch, pronounced decorations.....Set, **72c**

R3348—10¾x6⅝ tray, 3¼ in. covered puff jar, two 2½x1½ covered pomade jars, 4⅞x3¾ pin tray, 3¼x2 ring tray, extra thin china, melon paneled, purple flowers and green leaves all over each piece and cover, wreath and cluster design, combined gold lace and gold cloud wreath borders, gold edges...........Set, **79c**

R4911—11½x8 tray, 4 in. covered puff box, two 3½ in. covered pomade jars, 5x3¼ in. oval pin tray, 3¾x2½ in. ring branch, embossed rim borders, sponged gold edges, inner gold wreath with 4 large colored American Beauty roses and leaves, glazed white china....... ....Set, **95c**

Hair jewelry.

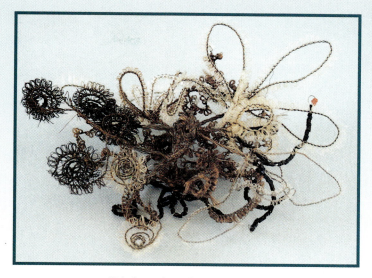

Hair decoration to be placed in hair.

Ladies were expected to brush their long hair twenty minutes in the morning, for ten minutes when it was dressed in the middle of the day, and for a like period at night. Women used hair receivers to store their hair after brushing or combing. In England, they are called "tidies," and this seems to be a good name for them as they tidied up the dressing area. As women cleaned their hairbrushes or combs, they tucked these combings into a two-piece hair receiver that had a lid with a circular hole. The collected hair was used for many purposes. Some was even knotted into jewelry.

This was also a period where infancy and childhood remained dangerous life stages, and many children succumbed at an early age. Pieces of hair were collected from a departed loved one and fashioned into a bracelet or necklace. These were worn to mark a period of mourning.

Victorians relished handicrafts and knotting and weaving hair was a popular pastime at that period in history. Hair wreaths were also made either with a living family member's hair or sometimes with a deceased relative's hair. Often times several family members' hair was used together.

Hairpieces or so-called "rats" were also made from these combings. Hair was added to a roll of wire mesh padding to make the rat. These monstrous hair-pads were placed on top of the head and held in place with the aid of hairpins and combs to give the hair fullness. Hair decorations were also made out of hair and placed in the hair for adornment.

This was a time when hats and bonnets were in fashion. No woman would think of going outside without her hat, and in fact some women even wore hats in the house! Many of the fashionable hats of this time period were often huge in size and covered

Victorian-era hat and hatpin.

Vanity organizers.

Hairpin holder, closed and open.

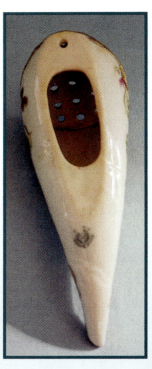

Hanging hatpin holder, front and back.

with flowers and/or feathers. During the Gay Nineties hats had become so bizarre that it's easy to imagine that the milliners were most likely laughing behind their customers' back.

Hats were secured with long elaborate hatpins that were necessary to skewer the hat to the coiffure. These could also be used as lethal weapons if needed, and laws were actually passed in some states banning them. Hatpin holders were invented to solve the problem of how to store the hatpins. Some were a three-in-one item (hatpin holder, pin tray, and ring tree), some just for hatpins and/or pins, and some could even be hung on the wall.

Hairpins were another necessity and hair pin cabinets and holders were placed on a lady's dressing table. Some hair pins were described as "invisible," while others could be found in colors. Nippon hair pin holders are extremely difficult to find and quite expensive considering their size.

Manicure sets complete with a tray, powder box, different size jars that could be used for cold cream, powdered pumice, cuticle-ice, etc. plus utensils for grooming the nails were a "must" in the Victorian era. Some of them even came in presentation boxes and the one shown in the photos on page 50 is an extremely rare item. The pieces are decorated in a moriage fashion and the fact that it is still in the original box adds greatly to its value.

Old ads for hair pin cabinets and hair pins.

Shaving mugs were popular utensils in the Victorian era that stretched from the 1860s to the early twentieth century. Men used straight razors that made shaving difficult and even perilous at times. In fact, many men preferred to be shaved at the local barbershop and some even kept a spare shaving mug there.

King Camp Gillette introduced the safety razor and disposable blade in 1903, and by 1906, his company was manufacturing nearly 250,000 razors and over one million blades annually. Soon after, straight razors fell into disfavor, and the shaving mug was no longer needed.

Some shaving mugs were sold separately while others could be purchased in gift sets. Items that might be found in a gift box were a brush or two, straight razor, mirror, comb, manicure scissors, razor holder, and corn knife as well as a shaving mug.

In the book *Manners Culture, and Dress* from 1891, a description of a gentleman's dressing room was given: "The arrangements of a gentleman's dressing-room are similar in most respects to those of the lady's dressing-room, the difference being only in small matters. In a gentleman's toilet — razors, shaving-soap,

During the Victorian era mustache cups were popular. Mustache cups were sold individually or with sets of dinnerware. They first became popular in the United States around 1850 and their popularity peaked around 1890.

Men's mustaches were waxed, curled, and even dyed! There were even mustache curlers and mustache spoons. The molded ledge on this special cup allowed the gentleman's mustache to rest there so that he could drink his beverage without letting his mustache touch the hot liquid.

Some of these cups have a decidedly masculine look while many are definitely feminine in appearance. Probably, the lady of the house wanted the cup to match her dinnerware at the table.

There are left-handed mustache cups but these are extremely rare to find.

Spittoons are another unusual item to find. Some people refer to them as cuspidors after the Portuguese word meaning "to spit." But the American term is usually spittoon. There was a time when one was found in most homes and public places. They were found in all sizes and in all kinds of material. Most of the Nippon marked ones are small in size and were preferred by the ladies.

There was chewing tobacco for men and snuff for ladies. Snuff was dried powdered tobacco that was inserted into the nostrils. This made expectoration a necessity, and ladies would carry a small spittoon or spit cup in their hand just for this purpose.

Manicure set: closed case (above left), open case (below left), close-up of items inside (above), close-up of detail on nail buffer (below).

An assortment of shaving mugs.

Boxed set with shaving supplies.

Two-piece shaving mug.

Two mustache cups, floral and scenic.

Ladies' spittoons.

Potpourri jars were also popular during the period when Nippon marked items were manufactured. A potpourri jar should always have two covers to be a complete item. The top cover has pierced holes while the inner cover is solid. A potpourri mixture is placed in the jar and when the solid cover is removed the aroma of spiced dried flower petals would permeate throughout the house.

Frequent bathing was not considered necessary during this time. Actually the Saturday night bath was just coming into vogue so potpourri jars were probably a necessity!

Another confusing collectible is the open salt dish. It is sometimes mixed up with a butter pat, nut cup, or coaster, each of which is bigger in size.

Years ago, celery and relish sets came complete with matching salts. However, it is also possible that individual salts could have been purchased. The open salt dish is just about the smallest and most inexpensive piece of Nippon you can purchase today and yet salt has been a valuable product to mankind throughout the ages.

Salt comes from the word salarium which is equivalent to our word salary. Salt was used as medium of exchange years ago; in fact, ancient Roman army troops were each given a salt allotment.

Salt is dug from the earth and harvested from the sea. Over time whole seas have dried up and salt was left behind. It is used to treat sore throats, absorb wine spills, it keeps sidewalks from freezing, it seasons our food, aids in digestion, and we can't exist without it. Salt is even used in religious rites.

Open salts are diverse and can be found with many different designs decorated on them: flowers, celery stalks, radishes, birds, scenes, and even the Capitol Building in Washington, D.C. Some are found with ball feet, a few have a pedestal base. And there are those that even have reticulated (cut out) handles.

Every time we buy a piece of Nippon we're buying a piece of history. There is a limited amount available and as more and more people collect it there will be fewer and fewer pieces to be found. But with each one we do find, there is a story about its beginning and where it's been for the last 100 years. If only our Nippon could talk.

Potpourri jar, open and closed (right).

Open salt.

Frequently Asked Questions

I receive many letters each month and many of the same questions appear time and time again. In this chapter, I would like to address some of them for collectors.

Q: Is there a difference in value between items marked with a green, blue, or red M-in-wreath?

A: I have found that the majority of items having a red, or so-called magenta mark usually are utilitarian pieces that are not so lavishly decorated as those bearing the blue or green M-in-wreath mark — hence they do not bring as high a price nor are they as much in demand. All the M-in-wreath pieces were manufactured by the Noritake Company. Both blue and green marks indicate high quality wares.

Q: What is the purpose of items referred to as tidies?

A: Hair receivers were called tidies years ago and that is still the term used in England, Australia, and New Zealand, I'm told. Tidies were used to store hair. The hair was brushed and wound around the finger and then pushed into the hole in the center of the lid. Hair accumulated in these receivers was used to make rattails to be used with one's own hair or pictures with hair flowers and jewelry.

Q: How can I tell if an item has a decal on it or is hand painted?

A: Whenever you see a pattern that is of a complex nature, it's a safe bet to assume it's a decal. Hold the item under a good light, use a magnifying glass, and if you see small dots making up the pattern, you have a decal (see photos). If you see brush strokes, then it's hand painted. Some items make use of both techniques. Most of the portrait pieces employed decals imported from France. The Noritake Company wanted to ensure that the people displayed would look European just in case the Japanese artist had difficulty painting these features. It was also a cost-effective measure.

Q: Do tea and chocolate sets always have sets of six and eight cups and saucers? I've seen them with four, five, and six.

A: I have hundreds of old Nippon ads and in checking them, I could only find where tea and chocolate sets were sold with six cups and saucers. It was also

Close-up of decals.

possible to buy pots separately, and cups and saucers were sold in half dozen and dozen size packages, so I guess you could have had a dozen cups if you wanted. Most likely the sets originally had six cups and saucers and one or two have been broken over the years. Of course, a tête-a-tête set would have had only two cups and saucers.

Q: Why do most moriage pieces have no backstamp?

A: There are many reasons why an item may not be stamped. It could predate the 1891 law, it could have been imported with a paper label which has been worn or washed off, the mark may have been scratched off, the piece may have been part of a set or in a box where only one item was marked, or perhaps the article was exported to a country where this ruling did not apply. There are some "newer" moriage type wares but the difference in texture is readily apparent to most collectors. I doubt that any company will be reproducing these wares; it would require considerably more time and effort for them than the ones they are now manufacturing. Today, we call the slip trailed items moriage, but years ago they were evidently referred to as moriago. Some of the dragon pattern pieces even had glass eyes attached. The glass crackled when it was fired.

Close-up of hand-painted work.

Ads from Butler Brothers 1907 catalog.

Q: Most pairs of urns are identical. Is it unusual to find them where the design on one is on the left and the other where it's on the right?

A: These are referred to as "mirror image" urns. Evidently this style was more in vogue in Great Britain in the early 1900s than the United States. Each pair I have ever found designed like this has had a backstamp indicating a Great Britain destination. They're unusual to find in the United States.

Q: Do all sugar shakers have a cork in the bottom?

A: They have either a cork in the bottom or a screw top. There are also those that have a cover; the holes in the top are concealed by it and it has a cork in the bottom. Sugar shakers are taller and wider than salt and pepper shakers.

Q: On the bottom of some of my items I have found a raised star or long raised bar. Is this an additional mark? Does it increase the value of the item?

A: Both of these raised marks are called spur marks and were added to the item only to give it strength when it was fired in the kiln. It adds no value to the item although some people think it does.

Q: I have two odd shaped vases. Neither will hold many flowers. Do you think they had another use?

A: Yes, decoration! One is referred to by collectors as a bottle vase and the other is a basket vase. One or two flowers would fit, but most likely they were used as cabinet pieces.

SUGAR SHAKERS.

L2480—4x4¾, paneled trailing blossom and leaf spray, conventional band border, gold lined edges and handle, gold starred top. 1 doz. in box............................Doz. 96c

SCREW TOP

L9421—5 in., ivory tinted, paneled, gold outlined pink lotus blossoms and green leaves beaded gold band, gold dec. top and line base. 3 in box.
EACH. 36c

Old ads from Butler Brothers catalogs.

Sugar shaker with cover.

Basket vases in different sizes.

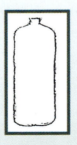

Bottle vase.

Basket vase.

Pancake warmer (notice steam holes in top).

Butter dish.

Q: How do you tell a covered pancake server from a covered butter dish?

A: *If you suspect that something warm was to be kept inside, check to see if it has a steam hole or two. A pancake warmer will, a butter dish will not.*

Q: How can I tell the difference between an open hatpin holder, a toothbrush holder, and a toothpick holder?

A: *An open hatpin holder is the tallest usually 5" in size, and narrower than a toothbrush holder which is about 4" tall and wider than a hatpin holder. A toothpick holder is about 2" in height. A glance at old ads will show the differences.*

Q: What's the difference between a stein and a mug?

A: *Height. A stein will be about 7" tall, a mug, 5" or less. Shaving mugs are about 4" tall.*

Q: What's the difference between a chamberstick and a candlestick?

A: *A chamberstick is usually shorter in height and has an attached plate and handle for holding the piece. Candlesticks are taller, generally 7 – 11" in height.*

Q: How do you tell a stickpin holder from a salt shaker?

A: *A stickpin holder will be about 1½" tall, and most salt shakers fall in the range of 2½" to 3½" tall.*

Q: What's a muffineer?

A: *A muffineer is just another name for a sugar shaker.*

TOOTHPICK HOLDERS.

L9121   L9123

L9121—2¼ in., clear white ribbed, small rose and leaf wreath, black border. Tokio red edge. 1 doz. in pkg. Doz. **32c**

L9122—1¾ in., clear white, hand painted rose and leaf cluster, gold ornamentation, cobalt edge. 1 doz. in box. Doz. **39c**

Toothpick holder.

HATPIN HOLDER

L7530—5½ in., forget-me-not decoration with spray and fancy gold trimming, gold lined edges. 1 doz. in pkg. Doz. **96c**

Hatpin holder.

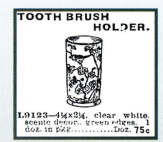

TOOTH BRUSH HOLDER.

L9123—4¼x2¼, clear white, scenic decor., green edges. 1 doz. in pkg........Doz. **75c**

Toothbrush holder.

SALT AND PEPPER SHAKERS.
Each with cork. 1 dz. box. 6 salts, 6 peppers.

L7032   L6181   L7743   L7165

L7032—3 in., 2 styles Japanese scene, floral border, Tokio red top and base.....Doz. **32c**

L6181—3½x2¼, allover Japanese decoration cobalt top & base, gold ornamented. Doz. **42c**

L7743—2 styles, 3½ in., ribbed, lt. green tints, current and grape decors., shaded green foliage, gold ornamented cobalt band, gold decorated top................Doz. **45c**

L7165—3½ in., paneled, pastel tints, cherry trees, gold line neck and base.........................Doz. **69c**

L8185—3 in., hexagon, clear white china, gold outlined pink roses and leaves, beaded gold scrolls, gold decorated top and line base. Doz. **85c**

Salt and pepper shakers.

SPOON TRAY OR PICKLE DISH.

L.2436--9¾ in., lt. tan border, gold outlined, red and lavender floral and leaf sprays with connecting stems, gold beaded edge, gold center medallion. ¼ doz. in box. .Doz. $3.60

Berry bowl and underplate.

Q: How do you distinguish between a celery dish and a pickle or relish dish?

A: A celery dish will generally be 9" to 11" long, whereas a relish dish will be smaller. Some of the so-called relish and pickle dishes we find today were once called spoon trays and used for spoons on the table. Many of the items had dual roles.

Q: Did all pierced berry bowls originally come with an underplate?

A: It only makes sense that they would have. When berries were placed in the bowl, they probably had just been rinsed with water and were wet. Without an underplate, drops of water would have been all over the table.

Q: What do you think is the finest Nippon chinaware and which do you think is inferior quality?

A: When we talk of fine wares, we mean those that are translucent, have a bell-like sound when tapped, are smooth to the touch, and have the whitest and thinnest porcelain. In my opinion, those that have the best porcelain bear the RC (Royal Crockery) mark. The most ornate and generally the best decorated pieces are those bearing the maple leaf mark; the M-in-wreath mark is next. Generally, pieces with the China E-oh mark and the pagoda mark were not made of the best quality porcelain. Items bearing the Royal Nishiki mark are usually of a softer paste material and do not have the fine quality of most of the other Nippon pieces. The rising sun mark is found on utilitarian pieces. The quality of the porcelain is fine but the decoration is very plain.

Q: Were all items backstamped with Nippon made by the Noritake Company?

A: The words Nippon and Noritake are not synonymous. Nippon is the name of the country of origin, so anything could have been backstamped with this word during the 1891 – 1921 period, musical instruments, lacquer boxes, etc. Noritake is the name of the company located in Nippon (Japan). If an item is marked Noritake that indicates that it was made by the Noritake Company in Japan, but if an item is marked Nippon, that does not necessarily mean that it was manufactured by the Noritake Company.

Q: I want to sell some Nippon items. How do I go about pricing them and finding buyers?

A: Check the Nippon books for similar items to get an idea of pricing. Keep in mind that prices shown in the books are retail prices and generally not what a dealer is willing to pay. Price your items fairly and run an ad in one of the antique trade papers on the Internet. Be prepared to send photos to prospective buyers and guarantee the merchandise. Always check over your pieces for chips, gold wear, etc., and describe them accurately.

Q: What does the M in the M-in-wreath stand for? An N would make more sense as they were produced by the Noritake Company.

A: The M stands for Morimura (Morimura Bros. was the forerunner of the Noritake Company) and the wreath was designed from the crest of the Morimuras. Morimura Bros. of New York City was also the importer

of Japanese wares to the United States from 1876 to 1941. The M-in-wreath is found under the glaze in green, blue, magenta, and gold colors. According to Noritake Company records, the letter N in the back-stamp was first registered in Japan in 1953 but used as early as 1952.

Q: When did the Noritake Company start making dinnerware sets?

A: Noritake Company records indicate that their first dinnerware pattern was Sedan in 1914. The registration date is unknown but the pattern number is listed as D1441. Since then the Noritake Company has manufactured more than 3,000 patterns of dinnerware.

Q: Did egg warmers ever have a cork as a stopper?

A: Egg warmers hold 4 – 6 eggs. The always came with a porcelain stopper. If one is found with a cork, you can be sure this is a replacement. The stopper was lifted out of the item, hot water was poured inside, the stopper was replaced, and the eggs were kept warm.

Q: Did ferners originally come with inserts?

A: Old ads indicate that most did. I have found a few where a metal container was still inside the ferner. Most are found without these items. One old ad I read stated that the china fern dish came with an inside perforated removable clay pot. I have never spotted one of these and it's doubtful that clay pots would have survived over the years.

Q: What's the difference between a chocolate pot, a teapot, and a coffee pot?

A: A coffee pot is tall, has a long spout and a cover; a chocolate pot, although tall in size, has a short spout at the top and a cover. Teapots are shorter and squatty with a long spout and cover. Milk pitchers are generally medium in height, some have a cover and some do not.

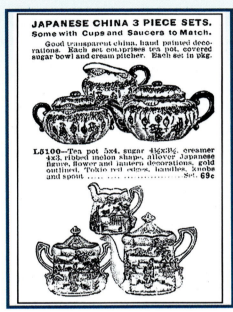

Ferner with metal insert.

Demitasse or after dinner coffee set.

Teapots.

Chocolate or mocha pot.

Demitasse or after dinner coffee pot.

Q: Sometimes you see a vase and a covered urn in the same decoration and size. When this happens, does this mean that the vase probably once had a cover?

A: Maybe yes and maybe no. It is possible that the cover is missing on the vase and it is also possible both type items were made bearing the same decoration. The covered urn may have a lip at the top for the cover to fit on. A covered urn should sell for more if both are in comparable condition.

Q: What is a tête-á-tête set?

A: It includes a teapot, covered sugar bowl, creamer, two cups, and two saucers — for more intimate talks!

Q: What's the difference between a snack set and a refreshment set?

A: Nothing. Old catalogs also called these items sandwich sets, dessert sets, and toast sets. These sets consist of a plate and matching cup. The plate has an indentation on it for the bottom of the cup.

Q: What pieces can I expect to find in a toy china tea set?

A: Often we find six tea plates, cups, and saucers; a covered teapot; covered sugar bowl; and a cream pitchers. Most collectors think that six plates make a complete set, but I've reviewed a number of old catalog ads and they show where some were originally sold with only three or four plates, cups, and saucers. So, if you find a set today with only three or four of each, it does not necessarily mean part is missing — that may be all there was originally.

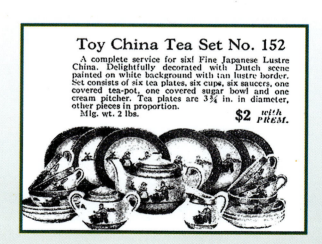

Q: What's a whip cream set?

A: A whip cream set consists of a small bowl, matching underplate, and a serving ladle. Collectors also call this a mayonnaise set.

Q: What's the difference between a bouillon cup and a tea cup?

A: A bouillon cup will either have two handles or no handle, a teacup, only one. Many bouillon cups are found with covers.

Q: How can I tell if an item is a wall plaque or just a rectangular tray or round plate?

A: Turn the item over. If it is a wall plaque there will be two or three holes on the back so wire could be threaded for hanging. Very large plaques are referred to as chargers.

Q: When I'm out shopping, I see dealers selling humidors without covers as ferners, and sugar bowls without tops as open sugars. How does a collector know the difference?

A: Many of the English manufactured chinaware sugar bowls were indeed "open" sugars, but I have yet to come across a Nippon one. Old ads indicate they came with covers. The lip found around the tops of many humidors and sugar bowls is a clue to the buyer that something sat on top of these items. However, a number of Nippon humidors do not have a lip, so I suppose a novice collector could be confused. Check the Nippon books and get to know what a ferner looks like and how it differs from a humidor.

Q: What's the difference between a syrup pitcher and an individual size teapot?

A: There will be a hole in the top of the teapot.

Q: Is a vanity set the same as a dresser set?

A: Not according to old catalog ads. A vanity set is made up of two perfume bottles and a powder dish. A dresser set might include a brush, comb, tray, hatpin holder, cologne or perfume bottle, pin tray, trinket dish, stickpin holder, powder box, hair receiver, ring tree, hairpin holder, and sometimes a pair of candlesticks. A manicure set was advertised with a tray, powder box, and different size jars that could be used for cold cream, powdered pumice, cuticle-ice, etc.

CONDENSED MILK JARS.

L6477 — 3¾x5, saucer 6¼, Japanese picture decorated, Tokio red edges, handles and knob. 3 in pkg....................Each, 33c

L6478 — Ht. 5½ in., saucer 6 in., blue tinted surface, rose clusters sides and cover, gold beaded edges and ornamented handles and cover. 3 in pkg....................Each, 39c

Jam Jar Set

No. 49010 GIVEN with a $2 purchase of Products or for $2 in Coupons.

Set consists of Jar, 3¾ in. high, Plate 6¾ in. in diameter, and Ladle. Decorated with pink, white and red roses, blended with shaded leaves. Edges are outlined in gold. Shipping weight 3 lbs.

Q: How do you tell the difference between a jam jar, condensed milk container, and a honey pot?

A: The honey pots I have found have all been in the shape of a bee hive; the top is ribbed and decorated with bees. There's a hole in the top for a spoon or ladle which originally came with it. Jam jars and condensed milk containers look a lot alike. Both come with covers and underplates. There will often be a notch in the cover of the jars and old ads indicate that porcelain spoons originally came with these items. A condensed milk container will have a hole in the bottom which was used to push up the can when you wanted to remove it.

Q: What do you know about companies other than Noritake that produced porcelain in Japan for export during the 1891 – 1921 period?

A: Very little, I'm afraid. It's believed that Nagoya, which is the home of the Noritake Company, was the source of most of our porcelain. My research indicates that over 90 percent of the items we find today can be traced to the Noritake Company in Nagoya. Most records were destroyed during World War II so little is even known about the Noritake Company. In the 1930s,

Nagoya's industrial growth accelerated due to its munitions and aircraft industries. This ultimately caused its ruin. American bombers virtually razed the city in WWII.

Q: What pieces make up an oatmeal set?

A: An oatmeal set is made up of a bowl, small pitcher, and matching plate. It's also called a child's breakfast set by collectors.

Q: Should collectors buy unmarked pieces of Nippon?

A: Absolutely, but not until they know what they are doing. There are a number of reasons why an item may not be marked, but I would suggest the beginner only buy marked pieces. Learn to identify the reproductions. They are marked Nippon but are not Nippon era wares!

Q: How do you tell a whiskey jug from a wine jug?

A: As a rule of thumb, the wine jug will usually be taller and will hold more liquid. Study the different shapes shown in this book and you will see what I mean.

The whiskey jugs are squattier, some are in the shape of the miniature barrel, some are bulbous, some are square, etc.; they can range in size from 5½" to 8" in height. The wine jugs run from 7½" to 11" in height, and there are several different shapes and sizes to be found in this category. In the interest of research, I filled several of these pieces with water. The tallest wine jug holds 46 oz. and a 7¾" triangular one holds 44 oz. The barrel-shaped whiskey jug will only hold 22 oz. and the 7" one holds 24 oz. So although one is only ¾" shorter than the other one, it holds 20 oz. less. The base part that holds the majority of the liquid is always larger on the wine jugs. Some of these can still be found with their original wicker basket. And remember a wine or whiskey jug is not complete without its porcelain stopper.

Q: How do you tell a humidor from a cracker jar?

A: When you take off the cover of the humidor, you will see a hollow space in which a sponge was placed. Some are even found today with the original sponge intact.

Q: What's the difference between a cookie jar and a cracker jar?

JAPANESE CHINA HIGH CRACKER JARS.

L5236   L5239

L5236—5¾x6½, allover hand painted Japanese figure and floral Kitani decoration. Tokio red edges and knob. 2 in pkg.....Each, 36c

L5239—Ht. 5½ in., elaborate Japanese decorations with colored figures, hand painted flowers and oriental effects with heavy gold trimmings, lid with solid gold fancy flower handle. 2 in pkg.........Each, 57c

L5238—6 x 7½, white china allover Japanese figures and landscape decoration gold illuminated, gold decorated maroon and cobalt blue edges, foot and knob. 1 in pkg. ....Each, 75c

L5238

JAP CHINA LOW CRACKER JARS OR COVERED TABLE DISHES.

L5240—6x4, allover characteristic Japanese figure & landscape & floral decoration, gold illuminated gold traced Tokio red edges, handles & knob. 2 in pkg., asstd ...Each, 39c

L5241—6x4½, allover floral leaf & gold filigree decoration, gold scroll traced scalloped cobalt edges, handles & knob. 1 in pkg. ....Each, 50c

L5243—7½ x 4, ribbed, elaborate floral and leaf decoration, shaded luster ground, gold traced and heavily beaded scalloped edges, fancy handles and knob. 1 in pkg.................Each, $1.00

A: Collectors get accustomed to referring to items in certain ways, and the taller cookie/cracker jar is usually referred to as a cookie jar. However, old catalog ads described them as high cracker or biscuit jars and low cracker or biscuit jars and even covered table dishes. Maybe we should return to the original terminology.

Q: What is a reticulated item?

A: Reticulation does not refer to a particular technique used, such as tapestry or gold overlay. It is merely a term collectors use for piercing. Holes or sections are cut in clay when it is at the leather hard stage (before it's fully dried out). An example might be a cel-

ery dish. At the edges there's a cutout space to make handles. The potter had to be very careful when doing this as it tends to weaken the clay piece.

Q: Does color variation affect the price of an item?

A: *It is amazing how different colors change the look of a piece! To the right, you see the same blown-out plaque painted in four different ways. The blue and white decor is referred to as wedgewood type — the others show the different artists' interpretations. Beauty is in the eye of the beholder, but many collectors have definite preferences and this can change the price somewhat. Good quality hand painting is always the most desirable.*

Holes at ends are handles.

Note the same dog plaque mold is painted three different ways. I have a favorite, but it just depends on which you prefer. Always buy what *you* like.

Q: What are so-called transitional pieces?

A: They are what Nippon collectors believe are in-between pieces, made at the end of the Nippon era. Because the backstamp had to bear the word Japan, the mark will have both names. Both the figural flower frog and the elephant creamer and sugar bear Nippon mark #37 plus the words "Made in Japan." Figural luster-ware pieces such as these do not usually bear the word Nippon in their backstamp.

Q: Is Nippon a type of porcelain?

A: Nippon is merely another name for Japan, the country of origin of our porcelain items. Many types of items can be found bearing a Nippon backstamp. The pottery vase shown in the photo was made by the Nori-take Company and bears a gold mark #47, green M-in-wreath backstamp. The other photos show paper Christmas lights, paper Easter eggs, a large satin type egg with painted decor, and wood and lacquer boxes with a gold and silver decor. All are stamped Nippon.

The following definitions are, for the most part, from a work on ceramic art by Jennie J. Young.

Pottery is from the Latin *potum*, a drinking vessel. It is applied in English usage to all opaque wares as distinguished from translucent porcelain — also to the place of manufacture. The French word *poterie*, however, is a general name for all vessels, both earthenware and porcelain.

Faience is a French word, and is applied to every kind of glazed earthenware.

Majolica is employed in very nearly the same significance. It is by some writers restricted to ware of Italian manufacture, and derived from the island of Majorca, "which lends its softened name to art."

Porcelain signifies a vitreous and translucent ware — standing in the ranks of the fictile art much higher than pottery. The name is derived from *porcella*, a little hog; the first ware of this kind seen in Europe was the egg-shell fabric of China, to which was given the name *pourcelaine*, its translucent delicacy suggesting the beautiful univalve shell familiar to dwellers along the Mediterranean coast. The shell, in turn was called *porcella*, from its fancied resemblance in shape to the back of pig. Porcelain is of two kinds, the natural, or pate dure, and the artificial, or pate tendre. The latter, "soft paste," was the first to be discovered in Europe by persistent chemical experiment. Evidences of the success of the potter's alchemy date back to 1580. It was not until 1709 that the accidental discovery of a bed of kaolin in Saxony led to the manufacture of hard porcelain. Two ingredients are necessary to its production: kaolin, a result of the decomposition of granite rock, and so called because found in great quantities in China, near a mountain named Kaoling; and petuntse, a pure feldspar. Kaolin is an infusible element and constitutes the body of the ware; fusible at high temperature, petuntse envelopes the kaolin and gives the translucency.

Glaze and enamel are terms often confused. Properly applied, "glaze" means transparent covering of the ware; "enamel" is a covering which obscures the body. Silicious or glass glaze is formed by fusing sand with an alkali. The addition of oxide of lead gives transparent plumbiferous glaze. When this is combined with oxide of tin, opaque stanniferous enamel is the result. Salt glaze, the only kind of glaze produced by fumes during baking, is also used on pottery. Another is a thin, plumbeous glaze called varnish.

Bone China or English artificial porcelain is composed largely of bone in combination with kaolin and feldspar.

Parian is a composition of silica, alumina, oxide of iron, lime, magnesia, potash, and soda.

Biscuit is a technical term applied to all kinds of ware before it is enameled or glazed. It literally means twice baked, but is invariably used as a name for pottery and porcelain when but once baked.

———————————

Q: Does an original box found with a Nippon doll or tea set add to the value of the item?

A: Definitely. It's the frosting on the cake in my opinion. Original stickers found on dolls also add to their value.

Q: Are the porcelain items from the 1891 – 1921 period made in the same way as today's wares?

A: Advances have been made over the years and certainly there is not the hand decoration found on today's items. I located a book advertising both blank and decorated pieces from the early 1900s and I am sure that our Nippon articles were made in a similar fashion. (See definitions.)

Q: Do some items have interchangeable names? Were they intended for several uses?

A: Going over old ads we note that jewel boxes were also called puff or powder boxes, also bonbon boxes or toilet boxes. Small nut dishes could also be used for salt dips, and spoon trays were the same as pickle and relish dishes; pin dishes and ashtrays were often interchanged. Chop plates and dessert plates were often the same, as well as olive, bonbon, and nut bowls.

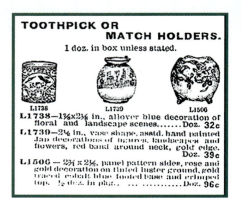

Recording and Insuring Your Collection

One thing every serious collector should do is keep accurate records on all items. This can be just for your own pleasure but more realistically as a help in case of fire, theft, or vandalism. Collectors should have photos and descriptions of each piece. Condition and backstamp should also be noted along with the price that was paid. A physical description should be included such as height, width, and diameter. Ideally, three sets should be kept, one at home, one in a safety deposit box, and one with your insurance company.

These records can either be kept in book form with individual inventory sheets in a three ring binder or perhaps a filing card system could be utilized. The records should be updated yearly. Remove the items you no longer own and jot down the current appraisal of all pieces.

Insurance can be costly but a fire or theft will be much more so. You can acquire a fine arts policy where most insurance compa-

nies will want individual photos of items plus an appraisal of each. Or another option is to take out a policy for a certain amount of money to cover all your pieces. Since insurance laws vary from state to state it would be advisable to speak with your local agent. Insure the items for their full value. Any new increases in value are not covered so amend your policy periodically. Household accidents such as breakage are often not included.

No one likes to think about thefts and fires but they do occur. First of all do not advertise the existence of your collection to everyone you meet. Good locks on doors and windows are a first step while many other collectors have preferred to install alarm systems. Check with your insurance company as these installations may give you a break on your premium.

Care and Cleaning of Your Nippon Porcelain

Don't leave items out where they can get knocked over or accidentally hit. Keep them out of the reach of small children and family pets. Stop accidents before they happen.

I would suggest washing your porcelain pieces carefully. Do not put a lot of pieces in the sink at one time. I use warm, softened water for both the washing and rinsing of my articles. If an item is very dirty a good long soaking in water and soap will usually correct the problem. A good spraying of Formula 409 can often be the answer. However, I would not leave moriage or coralene items in the water for a very long period. And I would never put a piece of cloisonné in a tub of water as the cloisons might fall out. I would also be extra careful cleaning a doll because much of the color on a doll's face has not been baked on and will disappear upon cleaning. Don't use abrasives or scouring pads because this can wear off some of the decoration. Use a stiff bottlebrush to clean the inside of a vase. And cotton swabs can be used to clean around moriage decoration.

Don't use chlorine bleach on your hand-painted items. I know that some people prefer this method but it stands to reason that the item might lose some of its vibrant colors when soaked. Discolored hairlines on white porcelain can sometimes be cleaned with a dab of chlorine on a cotton swab. Some of the discoloration may disappear but it will prove to only be a temporary measure. Some authorities believe that a crack can be boiled clean, however, I would not subject my items to great changes in temperature.

For the Pickard gold etched items, the company suggests that only simple care is needed to keep the piece in beautiful condition. One can remove stains simply by washing the piece thoroughly using a mild soap in warm water or an ammonia type glass cleaner. They state that one should not use silver polish, steel wool, or harsh cleaning powders.

Most of us have a multitude of dishes and we have to store them. Dishes should always be separated with napkins, paper, felt, or doilies, etc. Items that are unglazed on the bottom may not only scratch each other but our furniture as well, so it would be advisable to be careful when placing these pieces on your wood or glass furniture.

Cups should not be stacked on top of one another because there is always the risk of chipping. Also don't hang them on hooks by their handles; this is the weakest point of the cup.

When you store things in boxes or plastic containers, be extra careful. Disposable diapers, hospital pads, and bubble wrap make great wrappers and provide adequate protection. Whenever you are mailing items, be sure to use these wrappers and double box. Both boxes should be filled with styrofoam or sufficient newspaper to cut down on damage.

Porcelain wares are actually stronger and more durable than most people think, but accidents can happen. Use them and enjoy them but treat them with tender loving care.

Detection of Damage and Restoration

Ever get a piece of Nippon home only to discover a crack or hairline? Most of us are quick to buy and quick to trust when the person offering the piece tells us it is in "mint condition."

Looking before you leap is good advice. Buy quality and always buy the best you can afford because these items will hold their value. Knowingly buying damaged or restored items is a matter that should be left to each collector's judgment. There is really nothing wrong in buying either as long as it is identified as such and not misrepresented. But the piece should definitely be much less in price.

Know your dealer or else be very careful with your purchase. Never buy an item under poor lighting conditions, always hold the piece up to the light. You can often tell by touching the items if something is wrong. Check the most vulnerable places, areas that project, such as spouts, handles, rims, sprigged-on decoration, etc.

And dirt on the item can very well be hiding a hairline.

Gold wears off the quickest because it is the last to be fired and it is quite common to find touched-up gold. All one has to do is go to the local arts and crafts store and tubes of gold are just waiting on the shelf. Restorers are doing a great job of regolding items. Generally, when you see an item professionally restored it will look as though it just came out of the box. Sometimes when it looks too good there is another reason why. Those done at home with a tube of gold will generally look duller in color than the original. Part of a handle may be dull in color while the rest will be shiny. Droplets of color are another telltale clue along with pieces of lint or hair, which would never have survived firing in the kiln.

Some collectors have approached the problem of detecting hidden damage with the purchase of a long wave ultraviolet light. It can be a valuable aid in the detection of some repairs. When viewed under black light, hard to see cracks will fluoresce brightly. But there are also restorers who advertise that their work is invisible under black light. So it really is a buyer beware world.

Reproductions, Fakes, and Fantasy Pieces

Fake pieces seem to be everywhere: auctions, antique shows and shops, and even on eBay. Some are backstamped with a look-alike Nippon mark, some are found unmarked. Most of these items are manufactured in China but a number are known to have been exported from Japan.

The McKinley Tariff Act was passed in 1890 and states that as of March 1, 1891, all articles of foreign manufacture shall be marked in legible English words so as to indicate the country of their origin. This was to be done as indelibly and permanently as the nature of the article would permit.

On February 8, 1917, the Treasury Department decided that chinaware and porcelain not marked to indicate the country of origin at the time of importation may be released when marked by means of a gummed label or with a rubber stamp.

The Treasury Department further ruled that as of October 1, 1921, Nippon was a Japanese word (the English equivalent of which was Japan) and from that date on, all items now had to be marked Japan. Since Nippon is not considered the English name of a country at the present time, the fake backstamps under the glaze or just those stamped Nippon are allowed into this country when a paper label is affixed indicating the country of origin. If the item is made in China and has a label attesting to this fact, the piece is allowed into the United States. The mark under the glaze has no bearing with the importation ruling. After purchase, the paper label is easily removed and magically we now have a "Nippon" marked item.

How do you tell if an item is fake or not? One tip-off is when you find items at antique shops and shows far below the market price. Beware. It's always possible that this is a genuine item that the seller does not know the current price of, but it may also be a clue to you that the item is not genuine. Or perhaps you suddenly see a number of pieces in the same pattern in any one shop, booth, or auction. Be extra careful when you start seeing the exact same item time after time when you are out shopping. Seasoned Nippon collectors know this does not happen. Many of the fake pieces are not hand painted as most Nippon-era wares are. They feel rougher to the touch, the gold is more of a luster color, and the glazing on some of the Chinese pieces doesn't even extend into the whole interior. Buy from reputable dealers and ask for a written guarantee. If in doubt, don't buy.

What's the difference between a reproduction, a fake, and a fantasy piece? A reproduction duplicates an exact pattern or mold, a fake piece has a pattern on it that never existed on an original item or is in a different shape than a real piece, and a fantasy piece is one that never existed during the Nippon era such as an oyster plate, kerosene lamp, or a wine cooler.

Nearly 100 fake patterns have been found on a variety of pieces. Study the following pages showing a number of these bogus items. Another good reference is the International Nippon Collectors Club website: www.nipponcollectorsclub.com for pictures and information on these pieces. Knowledge is power. Don't pay Nippon-era prices for reproduction pieces.

Genuine Backstamps

Original M-in-wreath mark.

M-in-wreath. No stem.

Fake Backstamps

Hourglass in an upside down wreath.

K in an upside down wreath.

Genuine Backstamps	Fake Backstamps

M-in-wreath (blurred) Chinese mark.

M-in-wreath, word Nippon is straight across Chinese mark.

Plus, now the manufacturers in China have reproduced the M-in-wreath mark faithfully.

Genuine rising sun mark.

Japanese mark.

Chinese mark.

Genuine maple leaf mark. Original ¼" leaf.

Fake ½" leaf.

The words "hand painted" on original mark are in red, the rest is a green. Fake mark is all green.

Genuine RC mark.

Fake RC mark.

Genuine Backstamps

Genuine maruki mark.

Genuine cherry blossom mark.

Nippon

Fake Backstamps

Fake maruki mark.

On the genuine mark, "hand painted" is straight across.

Fake mark.

Stamped or incised on reproduction dolls or small figural items.

Milk pitcher, Texas Rose pattern, 6½" tall.

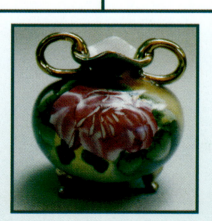

Vase, 4¼" tall.

Milk pitcher, 7½" tall.

Open hatpin holder, 5" tall.

Hatpin holder, 5" tall.

Hatpin holder, Pink Luster
pattern, 5¼" tall.

Hatpin holder, 5" tall.

Vase, 7½" tall.

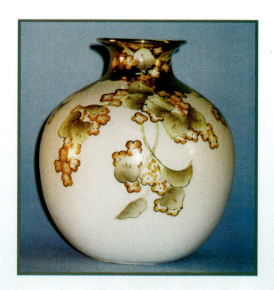

Vase, 7½" tall.

Sugar bowl, Green Mist pattern, 4¹/₂" tall.

Ring tree, 3¹/₂" wide.

Vase, 9" tall.

Vase, 14" tall.

Vase, 10" tall.

Vase, 8" tall.

Vase, 12¼" tall.

Left: Vase, 12" tall. Middle: Hatpin holder,
4" tall. Right: Vase, 10" tall.

Vase, comes in both
8" and 12" size.

Basket vase, 12½" tall.

Ewer, Texas Rose pattern, 8" tall.

Hatpin holder, 5¼" tall.

Small pitcher, tankard,
Antique Rose pattern, 12¼" tall.

Mug, Antique Rose pattern, 5" tall.

Tankard, Antique Spring
Song pattern, 11¼" tall.

Tankard, Antique Bouquet pattern, 11½" tall.

Hair receiver; bowl, 4" wide; hatpin holder, 4" tall.

Candlesticks, 9¼"; ferner, 6½" tall; hatpin holders, 5" tall.

Coffee pot, 9½" tall, reproduction.

Wall pocket, 8¼" tall, reproduction.

Hatpin holder, 4" tall.

Vase, 10" tall.

Bowl, 4¼" tall; vase, 4" tall; bowl, 4¼" tall; wallpocket, 5¾" long.

Hatpin holder, 6¼" tall.

Egg cup, 2½" tall.

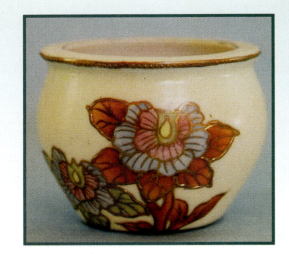

Small bowl, 2½" tall.

Wallpocket, 8½" long.

Hatpin holder,
6¼" tall.

Two-piece covered dish, reticulated (pierced)
decoration, 5½" tall.

Two-piece covered dish, 5³/₄" long.

After dinner coffee set, pot, 8" tall.

Shaving mugs, 3¹/₂" tall each.

Ferner, 8" tall.

Plate, 10" wide.

Hatpin holder, 6" tall.

Shaving mug, 3¹/₂" tall.

Wallpocket, 8¹/₂" long.

Covered jar, 6¹/₂" tall.

Small bowl, 4¹/₄" tall.

Vase, 8¹/₄" tall.

After dinner coffee set, Chantilly Rose pattern, pot, 7" tall.

Tea set, Orchid pattern, 7" tall.

Chocolate pot, 9¼" tall.

Candlestick, 10" tall.

Left: Genuine cracker jar.
Right: Cracker jar, 7½" tall, reproduction.

Hair receiver, 4" wide.

Wildflower pattern
cheese keeper: 4¼" tall, tray, 7¾" long, powder box.

Two-piece hair receiver, 4¾" wide.

Two-piece covered box, 4" wide.

Two-piece floral tea strainer; comes in two sizes: 6" long and 5" long.

Scenic tray, 9" long.

Two-piece covered box, Dogwood pattern, 4½" long.

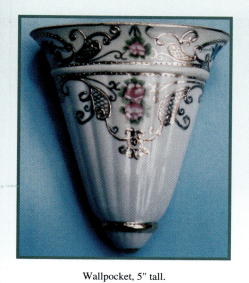

Wallpocket, 5" tall.

Hair receiver, 3" wide.

Fantasy item, kerosene lamp, 9½" tall.

Ladle, 11½" long.

Milk pitcher, 7" tall.

Cheese keeper, 7½" long, 4" tall.

Covered dish with 11" long underplate.

Vanity organizer, 6" long, 4" tall.

Hatpin holder, 5" tall.

Vase, 10½" tall.

Egg cup, 2½" tall.

Wallpocket, 9" long.

Hatpin holder, 5" tall.

Vase, 10¼" tall.

Tea set, teapot is 7¼" tall.

Vase, Antique Rose pattern, 5¾" tall.

Two-piece tea strainer, 5½" wide.

Sugar shaker, 5" tall.

Oyster dish, fantasy item, 9" wide.

Hatpin holder, 6" tall.

Hatpin holder, 6" tall. Looks like a domed
sugar shaker but there is no hole in the bottom.

Oyster dish, fantasy item, 9" wide.

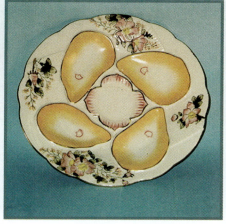
Oyster dish, fantasy item, 9" wide.

Wall plaque

Open hatpin holder, 4¾" tall.

Small bowl, 2½" tall; hair receiver, 5" wide.

Large hinged dresser box.

Hatpin holder, 6¹/₂" tall.

Vase, 4¹/₄" tall.

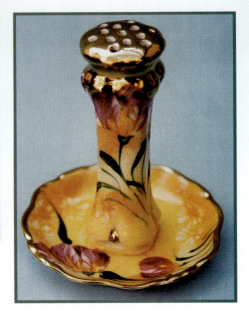

Hatpin holder, 5¹/₂" tall.

Open hatpin holder, 5" tall.

Covered box, 6" long. Has artist's signature written in gold.

Vase, 10¼" tall.

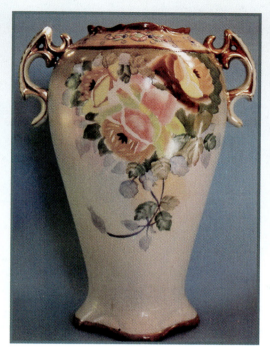

Vase, 12" tall.

Perfume bottle, 8" tall.

Wallpocket, 8" long.

Wine cooler, fantasy item, 7" tall.

Vase, 13" tall.

Covered box, 4¼" wide.

Covered box, 5½" diameter; milk pitcher, 7" tall; hatpin holder, 3½" tall.

Stickpin holder, 2½" tall.

Hatpin holder, 4" tall.

Wallpocket. 5½" tall.

Hair receiver, 3³/₄" wide.

Wallpocket, 5" long.

Wallpocket, 5¹/₂" tall.

Hair receiver, 4¹/₂" wide.

Rolling pin, opening on
each end for wooden han-
dles, 8¹/₂" long.

Hatpin holder, 6¹/₂" tall.

Hatpin holder, 6¼" tall.

Vase, 8" tall.

Vase, 8" tall.

Covered jar, 5¾" tall.

Vase, 3¾" tall.

Two-piece covered box, 4" wide.

Tray, 8¾" wide.

Tray, 11" long.

Tray, 11" long.

Reticulated bowl, 10¼" wide.

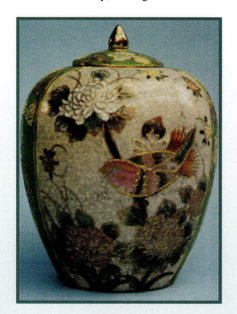

Covered jar, 6½" tall.

Two piece flask, 7" tall.

Bowl, 4¼" tall.

Covered container, 9½" tall.

Hatpin holder, 5" tall.

Doll.

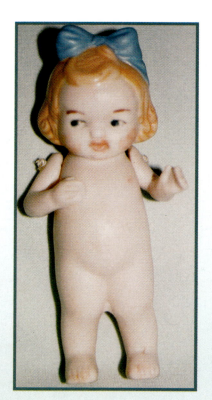

Doll.

Doll, 11" tall.

Figural boy on alligator, 5" long.

Figurine, 5" tall.

Figurine, 5" tall.

Toothpick holder, 3¼" tall.

Back of toothpick holder.

Nippon Backstamps

1. Baby Bud Nippon; incised on doll.

2. Bara hand painted Nippon.

3. The Carpathia M Nippon.

4. Cherry blossom hand painted Nippon; found in blue, green, and magenta colors.

5. Cherry blossom in a circle hand painted Nippon.

6. Chikusa hand painted Nippon.

7. China E-OH hand painted Nippon; found in blue and green colors.

8. Crown (pointed), hand painted Nippon; found in green and blue colors.

9. Crown Nippon (pointed) made in Nippon; found in green and blue colors.

10. Crown (square), hand painted Nippon; found in green and green with red colors.

11. Chubby LW & Co. Nippon; found on dolls. (Louis Wolf & Co.)

12. D Nippon.

13. Dolly sticker found on Nippon's Dolly dolls; sold by Morimura Bros.

14. Double T Diamond Nippon.

15. Double T Diamond in circle Nippon.

16. Dowsie Nippon.

17. EE Nippon.

18. Elite B hand painted Nippon.

19. FY 401 Nippon; found on dolls.

20. FY 405 Nippon; found on dolls.

21. G in a circle hand painted Nippon.

22. Gloria L.W. & Co. hand painted Nippon (Louis Wolf Co., Boston, Mass. & N.Y.C.).

23. Hand painted Nippon.

24. Hand painted Nippon.

25. Hand painted Nippon.

26. Hand painted Nippon.

27. Hand painted
Nippon.

28. Hand painted
Nippon with symbol.

29. Hand painted Nippon
with symbol.

30. Hand painted Nippon
with symbol.

31. Hand painted Nippon
with symbol.

32. Hand painted Nippon
with symbol.

33. Hand painted Nippon
with symbol.

34. Hand painted Nippon
with symbol.

35. Hand painted Nippon
with symbol.

36. Horsman No. 1
Nippon; found on
dolls.

37. IC Nippon.

38. Imperial Nippon; found
in blue and green.

39. J.M.D.S.
Nippon.

40. The Jonroth Studio
hand painted Nippon.

41. Kid Doll M.W. & Co.
Nippon.

42. Kinjo
Nippon.

43. Kinjo China hand
painted Nippon.

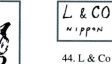

44. L & Co
Nippon.

45. LEH hand painted
Nippon.

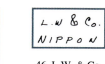

46. L.W. & Co.
Nippon (Louis Wolf
& Co., Boston,
Mass & N.Y.C.).

47. M-in-wreath, hand
painted (M stands for
importer, Morimura
Bros.); found in green,
blue, magenta, and gold
colors. Mark used since
1911.

48. M-in-wreath hand painted
Nippon, D.M. Read Co. (M stands
for importer, Morimura Bros.

49. M.B. (Morimura Bros.)
Baby Darling sticker; found on
dolls.

50. M. M. hand
painted Nippon.

51. Made in Nippon.

52. Maple leaf Nippon;
found in green, blue,
and magenta, dates
back to 1891.

53. Morimura Bros. sticker; found on Nippon items.

54. Mt. Fujiyama hand painted Nippon.

55. Nippon; found in blue, gold, and also incised into items.

56. Nippon 84.

57. Nippon 144.

58. Nippon 221.

59. Nippon with symbol.

60. Nippon with symbol.

61. Nippon with symbol.

62. Nippon with symbol.

63. Nippon with symbol.

64. Nippon with symbol.

65. Nippon M incised on doll (note N is written backwards); #12 denotes size of doll; M is Morimura Bros.

66. Noritake M-in-wreath Nippon; M is Morimura Bros., found in green, blue, and magenta.

67. Noritake Nippon; found in green, blue, and magenta colors.

68. Noritake Nippon; found in green, blue, and magenta colors. Mark dates from 1911, used on blank pieces (undecorated) of Nippon.

69. O.A.C. Hand painted Nippon (Okura Art China, branch of Noritake Co.).

70. Oriental china Nippon.

71. Pagoda hand painted Nippon.

72. Patent No. 30441 Nippon.

73. Paulownia flowers and leaves hand painted Nippon (crest used by Empress of Japan, kiri no mon); found in a green/red color.

74. Paulownia flowers and leaves, hand painted Nippon (crest used by Empress of Japan, kiri no mon).

75. Pickard etched china, Noritake Nippon; Pickard mark is in black; Noritake Nippon mark is blue in color.

76. W.A. Pickard hand painted china Nippon.

77. W.A. Pickard hand painted china, Noritake Nippon; Pickard mark printed in black, Noritake Nippon in magenta.

78. Queue San Baby sticker; found on Nippon dolls.

79. RC Nippon; RC stands for Royal Crockery (fine china).

80. RC hand painted Nippon (combination of both red and green colors). RC stands for Royal Crockery (fine china). Mark used since 1911.

81. RC Noritake Nippon hand painted; found in green and blue. RC stands for Royal Crockery (fine china). This mark has been in existence since 1911.

82. RC Noritake Nippon, registered in 1911. RC stands for Royal Crockery (fine china).

83. RE Nippon.

84. Rising Sun Nippon; mark used since 1911.

85. Royal dragon Nippon.

86. Royal dragon Nippon studio hand painted.

87. Royal Kaga Nippon.

88. Royal Kinran Nippon; found in blue, gold colors, made for domestic market in Japan since 1906.

89. Royal Kinran Crown Nippon; found in blue, gold, and green colors, made for domestic market in Japan since 1906.

90. Royal Moriye Nippon; found in green and blue colors.

91. Royal Nishiki Nippon; made for domestic market in Japan since 1906.

92. Royal Statsuma Nippon (cross within a ring, crest of House of Satsuma); made for domestic market in Japan since 1906.

93. Royal Sometuke Nippon; made for domestic market in Japan since 1906.

94. Royal Sometuke Nippon Sicily.

95. RS Nippon; found on coralene pieces.

96. S & K hand painted Nippon; found in green, blue, and magenta colors.

97. S & K hand painted Nippon; found in green, blue, and magenta colors.

98. Shinzo Nippon.

99. Shofu Nagoya Nippon.

100. SNB Nippon.

101. SNB Nagoya Nippon.

102. Spicer Studio Akron Ohio Nippon.

103. Spoke hand painted Nippon; mark in existence as early as 1911.

104. Studio hand painted Nippon.

105. Superior hand painted Nippon.

106. T Nippon hand painted (2 ho-o birds).

107. T hand painted Nippon.

108. T-in-wreath hand painted Nippon.

109. TN hand painted Nippon; mark is red and green.

110. T.S. hand painted Nippon.

111. TS hand painted Nippon.

112. Teacup, Made in Nippon.

113. Torri hand painted Nippon.

114. Tree crest hand painted Nippon (crest of Morimura family); also called Spider Mark.

115. Tree crest (also called Spider Mark) and maple leaf hand painted Nippon.

116. V Nippon, Scranton, PA.

117. The Yamato hand painted Nippon.

118. The Yamato Nippon.

119. C.G.N. hand painted Nippon; found in green.

120. F Nippon 03601 600; found incised on dolls.

121. F Nippon No. 76012 601; found incised on dolls.

122. F Nippon No. 76018 30/3; found incised on dolls.

123. FY Nippon No. 76018 403.

124. FY Nippon; found incised on dolls.

125. FY Nippon 301; found incised on dolls.

126. FY Nippon 402; found incised on dolls.

127. FY 9 Nippon 402; found incised on dolls.

128. FY Nippon 404; found incised on dolls.

129. FY Nippon 406; found incised on dolls.

130. FY Nippon 464; found incised on dolls.

131. FY Nippon No. 17604 604; found incised on dolls.

132. FY Nippon No. 70018 004; found incised on dolls.

133. FY Nippon (variation of mark) No. 70018 403; found incised on dolls.

134. FY Nippon No. 70018 406; found incised on dolls.

135. FY Nippon (variation of mark) No. 70018 406; found incised on dolls.

136. FY Nippon No. 76018; found incised on dolls, found in green.

137. Jollikid Nippon sticker (red and white), found on girl dolls; blue and white sticker found on boy dolls.

138. Ladykin Nippon sticker (red & gold); found on dolls.

139. Nippon (notice reversal of first N); found incised on items.

140. Nippon D13495; found in green.

141. Nippon E; found incised on dolls.

NIPPON 0

142. Nippon O; found incised on dolls.

5 NIPPON

143. Nippon 5; found incised on dolls.

97 NIPPON

144. Nippon 97; found incised on dolls.

98 NIPPON

145. Nippon 98; found incised of dolls.

99 NIPPON

146. Nippon 99; found incised on dolls.

101 NIPPON

147. Nippon 101; found incised on dolls.

102 NIPPON

148. Nippon 102; found incised on dolls.

105 NIPPON

149. Nippon 105; found incised on dolls.

123 NIPPON

150. Nippon 123; found incised on dolls.

151. Nippon 144 with symbol; found incised on dolls.

152. RE Nippon.

153. RE made in Nippon; found incised on dolls.

154. RE Nippon A9; found incised on dolls.

155. RE Nippon B8; found incised on dolls.

156. RE Nippon O 2; found incised on dolls.

157. Royal Hinode Nippon; found in blue.

158. Sonny sticker (gold, red, white, and blue); found on dolls.

159. Maruta Royal Blue Nippon.

160. Hand Painted Coronation Ware Nippon.

161. ATA Imperial Nippon.

162. Baby Doll, M.W. & Co. Nippon sticker; found on dolls.

163. BE, 4 Nippon.

164. Cherry blossom Nippon, similar to No. 4.

165. Cherry blossom (double) Nippon.

166. Louis Wolf & Co. Nippon.

167. C.O.N. Hand Painted Nippon.

168. FY Nippon 405; found on dolls.

169. FY Nippon 505; found on dolls.

170. FY Nippon 601; found on dolls.

171. FY Nippon 602; found on dolls.

172. FY Nippon 1602; found on dolls.

173. FY Nippon 603 No. 76018; found on dolls.

174. Happifat Nippon sticker; found on dolls.

175. Horsman Nippon, B9; found on dolls.

176. Horsman Nippon, B9; found on dolls.

177. James Studio China logo; used in conjuction with Crown Nippon mark.

178. JPL Hand Painted Nippon.

183. M Nippon F24.

179. Kenilworth Studios Nippon.

180. Maruki symbol, Hand Painted Nippon; since 1912.

181. Maruki symbol, Hand Painted Nippon No. 16034. Note: Japanese characters are fictitious.

182. M Nippon 10; found on dolls.

184. Manikin Nippon sticker; found on dolls.

185. Meiyo China Y-in-circle Nippon.

186. Nippon 3; found on dolls.

187. Nippon A3.

188. Nippon 144.

189. Nippon with symbol.

190. Nippon with symbol.

191. Nippon with symbol.

192. Nippon with symbol.

193. Nippon with symbol.

194. Nippon with symbol.

195. Nippon with symbol.

196. Nippon with symbol.

197. Hand painted Nippon with symbol.

198. Nippon with symbol, H in diamond, 14B, P.4.

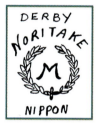

199. Noritake M-in-wreath Nippon; M is Morimura Bros.; found in green, blue, and magenta; Derby indicates pattern.

200. Noritake M-in-wreath Nippon; M is Morimura Bros.; Sahara indicates pattern.

201. Noritake M-in-wreath Nippon; M is Morimura Bros.; The Kiva indicates pattern.

202. Noritake M-in-wreath Nippon; M is Morimura Bros.; The Metz indicates pattern.

203. Noritake M-in-wreath Nippon; M is Morimura Bros. Registered in Japan in 1912.

204. Noritake M-in-wreath Hand Painted Nippon; M is Morimura Bros.; Marguerite indicates pattern.

205. Noritake M-in-wreath Hand Painted Nippon; M is Morimura Bros.; Sedan indicates pattern. First dinner set made in Noritake factory 1914.

206. Noritake M-in-wreath Hand Painted Nippon; M is Morimura Bros.; the Vitry indicates pattern.

207. NPMC Nippon Hand Painted.

208. RC Noritake Nippon; Waverly indicates pattern.

209. RE Nippon 1120; found on dolls.

210. RE Nippon B 9; found on dolls.

211. RE Nippon A4; found on dolls.

213. RE Made in Nippon A5; found on dolls.

214. RE Made in Nippon B9; found on dolls.

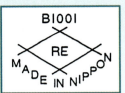

215. RE Made in Nippon B1001; found on dolls.

216. Royal Kuyu Nippon.

217. S in circle Nippon.

218. Sendai Hand Painted Nippon.

219. Stouffer Hand Painted Nippon.

220. Tanega Hand Painted Nippon.

221. Torii Nippon; similar to No. 113.

222. Nagoya N & Co. Nippon.

223. Old Blue Nippon Hand Painted.

These marks were used during the Nippon era but may have also been used after 1921.

224.* RC Noritake mark, used for domestic market in Japan by Noritake Co. since 1908. The RC stands for Royal Crockery (fine china). The symbol design is called Yajirobe (toy of balance). It symbolizes the balance in management.

225.* RC Noritake mark, used for domestic market in Japan by Noritake Co. since 1912. The RC stands for Royal Crockery (fine china). The symbol design is called Yajirobe (toy of balance). It symbolizes the balance in management.

226.* RC Nippontoki Nagoya mark, for export since 1911. The RC stands for Royal Crockery (fine china).

227.* Made in Japan mark, used by Noritake Co., registered in London in 1908.

232. Coalportia Nippon.

228.* Noritaké, made in Japan, for export to England, registered in 1908 by Noritake Co.

229.* Noritaké, registered in London in 1908 by Noritake Co.

230.* Noritaké, made in Japan mark, registered in London in 1908.

231.* RC Japan; Noritake Co. started using the mark in 1914. It was used on items sent to India and Southeast Asia. RC stands for Royal Crockery (fine china).

233. FY Nippon 302; found incised on dolls.

234. FY Nippon 303; found incised on dolls.

235. FY Nippon 501; found incised on dolls.

236. No. 700 Nippon HO6; found incised on dolls.

237. RE Made in Nippon C8; found incised on dolls.

238. RE Nippon M18; found incised on dolls.

239. SK Hand Painted Made in Nippon.

240. Patent No. 17705 Royal Kinjo.

241. RS Japan; found on coralene pieces.

242. U.S. Patent 912171; found on coralene pieces.

243. U.S. Patent 912171; found on coralene pieces.

244. Kinran U.S. Patent 912171; found on coralene pieces.

244. Kinran U.S. Patent 912971; found on coralene pieces.

245. Patent applied for No. 38257; found on coralene pieces.

246. Kinran Patent No. 16137; found on coralene pieces.

247. FY Nippon 401; found on dolls.

248. FY Nippon 409; found on dolls.

249. FY Nippon 15/4; found on dolls.

250. ESO hand-painted Nippon.

251. Miyako Nippon.

252. Royal Fuji Nippon.

253. RC Noritake, Nippon Toki Kaisha, circa 1912.

254. Maruki Nippon, circa 1906.

255. Noritake Howo, circa 1916.

256. Chikaramachi, made in Japan, circa 1912.

257. Noritake M, Japan, circa 1916.

258. Kokura, Japan, circa 1920.

259. FY Nippon No. 76018, 402; found incised on dolls.

260. FY Nippon, 11148; found incised on dolls.

261. L & Co. Nippon.

262. Yanagi Nippon, Louis Wolf & Co.

263. SK Hand Painted Nippon.

264. FY Nippon 106; found on dolls.

265. FY Nippon 203; found on dolls.

266. FY Nippon 304; found on dolls.

267. FY Nippon 1604; found on dolls.

268. Scrolled FY No. 76018 Nippon 30/3; found on dolls.

269. Scrolled FY NO 76018 Nippon 30/6; found on dolls.

270. Scrolled FY NO 76018 Nippon 30/8; found on dolls.

271. Scrolled FY NO 76018 Nippon 20/0; found on dolls.

272. Scrolled FY No 76018 103 Nippon; found on dolls.

273. Scrolled FY NO 70018 Nippon 301; found on dolls.

274. Scrolled FY NO 76018 Nippon 405; found on dolls.

275. Scrolled FY NO 76018 Nippon 502; found on dolls.

276. Scrolled FY NO 76018 Nippon 601; found on dolls.

277. Scrolled FY NO 76018 Nippon 603; found on dolls.

278. Scrolled FY NO 76018 Nippon 902; found on dolls.

279. Scrolled FY NO 76016 Nippon 2001; found on dolls.

280. BE in diamond, Nippon; found on dolls.

281. RE Nippon A1; found on dolls.

282. RE Nippon O2; found on dolls.

283. RE Made in Nippon A10; found on dolls.

284. RE Nippon M20; found on dolls.

285. BE Nippon B10; found on dolls.

286. Horsman Nippon NO1; found on dolls.

287. Horsman Nippon B.6; found on dolls.

288. Horsman Nippon NO-11; found on dolls.

289. JW Nippon 603; found on dolls.

290. H in diamond, Nippon 14B P.4.; found on dolls.

291. HS in an oval, Nippon 12A; found on dolls.

292. HS in an oval, Nippon 14C; found on dolls.

293. M in blossom Nippon 18; found on dolls.

294. M in blossom Nippon; found on dolls.

295. KKS in star, Nippon 3003 P.47; found on dolls.

296. KKS in star, Nippon 4003 P.53; found on dolls.

297. M in blossom, Nippon 4; found on dolls.

298. M in blossom, Nippon E20; found on dolls.

299. M Nippon 12; found on dolls.

300. M in circle, Nippon E24; found on dolls.

301. M in circle, Nippon W10; found on dolls.

302. Patent No. 30441 Nippon; found incised on dolls.

303. H Nippon; found incised on dolls.

304. 2 Nippon; found incised on dolls.

3 NIPPON

305. 3 Nippon; found incised on dolls.

NIPPON 20

306. Nippon 20; found incised on dolls.

NIPPON 21

307. Nippon 21; found incised on dolls.

NIPPON 22

308. Nippon 22; found incised on dolls.

NIPPON 23

309. Nippon 23; found incised on dolls.

NIPPON 24

310. Nippon 24; found incised on dolls.

NO. 32 NIPPON

311. NO. 32 Nippon; found incised on dolls.

NIPPON 50

312. Nippon 50; found incised on dolls.

NIPPON 77

313. Nippon 77; found incised on dolls.

NIPPON 80

314. Nippon 80; found incised on dolls.

NIPPON 81

315. Nippon 81; found incised on dolls.

NIPPON 82

316. Nippon 82; found incised on dolls.

NIPPON 86

317. Nippon 86; found incised on dolls.

NIPPON 88

318. Nippon 88; found incised on dolls.

NIPPON 89

319. Nippon 89; found incised on dolls.

A 3 NIPPON

320. A 3 Nippon; found incised on dolls.

A 13 NIPPON

321. A 13 Nippon; found incised on dolls.

NIPPON B1

322. Nippon B1; found incised on dolls.

NIPPON B5

323. Nippon B5; found incised on dolls.

NIPPON II3

324. Nippon B10; found incised on dolls.

NIPPON B11

325. Nippon B11; found incised on dolls.

C 02 NIPPON

326. C 02 Nippon; found incised on dolls.

X NIPPON

327. X Nippon; found incised on dolls.

PATENT NIPPON

328. Patent Nippon; found incised on dolls.

NIPPON D

329. Nippon D; found incised on dolls.

NIPPON 87

330. Nippon 87; found incised on dolls.

93 NIPPON

331. 93 Nippon; found incised on dolls.

NIPPON 96

332. Nippon 96; found incised on dolls.

I03 NIPPON

333. 103 Nippon; found incised on dolls.

NIPPON II3

334. Nippon 113; found incised on dolls.

NIPPON I22

335. Nippon 122; found incised on dolls.

222 NIPPON

336. 222 Nippon; found incised on dolls.

337. Sticker found on Crinoline ballerina dolls.

338. Sticker found on Pixie doll.

339. Sticker found on Sweetie doll; Louis Wolf & Co.

340. Sticker found on Baby Belle doll; Morimura Bros.

341. Sticker found on Cutie doll; Louis Wolf & Co.

342. Sticker found on Kewpie doll.

343. Sticker found on the feet of Nippon Kewpie doll.

344. N & Co Nagoya Nippon.

345. Orange Blossom, made in Nippon.

346. Noritake, Nippon.

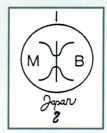

347. 1 MB (Morimura Bros.), Japan 8; found on dolls.

348. A9, RE Nippon; found on dolls.

349. No. 9 Horsman, Nippon; found on dolls.

350. No. 4, Horsman Nippon; found on dolls.

351. Royal Toya Nippon.

352. 03, RE in a diamond Nippon; found on dolls.

353. 14A, HS in an oval, Nippon.

354. M Nippon; found on dolls.

355. 2 MB (Morimura Bros.) Japan 7; found on dolls.

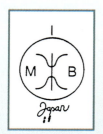

356. 1 MB (Morimura Bros.) Japan 11; found on dolls.

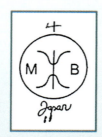

357. 4 MB (Morimura Bros.) Japan 11; found on dolls.

358. 01 RE in a diamond Nippon; found on dolls.

359. Wheelock hand painted Nippon.

Nippon from A to Z, Advertiques to Zig Zag Designs

ᔥ *Advertiques* ᔥ

Advertiques are a combination of advertising and/or promotional giveaways, gifts or advertising items that sold for very little. They were often given to tradesmen, vendors, salespeople, and sometimes the general public. They had messages written on them such as "Compliments of Eastern Outfitting Co.," "Compliments of Hammond Milling Co., Seattle, USA," or perhaps bear a sticker saying, "Compliments of Morimura Bros." Many of these stickers were washed off over the years and it is rare to locate one.

Fatima Turkish cigarettes are advertised on a combination matchbox holder and ashtray. A decal was placed on the item and features a veiled Turkish woman along with a red Maltese cross, a star, and a crescent. The words "Fatima Turkish Blend Cigarettes, Cameron & Cameron Co., Richmond, Va., Liggett & Myers Tobacco Co., Successor, No Gold Tips, Finest Quality" are also on the decal.

Morimura Brothers gave away a number of items over the years. One collector found a 1903 Morimura Brothers porcelain calendar. Then there's a calendar holder which says "Compliments of Hammond Milling Co. Seattle U.S.A.," shown on page 108.

Another advertique is a small nappy, which has a sticker on it bearing the words "Fair Week 1912 The D.M. Read Co. Bridgeport Conn." The D.M. Read Company is located in Bridgeport, Connecticut, and had an annual Houseware's Fair to which tradesmen, vendors, and salespeople were invited. They were presented with commemorative items made for the occasion including specialty pieces of china which were dated and which specified "Fair Week" on them. The general public attended because it was a big sale but did not receive any of the commemorative pieces.

The Nippon Nippers say souvenir on the pieces but Nipper is the main figure in the logo of the RCA trademark "His Master's Voice" so it is thought these were given out by the company years ago. Nipper is probably the most recognized dog in the world and has appeared on millions of records, phonographs, advertisements, etc. over the years. He is now over 100 years old.

According to the RCA Corp. little Nipper was a real fox terrier owned originally by the brother of an English artist. When the dog's owner died, the little animal became the pet of the artist.

One day in the late 1800s the artist, Francis Barraud, discovered the dog listening to an old-style horn-speaker phonograph with head cocked. The artist concluded the terrier thought he was hearing his original master's voice, hence the painting and the title *His Master's Voice*.

The painting became the property of the Victor Talking Machine Company in 1901 and the artist was permitted to paint a number of originals to supplement the annual royalty paid him by Victor to use the painting in various promotions.

These items are small in size, measuring 3 inches in height and 4 inches long. Most are found marked with Nippon, as the country of origin but several have been located that are marked Germany.

The reason I believe they were used as an advertising device is that numbers are found on them. Number 13 is Lowell, Massachusetts; number 20 is New London, Connecticut; number 24 is White Mountain, New Hampshire; number 27 is Scranton, Pennsylvania; number 35 is Watertown, New York; number 36 is Cincinnati, Ohio; number 42 is Syracuse, New York; number 221 is Burlington, Vermont; number 247 is Colorado Springs, Colorado; and number 920 is Westerly, Rhode Island. So far we know the numbers go to at least 920. Perhaps distributors in these various cities gave out these pieces to their customers. To date, the RCA Corp. has no idea about the distribution of these items.

Advertising tea strainer underplate, 4³/₄" wide. Strainer has three feet. Solitaire was a brand of the Morey Mercantile Company in Denver, Colorado. Rising Sun Mark, $150.00 – 200.00.

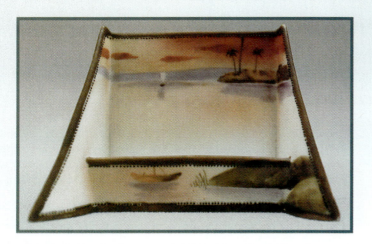

Calendar holder, 3" tall, green mark #47, back has printed "Compliments of Hammond Milling Co., Seattle, U.S.A.," $250.00 – 300.00.

Back view of calendar holder.

Novelty item, also souvenir piece from New London, Connecticut, 4" wide, mark #26, $175.00 – 225.00.

✎ *Airplane Décor Featured on Nippon* ✎

Airplane decoration is featured on a variety of Nippon items, from wall plaques to hanging ferners, double hanging matchbox holders, toothpick holders, covered boxes, powder jars, ashtrays, nappies, hatpin holders, vases, loving cups, shaving mugs, mustard pots, trivets, pitchers, demitasse sets, and tea sets. This decoration is found on items bearing the green #47 backstamp.

The pieces feature crudely drawn monoplanes and biplanes. A monoplane has one pair of wings whereas a biplane has two pairs of wings, one above the other. In 1909, aviator Louis Bleriot was the first to cross the English Channel in a powered airplane following the Wright Brothers success at Kitty Hawk, North Carolina, in 1903. During this period the world was filled with awe and wonder regarding these new flying machines and no doubt the Japanese wanted to feature these planes on Nippon wares because of their novelty.

Monoplane loving cup, 4" tall, green mark #47, $600.00 – 700.00.

Monoplane pin box, 3¹⁄₄" wide, green mark #47, $600.00 – 700.00.
Vase, 4¹⁄₄" tall, green mark #47, $600.00 – 700.00.

Monoplane hatpin holder, 5³⁄₄" tall, green mark #47, $600.00 – 700.00.
Matchbox holder, 3" tall, green mark #47, $600.00 – 700.00.

Close-up of monoplane decoration.

Bi-plane smoke set, green mark #47, $2,100.00 – 2,500.00.

American Indians Featured on Nippon

American Indians are the decoration for numerous pieces of Nippon porcelain. Although some are hand painted, many of these items bear decals as their decoration and probably the most popular are three Indian chiefs featured on some of the wares. Their portraits are surrounded with applied moriage trim of crossed arrows and the staff of power, which is entwined with tossled rope and buffalo horns. In the so-called Indian Chief series, all are wearing medals awarded to them by the United States government as a means to pacify the Indians and to encourage them to turn to farming. During President Ulysses S. Grant's term (1869 – 1877) the medal given to the Indian chiefs featured a likeness of President Grant on one side and a globe surrounded by farm implements on the reverse. The three Indian chiefs are Chief Sitting Bull (1834 – 1890) from the Hunkpapa Sioux tribe, Chief Joseph (1840 – 1904) from the Nez Perce tribe, and Chief Red Cloud from the Oglala Sioux tribe. Backstamps found on these pieces indicate that most were manufactured after 1910. All kinds of items can be found, from vases to humidors, wall plaques, ashtrays, bookends, cigarette boxes, pitchers, matchbox holders, steins, bowls, and relish dishes. These pieces can be found utilizing many of the techniques employed on Nippon wares such as molded in relief, coralene, and moriage trim. Some were even copies of famous paintings of that era.

Humidor, molded in relief, 7" tall, green mark #47, $4,000.00 – 5,000.00.

Ashtray, molded in relief, 6½" long, green mark #47, $900.00 – 1,000.00.

Wall plaque, molded in relief, 10½" wide, green mark #47, $1,200.00 – 1,500.00.

Humidor, molded in relief, 7½" tall, green
mark #47, $3,000.00 – 3,500.00.

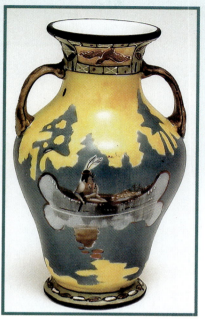

Vase, 7" tall, mark #38, $300.00 – 400.00.

Pitcher, 4¾" tall, mark scratched off, $150.00 – 200.00.

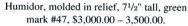

✒ *American Indian Designs* — **Coming to the Call** ✒

Frederic Remington (1861 – 1909) painted the original painting *Coming to the Call* in 1905. Remington was an illustrator, painter, and sculptor. His field sketches were often done in watercolors and he is known for his paintings of soldiers, cowboys, Indians, and toughs. *Coming to the Call* was published as a full-color double page for the August 19, 1905 *Collier's Weekly* spread. It's been advertised as one of his four best paintings. The Japanese copied his work on a number of Nippon wares, however the design featured on Nippon wares varies a little from the original.

This décor is growing in popularity and features an Indian at dusk riding in a canoe. Pieces having this decoration feature both a plain and geometric border. It is found on plaques, humidors, vases, and various utilitarian items. Pieces carry the green #47 backstamp.

Wall plaque, 10" wide, green mark #47, $500.00 – 600.00.

Humidor, 7" tall, green mark #47,
$1,300.00 – 1,500.00.

Bowl, 7½" wide, green mark #47,
$250.00 – 300.00.

Close-up of design.

Ferner, 7¼" wide, green mark #47, $600.00 – 700.00.

ᴥ *American Indian Designs* — In the Crystal Depths ᴥ

W.C. Wyeth (1883 – 1945) painted *In the Crystal Depths* in 1906. It is an oil on canvas and was used for an illustration for the series *The Indian in His Solitude*. It was featured on the cover of *Outing* magazine in June of 1907. It is a primitive looking scene of an Indian in his canoe looking intently at the water in what appears to be a river running through a gorge. The scene featured on Nippon pieces varies a little from the original.

Wall plaque, 10³/₄" wide, green mark #47, $800.00 – 1,000.00.

ᴥ *American Indian Designs* — Incised Indian ᴥ

Incised Indian pieces are decorated with a stylized Indian done in earth tones and this decoration is known to exist on humidors, candlesticks, wall plaques, steins, and various smoking pieces. These items carry the green #47 backstamp.

Humidor, 6" tall, green mark #47,
$800.00 – 900.00.

Stein, 7" tall, green mark #47,
$800.00 – 900.00.

⇜ *American Indian Designs* — *Molded Indian on Horseback* ⇝

Molded Indian on horseback depicts an Indian on horseback riding into battle. This décor is most often found on 10" wall plaques, but is occasionally seen on chargers, ferners, and humidors. Pieces are marked with the green #47 backstamp.

Wall plaque, molded in relief, 10¹⁄₂" wide, green mark #47, $900.00 – 1,000.00.

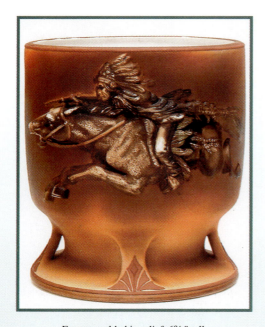

Ferner, molded in relief, 6³⁄₄" tall, green mark #47, $1,200.00 – 1,500.00.

⇜ *American Indian Designs* — **Shadows at the Waterhole** ⇝

Shadows at the Waterhole is a painting by artist, Frederic Remington. It was painted in 1907 and was featured in the August 24 issue of *Collier's Weekly*. This painting has been advertised as one of his four best paintings. The original painting features three Indians and two horses at sunset. Nippon artists varied this scene somewhat from the original.

Nippon pieces feature a scene done in rich vibrant primary colors. This décor has been found on humidors and wall plaques and they carry the green #47 backstamp.

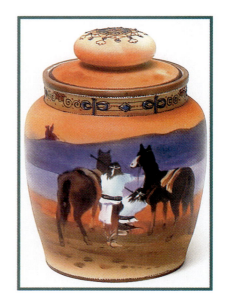

Humidor, 7¹⁄₄" tall, green mark #47, $1,300.00 – 1,700.00.

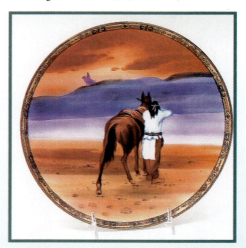

Wall plaque, 10¹⁄₄" wide, green mark #47, $800.00 – 950.00.

☙ *American Indian Designs — The Hunter* ☙

The Hunter is an oil on canvas painted by the artist, W.C. Wyeth, circa 1906. It was the cover illustration for the June 1906 issue of *The Outing* magazine. It features an Indian out hunting with bow and arrow in his hand and a dead bird slung over his back. The version featured on Nippon pieces varies slightly from the original.

Wall plaque, molded in relief, 10½" wide, green mark #47, $850.00 – 950.00.

☙ *American Indian Designs — Three Chief Series* ☙

Probably the most popular of the Indian designs are those of the three Indian chiefs featured on some of the Nippon wares. All the three chiefs are wearing medals awarded to them by the United States government as a means to pacify the Indians and to encourage them to turn to farming. During President Ulysses S. Grant's term (1869 – 1877) the medal given to the Indian chiefs featured a likeness of President Grant on one side and a globe surrounded by farm implements on the reverse. The three Indian chiefs are Chief Sitting Bull (1834 – 1890) from the Hunkpapa Sioux tribe, Chief Joseph (1840 – 1904) from the Nez Perce tribe and Chief Red Cloud from the Olgala Sioux tribe.

The so-called enameled Indian design has decalcomania medallions featuring the Indian chiefs' heads with enamel moriage trim work. This décor is only seen on smoking items such as humidors, ashtrays, and cigarette boxes.

The other three chiefs' pieces have their decalcomania (decal) portraits surrounded with applied moriage trim of crossed arrows and the staff of power, which is entwined with tossled rope and buffalo horns.

Wall plaque featuring Chief Joseph, 10½" wide, blue mark #47, $2,000.00 – 2,400.00.

Humidors, 5½" tall each,
Left: Chief Joseph, blue mark #47.
Middle: Chief Sitting Bull, green mark #47.
Right: Chief Red Cloud, green mark #47.
$1,500.00 – 1,800.00 each.

Wall plaque featuring Chief Sitting Bull, 10½" wide,
blue mark #47, $2,000.00 – 2,400.00.

Wall plaque featuring Chief Red Cloud, 10½" wide,
blue mark #47, $2,000.00 – 2,400.00.

Humidors, 7½" tall each,
blue mark #52.
Left: Chief Joseph.
Middle: Chief Red Cloud.
Right: Chief Sitting Bull.
$2,400.00 – 3,000.00 each.

⌒ *Angelus Design* ⌒

Jean Francois Millet (1814 – 1875) painted *The Angelus* in 1859. Millet was a master painter in France and this scene features two peasants in a field giving thanks for their crops. This painting appears to be a romantic veneration of peasant life and rural simplicity painted in soft colors. The scene displayed on Nippon wares is a decal that is an adaptation of the original painting.

Vase, 11½" tall,
green mark #47, $1,700.00 – 2,000.00.

ᴥ *Animals Found on Nippon Porcelain* ᴥ

Many different animals have been found on Nippon. All types of techniques were used including molded in relief, hand painting, moriage, figural, coralene, tapestry, and decals. Some have even been copied from famous artists such as Sir Edwin Landseer, Frederic Remington, and Anton Mauve. Bats, bears, buffalos, camels, cats, cows, deer, dogs, elephants, elk, foxes, giraffes, goats, horses, kangaroos, lions, mice, moose, mules, rabbits, raccoons, seals, sheep, squirrels, tigers, and oxen all adorn Nippon wares.

Two-piece mayonnaise set, underplate: 5¼" wide, Bowl: 4½" wide, $150.00 – 200.00.

Smoke set, tray: 9¾" wide, green mark #47, $600.00 – 700.00.

Humidor, 7¼" tall, green mark #47, $800.00 – 1,100.00.

Humidor, molded in relief, 6½" tall, green mark #47, $3,000.00 – 4,000.00.

Humidor, 6" tall,
green mark #47, $500.00 – 600.00.

Wall plaque, molded in relief, 10¹/₂" wide,
green mark #47, $800.00 – 950.00.

Mug, 5¹/₂" tall,
green mark #47, $250.00 – 300.00.

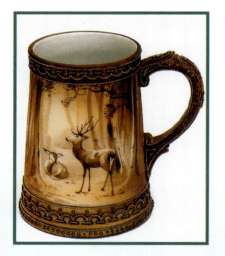

Mug, 5¹/₂" tall,
green mark #47, $300.00 – 400.00.

Wall plaque, 10" wide,
green mark #47, $600.00 – 700.00.

Vase, 9¹/₂" tall,
green mark #47, $350.00 – 450.00.

Wall plaque, molded in relief, 10½" wide,
green mark #47, $700.00 – 900.00.

Matchbox holder/tray, 5¼" wide,
green mark #47, $250.00 – 300.00.

Wall plaque, 9" wide,
green mark #47, $425.00 – 500.00.

Wall plaque, molded in relief, 10½" wide,
blue mark #47, $900.00 – 1,200.00.

Wall plaque, molded in relief, 10¾" wide,
green mark #47, $700.00 – 900.00.

Wall plaque, molded in relief, 10½" wide,
green mark #47, $900.00 – 1,200.00.

Ashtray, molded in relief, 5½" wide,
green mark #47, $600.00 – 700.00.

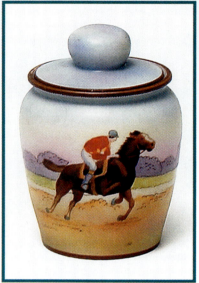

Humidor, 5¼" tall,
green mark #47, $350.00 – 400.00.

Wall plaque, molded in relief, 10½" wide,
green mark #47, $1,500.00 – 1,800.00.

Wall plaque, 10½" wide,
blue mark #47, $1,000.00 – 1,200.00.

Wall plaque, 10½" wide,
blue mark #47, $1,000.00 – 1,200.00.

Humidor, molded in relief, 7" tall,
blue mark #47, $1,200.00 – 1,500.00.

Humidor, 6" tall,
green mark #47, $500.00 – 600.00.

Ashtray, molded in relief, 5¼" wide,
green mark #47, $500.00 – 600.00.

Humidor, 6" tall,
green mark #47, $1,200.00 – 1,500.00.

Wall plaque, 12¼" wide,
green mark #47, $1,800.00 – 2,200.00.

Wall plaque, 12" wide,
green mark #47, $1,800.00 – 2,200.00.

Humidor, 5¾" tall,
mark #351, $300.00 – 350.00.

Humidor, molded in relief, 7" tall,
green mark #47, $1,200.00 – 1,500.00.

Humidor, molded in relief, 7¼" tall,
green mark #47, $1,800.00 – 2,200.00.

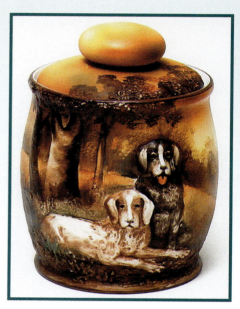

Humidor, molded in relief, 7" tall,
green mark #47, $1,800.00 – 2,200.00.

Wall plaque, 11" wide,
green mark #47, $800.00 – 1,000.00.

Stein, molded in relief, 7¼" tall,
green mark #47, $1,500.00 – 1,800.00.

Ashtray, 6¾" wide,
green mark #47, $250.00 – 300.00.

Wall plaque, 10" wide,
green mark #47, $400.00 – 475.00.

Wall plaque, 8³/₄" wide,
green mark #47, $250.00 – 300.00.

Wall plaque, 9¹/₂" wide,
mark #109, $550.00 – 650.00.

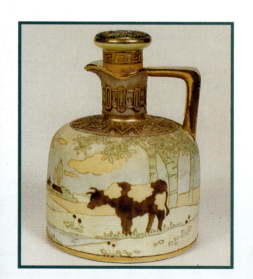

Whiskey jug, 6" tall,
green mark #47, $850.00 – 950.00.

Ashtray, 5¹/₄" wide,
mark #17, $225.00 – 275.00.

Humidor, molded in relief, 7¹/₂" wide,
green mark #47, $2,100.00 – 2,400.00.

⌒ *Animal Scenes* — **African Monarch** ⌒

African Monarch features a beautiful lion that is a copy of a painting by Herbert Dicksee (1862 – 1942). The decal found on Nippon pieces is usually decorated with hand-painted work as well as some moriage decoration in the form of leaves and acorns. Dicksee came from an artistic English family. He used to visit the Zoological Gardens and many of his wild animal etchings were drawn there. He had a fascination with lions, tigers, and leopards. He also drew domestic scenes and dogs. Early on, he painted in oils and watercolors but eventually turned to etchings. He paid painstaking attention to the anatomy of animals.

Ferner, 5³/₄" wide,
green mark #47, $600.00 – 725.00.

Shaving mug, 3³/₄" tall, green mark #47, $350.00 – 450.00.

Humidor, 5¹/₂" tall, green mark #47,
$600.00 – 725.00.

Close-up of *African Monarch.*

ᔒ *Animal Scenes — Anton Mauve's* **Spring** ᔒ

Anton Mauve (1838 – 1888) was a Dutch landscape painter who excelled in painting scenes featuring the green meadows of Holland and the peaceful rural life of the fields and country lanes.

He was a cousin of Vincent van Gogh and also his mentor. The version found on Nippon wares was adapted from the painting *Spring*.

Wall plaque, 10¼" wide, green mark #47, $350.00 – 450.00.

ᔒ *Animal Scenes — Apollo and Dogs* ᔒ

The Apollo and dogs design is found on three molded-in-relief Nippon items: a vase, humidor, and a 12" wall plaque. Apollo was the son of Zeus and was considered the Greek god of the sun. He was born on the sunny Greek island of Delos with his twin sister Artemis who was the virgin goddess of the hunt and

the moon. Apollo supposedly drives his chariot across the sky daily. He was considered one of the greatest of the Olympia gods and the perfection of youthful manhood. Many of the Greek gods were associated with dogs, and Apollo is no exception.

Humidor, molded in relief, 6" tall, green mark #47, $2,000.00 – 2,500.00.

Wall plaque, molded in relief, 12" wide, green mark #47, $2,500.00 – 3,000.00.

♒ *Animal Scenes — Artemis and Horse* ♒

Artemis and one of her horses are featured on one of the rarest Nippon pieces known to exit. She is found on a 14" wide rectangular wall plaque that is molded in relief. Artemis is the twin sister of Apollo who is depicted on other Nippon items. Artemis is known as the virgin goddess of the hunt and the moon. She has long, flowing, gold hair and her horse is pulling her chariot across the sky. Artemis was born on the floating island of Delos.

Wall plaque, 14" wide, green mark #47, $10,000.00 – 13,000.00.

♒ *Animal Scenes — Captive Horse* ♒

Captive horse is the name given to a décor that features two dogs and a horse communing. These stylized pieces are generally trimmed with some type of heavy clay moriage. This decoration is known to exist on wall plaques, both round and rectangular, inkwells, mugs, and humidors. Pieces are marked with the green #47 backstamp.

Wall plaque, 10½" wide,
green mark #47, $500.00 – 600.00.

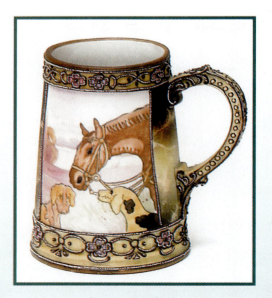

Mug, 5½" tall,
green mark #47, $350.00 – 400.00.

❧ *Animal Scenes — Cows at Water's Edge* ❧

Cows at water's edge is a popular pattern, which features one or more cows resting at the edge of a pond. It is known to exist on vases, urns, cracker jars, and rectangular plaques. These items carry the green #47 backstamp.

Wall plaque, 10¼" wide, green mark #47, $2,400.00 – 2,800.00.

❧ *Animal Scenes* — **Fathers of the Pack** ❧

William Barraud (1810 – 1850) painted *Fathers of the Pack* and it is this painting that inspired the molded in relief wall plaque featuring three dog heads. The Nippon era ones have a matte finish whereas the ones that were made after this period have a shiny appearance and bear the M in wreath, Made in Japan backstamp.

Barraud painted mostly horses and dogs and studied animal painting with Abraham Cooper. He exhibited at the Royal Academy and this English painter also collaborated on a number of paintings with his brother, Henry. He is also known for his many sports and hunting scenes.

The three dogs featured in the painting are hunting hounds that were owned by Mr. Richard Hill and were used in the Pytchley hunt. At first Barraud painted in oil and watercolors and then switched to etchings. It often took up to three to four months to etch a plate and it is believed that he produced about 140 artistic works over his lifetime.

Wall plaque, 10½" wide, green mark #47, $1,500.00 – 1,900.00.

⤳ *Animal Scenes — Fighting Frogs* ⤳

Fighting frogs is a design featuring frogs that appear to be hitting each other with sticks. The frogs are executed in a moriage technique on a green background. Three frogs are depicted on the front of the item and a single frog is featured on the reverse side. Fighting frogs are found on various Nippon items including wine jugs, vases, ferners, mugs, and ewers. Most pieces are unmarked as are a lot of those decorated in the moriage technique, however, a few do bear the maple leaf mark. Today, these items are difficult to find and generally expensive to purchase.

This design is similar to work produced by the Japanese artist Toba Sojo, also called Kakuyu (1053 – 1140), a monk of a Buddhist sect near Kyoto. *Scrolls of Frolicking Animals* are ink paintings on paper attributed to him and are considered national treasures of Japan. They are housed in the Kosan-Ji Temple in an area west of Kyoto. Kozan-Ji sits high on the slopes of Mt. Takao. The four scrolls feature animals and birds shown amongst autumn grasses in situations that are both humorous and deriding the Buddhist clergy. The paintings are a satire of the life of people disguised as animals. The animals are dancing, swimming, wrestling, there is even a monkey dressed as a monk worshipping a frog. At that time there was decadence among the monks and nobles and these animals are depicted as nobles, soldiers, monks, and other people. They were an attempt to get around censorship. The Japanese have long enjoyed art where animals engage in human behavior and fighting frogs appears to be an attempt to emulate some of this earlier art.

On a recent trip to Kyoto I visited this museum and viewed copies of these picture scrolls and received permission to photograph them. These scrolls are very famous in Japan and it is presumed that these scrolls are the source of inspiration for this particular design.

Moriage vase, 6" tall, unmarked, $2,600.00 – 3,000.00.

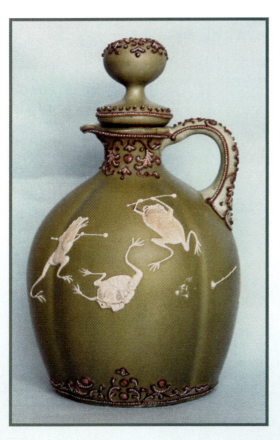

Wine jug, 8¼" tall, unmarked, $3,000.00 – 3,500.00.

Back of vase.

Photo taken at Kosan-Ji Temple of part of picture scroll.

Photo of part of picture scroll of frolicking birds and animals.

➬ *Animal Scenes — French Bulldog Head* ➬

Herbert Dicksee (1862 – 1942) painted the French bulldog head. The dog is found on molded-in-relief wall plaques in three-color variations, see page 63. The Nippon pieces are an adaptation of this old painting. The dog is wearing a collar and appears to be quite dignified. Herbert Dicksee came from an artistic English family and was famous for his dog paintings as well as those that featured lions, tigers, and leopards. Early on, he painted in oils and watercolors but eventually turned to etching. He paid painstaking attention to the anatomy of animals.

Wall plaque, 10" wide, green mark #47, $1,000.00 – 1,200.00.

Animal Scenes — Landseer's Newfoundland

Sir Edwin Landseer (1802 – 1873) painted *A Distinguished Member of the Humane Society* in 1838 and it became one of his most famous paintings. It features a Newfoundland dog named Paul Pry who is sitting proudly and nobly on a dock by the water's edge. Landseer's dog paintings of the 1830s constitute one of the high points of his art. Many prints of this famous dog were made and sold for just pennies. The Nippon version is done in sepia tones and is known to exist on wall plaques, both round and rectangular, and humidors. These items carry the green #47 backstamp, which indicates that they were manufactured after 1910.

Wall plaque, 10¼" wide, green mark #47, $2,400.00 – 2,800.00.

Animal Scenes — Lion's Head

Lions Head was painted by Herbert Dicksee (1862 – 1942) and was one of his early works. Dicksee came from an artistic English family and he had a fascination with lions, tigers, leopards, and also domestic scenes and dogs. He paid painstaking attention to the anatomy of animals and used to visit the Zoological Gardens where he drew many of his animals.

Wall plaque, molded in relief, 10½" wide,
green mark #47, $1,500.00 – 2,000.00.

Wall plaque, 12¼" wide,
green mark #47, $1,900.00 – 2,100.00.

☙ *Animal Scenes* — **Monarch of the Glen** ☜

Monarch of the Glen is one of Sir Edwin Landseer's most famous paintings. Landseer (1802 – 1873) was an English painter trained by his father. He was a boy prodigy and is the most celebrated of Victorian England's animal painters. Each year he traveled to the Highlands in Scotland to rest, draw, and get inspiration for his paintings. The design used on Nippon pieces is evidently an adaptation of this work of art.

Wall plaque, 10³/₄" wide, green mark #47, $225.00 – 275.00.

☙ *Animal Scenes* — **Moose in the Woods** ☜

Georges Frederic Rotig painted *Moose in the Woods* and this design is found on molded relief Nippon era pieces. Rotig (1873 – 1961) was a Parisian painter of animals. He had the good fortune to study with some of the most talented instructors of his time: Jules Lefebvre, Benjamin Constant, and Jean Paul Laurens. He exhibited at the Salon des Artistes Francais in 1894 and received medals in 1902 and 1904. He also received the Rose Bonheur prize in 1913. Some of his paintings can be found in the collections of museums in Le Havre, Cambria, and Amiens.

Moose in the Woods, also referred to as *The Moose*, appears on two different size wall plaques, the 10¹/₂" one and the charger size which is 14" wide. The design is also found on a vase. This adaptation is almost an exact copy of the original work of art except for the background area which contains several more moose.

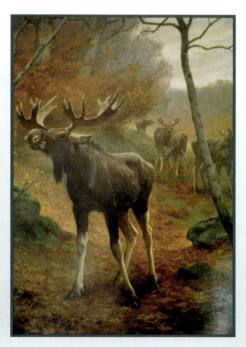

Wall plaque, molded in relief, 10³/₄" wide, green mark #47, $700.00 – 900.00.

Original painting by Georges Frederic Rotig.

Close-up of painting.

ᔟ *Animal Scenes* — The Raiders ᔟ

The Raiders also known to Nippon collectors as the lion and lioness was painted by Herbert Dicksee (1862 – 1942) in 1905. Dicksee came from an artistic English family and had a fascination with lions, tigers, and leopards. He also painted domestic scenes and dogs. He was known for his painstaking attention to the anatomy of animals. This particular scene is found on molded in relief humidors and wall plaques.

Wall plaque, molded in relief, 10½" wide,
green mark #47, $600.00 – 800.00.

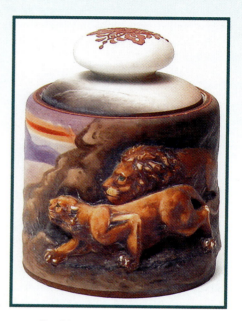

Humidor, molded in relief, 7¼" tall,
green mark #47, $800.00 – 1,000.00.

ᔟ *Animal Scenes* — To Ho, To Ho ᔟ

To Ho, To Ho, was painted by Sir Edwin Landseer and features two sporting dogs. It is believed that the scene found on Nippon wares is an adaptation of this painting. Landseer (1802 – 1873) was the most famous English artist of his generation and the most celebrated of Victorian England's animal painters. He was a boy prodigy who sketched animals from early in his lifetime. His father trained him to paint and Landseer used to go to the Highlands in Scotland every year to rest, draw, and get inspiration for his paintings.

Smoke set, tray: 11½" long, blue mark #3, $1,800.00 – 2,100.00.

⌒ *Animal Scenes — Two Different Dog Series* ⌒

There are two series of dogs featured on Nippon wares. The one series features six different dogs showing just head and neck views. All the dogs are decalcomanias (decals). In this series there are three sizes of wall plaques, 8", 9", and 10". The 8" and 10" ones have a green border trimmed with heavy enameling. The 9" size has a different border and the dog is framed in a medallion type center.

Four champion dogs are featured on a limited number of Nippon pieces. All are decals and include L'Ambassadeur (white in color), Katerfelto (white with dark spots), Rodney Stone (dark brown with a white chest), and Bromley Crib (brown with white nose band). All are champion bulldogs. The English bulldog

breed was developed in England in the thirteenth century. They were known for their courage and ferocity in the sport of bull-baiting. Bullbaiting became illegal in 1835 and the dog was then bred to eliminate viciousness. The bulldog has a massive head, wide shoulders, and short, stout and straight forelegs. It has a large broad nose and a deep, broad and full chest. These dogs are found on 10" plaques, 7" whiskey jugs, 5½" tall humidors, 5½" wide cigarette boxes, 5" round ashtrays, and 6½" wide ashtrays with match holders. The series has a cream background with brown and rust geometric designs except the jugs, which have a marbled background. The dogs are featured in a panel or reserve.

Wall plaques, blue mark #52. 10" wide, $900.00 – 1,000.00.
9" wide, $800.00 – 900.00. 8" wide, $700.00 – 800.00.

Wall plaques, blue mark #52.
Left: 10" wide, $900.00 – 1,000.00.
Right: 8" wide, $700.00 – 800.00.

Wall plaques, blue mark #52.
Left: 10" wide, $900.00 – 1,000.00.
Right: 8" wide, $700.00 – 800.00.

Wall plaque, 10" wide, green mark #47, $900.00 – 1,000.00.

Humidor, 5½ tall", green mark #47. $1,100.00 – 1,300.00.

Close-up of name.

Back of humidor.

Whiskey jug, featuring Rodney Stone, 6¾" tall, green mark #47. $1,100.00 – 1,300.00.

Combination ashtray and matchbox holder, 6½" long, green mark #47, $750.00 – 850.00.

✑ *Animal Scenes — Victory* ✑

Victory is a scene painted by Herbert Dicksee (1862 – 1942) and features a lion killing a snake. This particular adaptation is found on molded-in-relief pieces on Nippon ware. The ferner has been found in two color variations. Dicksee came from an artistic English family and used to visit the Zoological Gardens to study the animals. He had a fascination with lions, tigers, and leopards although he did paint some domestic scenes and dogs. He paid painstaking attention to the anatomy of animals.

Ferner, molded in relief, 8¼" long,
green mark #47, $600.00 – 800.00.

Humidor, molded in relief, 6¾" tall,
green mark #47, $800.00 – 950.00.

Ferner, molded in relief, 8¼" long,
green mark #47, $600.00 – 800.00.

✑ *Arrival of the Coach* ✑

The arrival of the coach is a stylized scene of an English coach. There is a footman riding on the back of the carriage and he's blowing a horn, perhaps as a warning or an announcement to others that the coach is arriving. In the 1500s, the first coaches were introduced in England. They belonged mainly to royal families and the aristocracy and were a mark of rank and/or wealth. During the seventeenth century they were used as public transportation between towns and eventually became known as the stagecoach.

This design is known to exist on vases, jugs, and wall plaques. These pieces carry the green #47 backstamp.

Vase, 5½" tall,
green mark #47, $700.00 – 800.00.

Vase, 7½" tall,
green mark #47, $700.00 – 800.00.

Wall plaque, 11" wide,
green mark #47, $700.00 – 800.00.

✎ *Art Nouveau Style* ✎

Art Nouveau designs feature twisting, long flowing lines. This art style was popular in both the United States and Europe from approximately 1890 to 1910. It took its inspiration from nature and women. Depictions of flowers, leaves, and insects in a swirling motif style were now the modern style or so-called new art. After World War I it went out of favor and was replaced by the Art Deco movement.

Moriage portrait vase, 10" tall,
blue mark #52, $4,000.00 – 5,000.00.

Humidor, 6½" tall,
green mark #47, $2,200.00 – 2,400.00.

View of humidor open.

Covered jar, 9¾" tall,
blue mark #47, $450.00 – 550.00.

Vase, 15½" tall, green mark
#47, $800.00 – 950.00.

⤺ *Artist Signed Items* ⤻

Artist signatures or initials are found on a few Nippon pieces and many collectors feel that this adds to the value of the item. Seasoned collectors know that this is not true. Sometimes blank items entered the United States and were painted at a decorating studio or by an individual, most likely a woman whose hobby was china painting. Sometimes we find just initials or a Japanese name written in English. Why this was done is unknown. A few Nippon pieces were decorated at the Pickard Company and the artist's name might be found on one of these items. Signatures mean little to collectors. Quality of workmanship means everything. If the item is poorly executed, as is the case with some of the decorating studio pieces it can be worth very little. If the piece has a beautiful design and the artwork is superb no one cares if there is signature or not. Collectors should try to buy the best quality Nippon porcelain they can afford. One good item is better than three or four mediocre pieces.

Artist signed item.

Artist signed item.

⌇ *Beading* ⌇

A number of pieces are found with allover beading while others might just have a trim of beadwork. Clay slip was used to actually make tiny beads on the items that were produced. After the firing, the beads were painted over in gold or other colors. Many of the later pieces, however, merely had dots of enameling applied to acquire this effect.

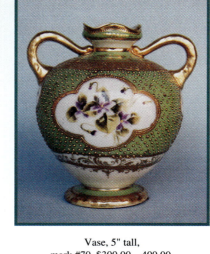

Vase, 5" tall,
mark #70, $300.00 – 400.00.

Pin dish, 2¼" wide,
green mark #52, $200.00 – 250.00.

Vase, 12" tall,
blue mark #52, $1,000.00 – 1,200.00.

Chocolate pot, 9½" tall,
mark #89, $700.00 – 900.00.

Covered urn, 10¼" tall,
blue mark #52, $1,200.00 – 1,400.00.

Beading — Aqua Beaded Items

Aqua beading is found on a number of Nippon items. The aqua beads are placed on a gold background generally surrounding a center medallion of pink, white, and red roses. Paintings of more roses are interspersed over the gold area. This particular pattern is a favorite with many collectors. Numerous items can be found, cups and saucers, creamers and sugar bowls, etc. but this pattern is more often found on vases of various shapes and styles.

Vase, 9" tall,
blue mark #52, $900.00 – 1,200.00.

Vase, 7" tall,
blue mark #52, $800.00 – 1,000.00.

Beaded — Beaded Mum Designs

The beaded mum design features gold beads of different sizes placed all over the background of the piece. Lush, hand-painted lavender and white mums and green leaves complete the pattern. Collectors find this to be an extremely desirable design.

Vase, 5" tall,
green mark #52, $1,000.00 – 1,200.00.

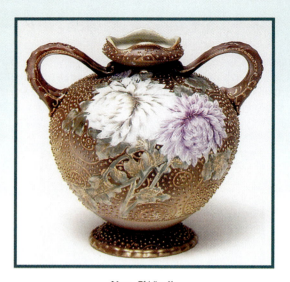

Vase, 7¼" tall,
blue mark #52, $1,200.00 – 1,500.00.

Vase, 11¼" tall,
blue mark #52, $2,000.00 – 2,500.00.

ᔥ *Beverage Items* ᔥ

The Japanese made all kinds of items for beverages. One can find wine and whiskey jugs, steins and mugs, chocolate sets, tea sets, demitasse sets, cordial sets, lemonade sets, tankard and mug sets, pitchers, saki containers, carafe sets, punch sets, mustache cups, and invalid feeders.

Invalid feeder, 6½" long, blue mark #84,
$50.00 – 65.00.

Tankard, 11½" tall,
blue mark #52,
$800.00 – 1,000.00.

Stein, 7¼" tall, green mark #47,
$800.00 – 950.00.

Chocolate set, pot: 10½" tall, set comes with six cups
and saucers, mark #109, $300.00 – 350.00.

Chocolate set, pot: 10½" tall, set comes with six cups
and saucers, blue mark #52, $1,400.00 – 1,800.00.

Chocolate set, comes with six cups and saucers,
blue mark #52, $2,000.00 – 2,400.00.

Chocolate set, pot: 10¼" tall, set comes with six cups and saucers,
green mark #52, $1,800.00 – 2,300.00.

Carafe set, mark #47, $1,000.00 – 1,300.00.

Saki container, 6¾" tall, mark #89, $350.00 – 400.00.

Whiskey jug, 6" tall, green mark #47,
$850.00 – 1,000.00.

Tea set, mark #47, comes with six cups and saucers, $400.00 – 500.00.

Mustache cup and saucer, mark #84, $200.00 – 250.00.

Punch set, Bowl: 17" wide including handles,
green mark #47, $3,000.00 – 3,500.00.

Cordial set, container: 8" tall,
green mark #47, $1,000.00 – 1,200.00.

⚞ *Bird Scenes* ⚟

Birds can be found on all types of items and in all types of decoration; hand painted, molded in relief, coralene, tapestry, moriage, figural, and decals. There are many types of birds portrayed from the kingfisher to the swan, ostrich, pheasant, bluebird, robin, eagle, chicken, duck, cockatoo, crane, canary, turkey, owl, pelican, stork, swallow, wren, and mythological hoo bird.

Pin box, 2¾" tall, blue mark #47, $400.00 – 500.00.
Pin tray, 4¼" wide, blue mark #47, $250.00 – 300.00.
Powder shaker, 4¼" tall, blue mark #47, $400.00 – 500.00.

Baby items, green mark #47.
Tray, 9" long, $350.00 – 400.00.
Powder shaker, $300.00 – 350.00.

Wall plaque, 8¾" wide, green mark #47, $350.00 – 400.00.

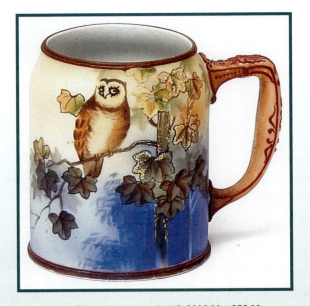

Mug, 4¾" tall, green mark #47, $325.00 – 375.00.

Mug, 5½" tall, green mark #47,
$375.00 – 450.00.

Stein, molded in relief, 7" tall, green mark #47,
$1,500.00 – 1,800.00.

Vase, 11½" tall, green mark #47,
$450.00 – 550.00.

Wall plaque, 10" wide, green mark #47,
$350.00 – 400.00.

Wall plaque, 8³/₄" wide, green mark #47,
$350.00 – 400.00.

Wall plaque, 7³/₄" wide, green mark #47,
$250.00 – 325.00.

Matchbox holder, 3¹/₂" tall, green mark #47,
$350.00 – 400.00.

Humidor, molded in relief, 6³/₄" tall, green mark #47,
$1,800.00 – 2,000.00.

Humidor, 5½" tall, green mark #47,
$400.00 – 475.00.

Figural owl vase, 9¼" tall, green mark #47,
$1,800.00 – 2,200.00.

Figural ashtray, 5½" wide, green mark #47,
$800.00 – 1,000.00.

Humidor, 6½" tall, green mark #47,
$550.00 – 650.00.

Humidor, 3¾" tall, green mark #47,
$400.00 – 475.00.

Humidor, 6¾" tall, green mark #47,
$550.00 – 650.00.

Humidor, 6½" tall, green mark #47,
$600.00 – 700.00.

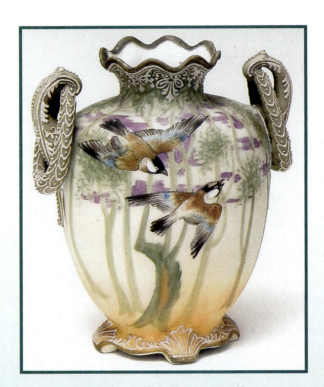

Moriage vase, 8½" tall, blue mark #47,
$1,100.00 – 1,300.00.

Vase, 9" tall, blue mark #47,
$400.00 – 450.00.

Vase, 10" tall, green mark #47,
$600.00 – 700.00.

Vase, 7¾" tall, blue mark #47,
$200.00 – 250.00.

Vase, 15½" tall, blue mark #47,
$1,800.00 – 2,200.00.

Wall plaque, 9¾" wide, blue mark #47,
$400.00 – 450.00.

Wall plaque, 9" wide, green mark #47,
$150.00 – 200.00.

Wall plaque, 8½" wide, blue mark #47,
$200.00 – 250.00.

Wall plaque, 11¼" wide, green mark #47,
$800.00 – 1,000.00.

Wall plaque, 10" wide, green mark #47,
$600.00 – 750.00.

Wall plaque, 10¼" wide, green mark #47,
$450.00 – 550.00.

Moriage vase, 8½" tall, blue mark #52,
$800.00 – 1,000.00.

Wall plaque, molded in relief, 10½" wide,
green mark #47, $2,500.00 – 3,000.00.

Vase, 5¼" tall,
green mark #47, $200.00 – 250.00.

Humidor, 7" tall, green mark #47, $725.00 – 825.00.

Wall plaque, 11" wide, blue mark #52, $750.00 – 850.00.

Wall plaque, 10" wide, blue mark #52, $600.00 – 700.00.

Covered urn, 14¹/₄" tall, blue mark #52,
$2,000.00 – 2,400.00.

Vases.
Left: 3¹/₂" tall, blue mark #47, $125.00 – 150.00.
Right: 5" tall, unmarked, $75.00 – 100.00.

Vase, 7³/₄" long, green mark #47, $150.00 – 200.00.

⤳ *Bird Scenes — Aqua Flying Swan Design* ⤳

Items decorated with the aqua flying swan design are trimmed in heavy gold and enameled jewelling. The hallmark of these pieces is the swans flying through marsh reeds. This pattern is known to exist on a variety of molds including chocolate and tea sets, dresser sets, vases, ferners, candlesticks, and urns. Pieces are backstamped with the blue or green #52 or green or blue #47 mark. This scene was copied from Royal Worcester pieces which Charles Baldwyn designed.

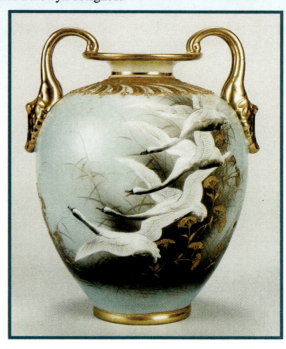

Tankard set, green mark #47, $3,000.00 – 3,500.00.

Vase, 8¾" tall, green mark #47, $800.00 – 950.00.

Vase, 7¾" tall, blue mark #52,
$800.00 – 950.00.

Chocolate set, pot: 9¼" tall, comes with six cups and saucers,
blue mark #47, $1,200.00 – 1,400.00.

✍ *Bird Scenes — Audubon's Eagle* ☞

John James Audubon dedicated his life to the work he loved. He began studying birds in his own backyard while still a young boy. In 1820, he gave up his business career to dedicate his life to painting all the known birds in North America. He published *The Birds of America* in 1838 and the eagle featured on Nippon items is a variation of his eagle print shown in his book. The eagle is perched on a ledge overlooking a body of water.

Wall plaque, molded in relief, 10¼" wide, green mark #47, $2,800.00 – 3,200.00.

✍ *Bird Scenes — Golden Eagle Border* ☞

Items having the golden eagle border also feature heraldry shields in gold. The eagle is placed on a blue background and the rest of the design features plush peach and white flowers. Several items are known to exist with this decoration.

Sugar and creamer set, green mark #47, $160.00 – 200.00.

Close-up of border.

Bowl, 8½" wide, green mark, #47, $175.00 – 225.00.

✍ *Bird Scenes — Green Swan Scene* ✍

The green swan scene features a soft pastel décor scene of two swans on a lake and has a light green background. Gold leaves in overlay complete this decoration. It is found on a large number of molds including vases, plaques, chocolate sets, and urns and these items carry the blue #52 backstamp.

Wall plaque, 10" wide, blue mark #52, $450.00 – 550.00.

Close-up of green swan scene.

Chocolate set, blue mark #52, $2,500.00 – 3,000.00.

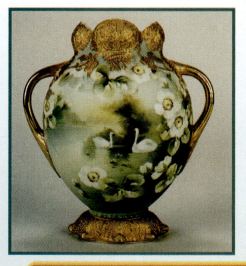

Vase, 8¹/₂" tall, blue mark #52, $900.00 – 1,100.00.

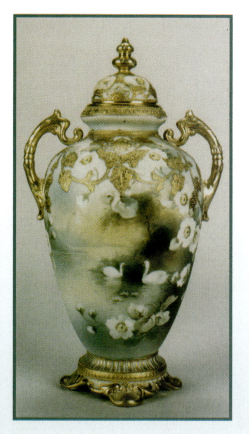

Covered urn, 14¹/₂" tall, blue mark #52, $3,000.00 – 3,500.00.

✑ *Bird Scenes — Midnight Swan Design* ✑

The midnight swan design is a beautifully painted scene of two swans swimming on a moonlit pond. It is found on vases, humidors, and wall plaques and they carry the blue #47 backstamp, which indicates that they postdate 1910.

Wall plaque, 10" wide, blue mark #47, $400.00 – 475.00.

✑ *Black Collectibles* ✑

Black collectibles are among the rarer pieces found by Nippon collectors today. There are only a few designs known to exist, and of those, the black man playing the banjo is probably found the most often. Items that have been found bearing this pattern are a wall plaque, humidor, and two different shapes of ashtrays. Another wonderful humidor has a mottled brown background and a black man wearing a tall hat. Other known pieces are a trivet, novelty dish, and a few black dolls.

There was a noticeable interest in black collectibles in the late 1800s and it was probably this interest that spurred Noritake artists to create some of these wonderful wares. They are truly artifacts of history and very desired by Nippon collectors today. They were so popular in fact, that reproduction wholesalers have even manufactured a black boy on an alligator figural and a black mammy toothpick holder. No such real Nippon items ever existed and yet when they were first sold, collectors thought that they had discovered rare undocumented pieces. They were offered by the reproduction wholesalers for $2.00 to $3.00 and were often sold by dealers for over $100.00!

Ashtray, 6¾" wide, green mark #47, $750.00 – 850.00.

Ashtray, 6½" wide, $750.00 – 850.00.

Humidor, 5¾" tall, green mark #47,
$800.00 – 1,000.00.

Wall plaque, 7¼" wide, green mark #47, $700.00 –800.00.

Doll, 4¾" tall, mark #55,
$125.00 – 165.00.

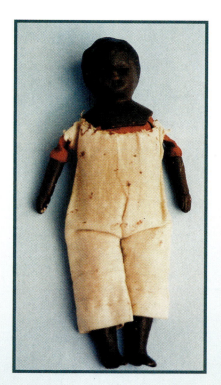

Doll, 7" tall, mark #302, $175.00 – 225.00.

Humidor, 4" tall, green mark, #47, $800.00 – 1,000.00.

☙ *Burnished Stoneware Design* ❧

Burnished stoneware décor is unusual to find and is decorated with low relief moriage. It features numerous floral and howo bird treatments and is finished with a gold wash. It is known to exist on ashtrays, vases, humidors, match holders, and trays. Pieces are marked with the green #47 backstamp.

Vase, 6" tall, green mark #47, $600.00 – 700.00.

☙ *Children's Items* ❧

Years ago, girls were expected to learn the art of good housekeeping and social graces from their mothers. There were items made specifically for children to prepare them for adult life. There were tiny tea sets for this purpose and there were also ones made small enough for dolls to have tea parties with each other. Mothers would instruct their daughters on the proper etiquette for having such parties. In addition, there were miniature salt and pepper shakers, tureens, chambersticks, egg cups, and dresser items. There were also items made specifically for use by the child when dining. These would include feeding dishes, mugs, and oatmeal sets.

Child's play teapot, 2½" tall, blue mark #47, $35.00 – 50.00.

Child's play tea set, pot is 4" tall, mark #84, $250.00 – 325.00.

Child's play tea set, blue mark #84, $275.00 – 350.00.

Child's feeding set, plate: 6½" wide, mark #84.
Plate, $65.00 – 85.00. Cup and saucer, $85.00 – 110.00.

Child's dresser jar, 3" tall, blue mark #47,
$125.00 – 150.00.

Child's plate, 6" wide, mark #10, features
three kewpies hand painted in United States,
signed Marie Chandler Tenhaaf,
$150.00 – 200.00.

ᔆ *Children's Items — Children's Face Design* ᔆ

Pieces in the so-called child's face design are molded in relief and feature both a girl and boy. Some collectors also call this pattern doll face or googly. The children are wearing green shirts, girls have red bows in their hair and red hats serve as finials on some items. We can find tea sets for children, some even small enough for dolls to use, hanging plaques, trinket dishes, powder boxes, feeding dishes, plates, pitchers, salt and pepper sets, cereal bowls, mugs, and even egg cups.

Child's tea set, teapot: 2⅞" tall, mark #55, $75.00 – 100.00.

Wall plaque, 6" wide, blue mark #84, $75.00 – 100.00.

❧ *Children's Items — Sunbonnet Babies* ❧

Bertha L. Corbett drew the original Sunbonnet Babies. The *Sunbonnet Babies Book* was written by Eulalie Osgood Grover in 1902 and illustrated by Corbett. Other Sunbonnet Baby books were published in 1907. The Sunbonnet Babies were named Molly and May and were popular during this time period. They could be found on postcards and postcard albums, advertising items, china (especially Royal Bayreuth), and other items of the day. Nippon Sunbonnet Babies can be found on two different wall plaques, a Dutch shoe, an inkwell, a child's tea set, and a child's breakfast set. Bertha Corbett also created the *Over-all Boys* who were sent out to accompany the ladies in the sunbonnets. The boys are dressed in overalls and big straw hats, which serve largely to conceal their faces.

Wall plaque, 8" wide, green mark #47, $300.00 – 375.00.

Small pitcher, 3¼" tall, $100.00 – 150.00.

Small pitcher, back side.

Child's tea set consisting of teapot, sugar bowl, creamer, four cups, saucers, and plates,
pot: 3½" tall, green mark #47, $600.00 – 700.00.

Postcard, found on plaque with moriage wheat.

Moriage wall plaque, 10" wide, blue mark #52, $500.00 – 600.00.

Postcard, boy and cow are found on Dutch shoe and inkwell.

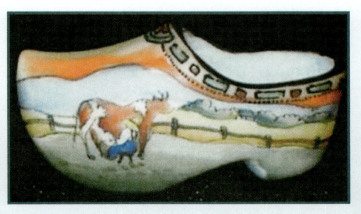

Dutch shoe, 3" long, green mark #47, $175.00 – 225.00.

ᔒ *Cloisonné Pieces* ᔒ

Nippon cloisonné pieces are difficult to find. Not a lot of these items were produced because the technique was rather difficult. Another term for this type of decoration is inlaid enamel. The patterns often look like a mosaic, set stones, or tree bark. It is a unique style using a combination of porcelain and metal.

The decoration was originally divided into cells called cloisons. Strips of soft metal separated the cloisons keeping the colors separated during firing. The metal is soldered or glued to the base. The metal often outlined shapes such as butterflies, flowers, and fruit. Enamel glaze is colorless and transparent and various metallic oxides had to be added to give it color. Different colors of enamel were placed in between the wires. When fired, the enamel and metal fused to the body of the item. These pieces resemble traditional cloisonné pieces except that they were produced on porcelain rather than a metal background.

For years, the Japanese had created cloisonné items on copper or bronze. They had learned this technique from the Chinese who had been producing cloisonné pieces for years. In fact, Beijing is called the cradle of the cloisonné technique. During the Meiji period in Japan, the government invited chemists and technicians from the West to help them perfect the cloisonné on porcelain technique.

Collectors should be very careful when cleaning these items. If these pieces are submerged in water the cloisons can dislodge from the background so this type of cleaning should be discouraged.

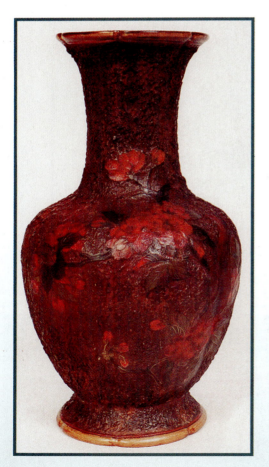

Vase, 10" tall, green mark #47,
$750.00 – 850.00.

Mantle set consisting of a pair of candlesticks, 8" tall; and a vase, 8" tall; green mark #47; candlestick pair; $700.00 – 900.00; vase, $650.00 – 750.00.

⋙ *Cobalt Blue* ⋘

Cobalt blue can be found on every type of Nippon marked item, from relish dishes to bolted urns. Within the cobalt blue field, there are many areas to choose from, if one wishes to further delineate a collection. For example, one may find pieces that are all cobalt with gold decoration, cobalt with scenes, cobalt with roses, cobalt with any other flower, prized pieces of cobalt with portraits, and even the rare cobalt blue and coralene pieces.

Cobalt blue may be used as a trim or border color on Nippon. Some pieces have scenes or flowers within various shaped medallions and the cobalt is the background color. There are also very desirable pieces that are all cobalt blue, overlaid with intricate gold designs.

Until 1869, the Japanese used "gosu" to obtain the cobalt color. Gosu is a pebble found in riverbeds. It had to be ground up and mixed with green tea before it could be applied to the porcelain. The tannin in the tea prevented the color from spreading where it didn't belong when the glaze was applied.

In 1869, the Japanese began using imported cobalt oxide for the blue coloring. It was first used at the kilns in Narita. The imported cobalt oxide was more reliable than gosu and much easier to obtain.

The color comes out strong and the application is even. This means less possibility of streaking in the color.

Using the native gosu results in a soft, grayish-blue color, whereas using cobalt oxide results in the strong blue with which we are familiar. It does not take much imagination to assume that Japanese exporters preferred this eye-catching color to enhance their wares.

Most cobalt blue pieces are found with gold decoration. Some of it is quite elaborate. Even if the gold only consists of a little trim around the border, it is usually there. Because gold is expensive and cobalt oxide gives reliable results, it is understandable that these were used together.

Because cobalt blue is a rich color, suggesting the purple of royalty, pieces adorned with it usually have a formal appearance. A cobalt and gold chocolate set would be used for company, not for the family's everyday use.

Cobalt is a rich and brilliant color that gives a substantial "air" to a piece. The regal color adds a certain elegance to any decoration. Nippon pieces decorated in cobalt blue do not hide on the shelf.

Plate, 7½" wide, unmarked, $150.00 – 200.00.

Vase, 6" tall, blue mark #47, $400.00 – 475.00.

Chocolate pot, 10" tall, blue mark #52,
$550.00 – 650.00.

Vase, 8¾" tall, blue mark #52,
$450.00 – 550.00.

Vase, 9" tall, green mark, $1,000.00 – 1,200.00.

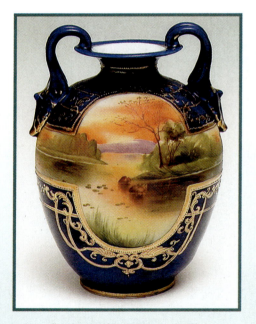

Scenic vase, 9" tall, blue mark #52,
$850.00 – 950.00.

Vase, 10¼" tall, mark #228, $850.00 – 950.00.

Bowl, 10¼" wide, green mark #47, $300.00 – 400.00.

Vase, 7¼" tall, blue mark #52, $750.00 – 850.00.

Chocolate set, comes with six cups and saucers, mark #89, $700.00 – 900.00.

Vase, 5¾" tall, green mark #47, $275.00 – 300.00.

Tea set, mark #228, $350.00 – 425.00.

ᔧ *Cobalt Blue — Cobalt and Gold Scroll Design* ᔧ

Cobalt and gold scroll is a long time popular pattern among collectors. This décor has a background painted a stunning cobalt color and the design is made up of gold scrolling along the top and bottom. It is known to exist on chocolate sets, tea sets, demitasse sets, vases, dresser sets, bouillon cups, humidors, cake sets, and dinner and luncheon plates. This décor carries the green or blue #52 or the green #47 backstamp.

Cobalt and gold bouillon cups and saucers, blue mark #52, $1,700.00 – 2,000.00.

Vase, 9½" tall, green mark #47, $900.00 – 1,000.00.

Plate, 8½" wide, green mark #47, $200.00 – 250.00.

⤜ *Cobalt Blue — Cherry Tree Design* ⤛

Cobalt cherry tree design features cobalt and silver overlay trim on Nippon pieces. The design's focus is that of a cherry tree in full blossom. The scene features a number of other trees in the background as well as a body of water. This pattern is known to exist on various molds of vases, humidors, and tea sets. The items carry the RC mark.

Vase, 6" tall, mark #79, $700.00 – 800.00.

⤜ *Cobalt Blue — Golden Forest* ⤛

Cobalt golden forest features a medallion of heavily gilded gold trees with a gold-tone forest in the background. The background is cobalt with gold swags. Pieces known to exist with this decoration are vases and urns that carry the blue #52 backstamp or the #47 marks.

Vase, 18" tall, green mark #47, $4,500.00 – 5,000.00.

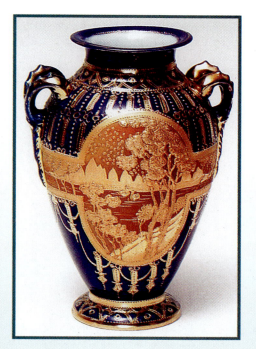

Vase, 8¼" tall, blue mark #47, $1,200.00 – 1,400.00.

Vase, 7½" tall, blue mark #52,
$1,000.00 – 1,200.00.

Covered box, 6¼" wide, green mark #47,
$600.00 – 800.00.

⟨ *Cobalt Blue — Jeweled Country Road* ⟩

Cobalt jeweled country road is one of the more stunning cobalt decors. These pieces feature a rust tone scene of a country road over a field of cobalt and gold. This design is known to exist on urns, vases, chocolate and tea sets, and wall plaques. They carry the blue #52 backstamp.

Vase, 9" tall, blue mark #52,
$1,100.00 – 1,300.00.

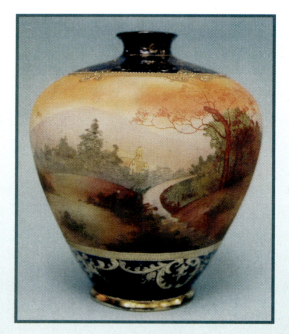

Vase, 7" tall, blue mark #52,
$950.00 – 1,100.00.

ᔓ *Cobalt Blue — Jeweled Roses* ᔒ

This pattern is a favorite with collectors and features large plushy light and dark pink roses on a cobalt background. There is a lot of gold decoration and also jewelling on these pieces.

This design is found on many different items including vases, pitchers, pancake dishes, bowls, cake plates, shaving mugs, compotes, punch bowls, etc.

Plate, 10¼" wide, blue mark #52, $700.00 – 900.00.

Pitcher, 8½" tall, blue mark #52,
$1,800.00 – 2,200.00.

Vase, 12" tall, blue mark #52, $1,600.00 – 1,800.00.

Shaving mug, 3¾" tall, green mark #52, $500.00 – 600.00.

⌒ *Cobalt Blue — Mums* ⌒

Cobalt mums design features a variety of mums in white, light blue, and light or dark pink colors. The flowers are found on medallions on the item and are surrounded by gold decoration and gold beads on a beautiful cobalt background. Many different items are found with this decoration including vases, chocolate sets, wall plaques, ferners, pitchers, plates, bowls, and cracker jars.

Serving tray, 10" wide, blue mark #52, $900.00 – 1,100.00.

Calling card tray, 7½" long, blue mark #52, $500.00 – 600.00.

Celery dish, 13¼" long, blue mark #52, $800.00 – 1,000.00.

✎ *Cobalt Blue — Orchid* ✎

Cobalt orchid pattern features large plushy pink orchids in a medallion. It is known to exist on various molds of vases. These pieces carry the blue #47 and #52 backstamps.

Gold overlay vase, 7½" tall, blue mark #47,
$1,200.00 – 1,400.00.

Vase, 12¼" tall, blue mark #52, $2,200.00 – 2,600.00.

✎ *Cobalt Blue — Ostriches* ✎

Cobalt ostrich décor features two ostriches with palm trees on a magnificent cobalt and gold background. Ostriches live on the savannas and semi-deserts of Africa. They are very large birds and reach eight feet in height. They have long necks, long and strong legs, and two toes. Their short wings make them incapable of flight but they are fast runners. This particular design is a favorite with collectors.

Vase, 12" tall, blue mark #47,
$1,700.00 – 2,100.00.

⤳ *Cobalt Blue — Red Mountain Scene* ⤳

Cobalt red mountain is possibly one of the most beautiful scenes done in cobalt. This decor features a beautiful mountain and river scene on a cobalt background. Trim work is cobalt with heavy gold and green jewelling. This scene is known to exist on vases, urns, plaques, and chocolate sets. These pieces carry the blue #52 backstamp.

Vase, 10" tall, blue mark #52, $1,500.00 – 2,000.00.
Plate, 7³/₄" wide, blue mark #52, $800.00 – 950.00.

Vase, 8' tall, blue mark #52, $1,200.00 – 1,500.00.

⤳ *Cobalt Blue — Roses and Mums* ⤳

Cobalt roses and mums is a decoration of pink and blue roses and blue mums on a cobalt background. This decoration is found in a medallion surrounded by lots of gold and gold beads. It is found on many Nippon molds.

Wall plaque, 12¹/₂" wide, blue mark #52,
$1,000.00 – 1,200.00.

Close-up of roses and mums design.

Sandwich tray, 10¹/₂" wide, green mark #52,
$1,000.00 – 1,200.00.

⤙ *Cobalt Blue — Roses and Pendants* ⤚

This design features light to dark pink roses on a cobalt background. There is a lavish use of gold decoration and gold pendant type buds are featured in the background. The number of pendants varies with the size of the piece but they are generally found in groups of three or five. This decoration can be found on bowls, pitchers, sugar shakers, etc.

Plate, 8¾" wide, blue mark #52, $600.00 – 700.00.

Bowl, 7" wide, blue mark #52, $450.00 – 550.00.

Close-up of roses and mums design.

⤙ *Cobalt Blue — Swan* ⤚

Cobalt swan is a décor sought after by many collectors. This scene features a medallion of two swans on a lake over a background of cobalt and gold. Items known to exist with this decoration are chocolate and tea sets, vases, urns, wall plaques, dresser sets, bowls, cake sets, and cracker jars. These pieces carry the blue or green #52 backstamp.

Vase, 9" tall, green mark #52, $1,100.00 – 1,300.00.

ᔕ *Coralene* ᔕ

Nippon marked coralene pieces are unusual to find but do exist. The mark is a semicircle rising sun above the words RS NIPPON. Most Japanese coralene items, however, are stamped "Patented 2/9/1909 Japan 912171," others are marked "Patent Applied For No. 38257" with Japanese markings included. "Kinran Patent No. 16137 Japan," or the RS mark is often found backstamped on items with the word Japan instead of Nippon appearing.

There is a wide variety of pieces to be found, vases, ferners, lamps, ewers, teapots in an assortment of designs, florals, scenics, geometrics, even birds and dragons to mention a few. Most backgrounds have a matte finish.

Collectors should be careful to check the items for missing beads and it is advisable to not soak the pieces in water when cleaning as the beading may fall off.

A.L. Rock, an American living in Yokahama, Japan, was the first to perfect this technique and apply for a patent.

There has been a lot of confusion as to what constitutes coralene beading and how it was manufactured and in an attempt to clean up any misconceptions regarding these pieces a copy of the original patent has been secured and is included for reference.

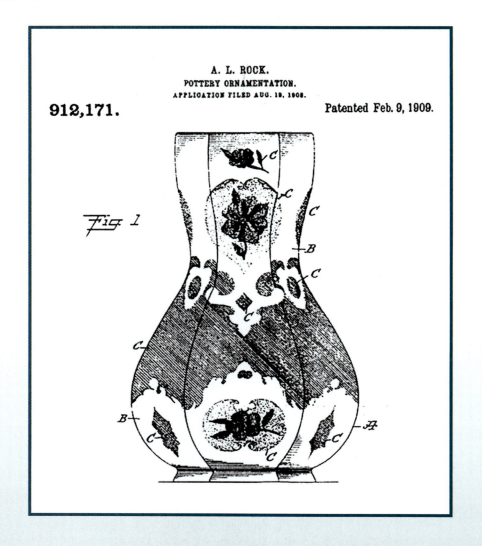

UNITED STATES PATENT OFFICE.

ALBAN L. ROCK, OF YOKOHAMA, JAPAN, ASSIGNOR TO A. A. VANTINE & CO., OF NEW YORK, N. Y., A CORPORATION OF NEW JERSEY.

POTTERY ORNAMENTATION.

No. 912,171. Specification of Letters Patent. Patented Feb 9, 1909

Application filed August 19, 1908. Serial No. 449,223.

To all whom it may concern;

Be it known, that I, ALBAN L. ROCK, a citizen of the United States, at present residing in Yokohama, Japan, have invented
5 a new and Improved Pottery Ornamentation, of which the following is a full, clear, and exact description.

The object of the invention is to provide a new and improved pottery ornamentation, the
10 ornamentation being arranged to produce a permanent glass bead effect on porcelain vases and other pottery articles, in such a manner that the colorless transparent glass beads are fused in position on the body of the
15 pottery article by a fusing pigment which produces color effect in any predetermined design.

The invention consists of novel features and parts and combinations of the same, which
20 will be more fully described herein-after and then pointed out in the claim.

A practical embodiment of the invention is represented in the accompanying drawings, forming a part of this specification, in which
25 similar characters of reference indicate corresponding parts in all the views.

Figure 1 is a side elevation of a vase showing the improvement and produced according to my method; Fig. 2 is an enlarged side
30 elevation of part of the same; and Fig. 3 is a transverse section of the same.

A portion of the surface of the body A of the base shown in Fig. 1, is ornamented by a suitable gold ornamentation B, and the
35 remaining surface portion is covered by a glass bead ornamentation C, which consists of a fusing and carrying medium C′ and colorless transparent glass beads C^2 fused to the surface of the body A by the said fusing and carrying
40 medium C′. The beads C^2 are comparatively small and are preferably spherical in shape, and the fusing and carrying medium C′ maybe in a plain uniform color or in many colors, according to predetermined design, as
45 indicated at the portions representing the flowers on the vase shown in Fig. 1. The fusing and carrying medium C′ consists of porcelain pigments and a fusible matter, either mixed together prior to the application on the body,
50 or applying the said pigments first and then the fusible matter. Sometimes both methods are used on the same article. As a rule, color work on porcelain showing bead decorations,
55 is done in a dull color effect by means of mixing shiroye, balsam copaiba with oil of turpentine, and then the outline of the bead design is done by a specially prepared pigment which when fired results in the gold-moriage.
60 The principal components of the fusible matter are 248 grains of silicate of albumen (shiroye) and 192 grains of flux (hakukyoku) to which is added as a carrying medium about
65 9.6 grains of a dry procelain pigment or color, the several ingredients being mixed with a certain percentage of water and all parts are well ground together. The porcelain color or pigment used with the fusible matter to form the fusible and carrying medium C′ must be
70 of such a shade as can be fired satisfactorily at a uniform degree of heat, as otherwise some of the colors will not be fired enough while other shades may be fired too much, and the
75 slightest mistake in the selection of color shades in this respect tends to spoil the article.

In practice, the fusing and carrying medium
80 C′ is applied to the body of the vase in a wet state, and then the colorless transparent glass beads C^2 are placed onto the said wet fusing and carrying medium, which holds the beads in position one alongside the other, as the rear
95 portions of the beads are pressed into the wet medium. The vase or other article thus decorated is then fired in the usual manner, so that the beads are fused with their rear portions onto the porcelain body by the fusing
90 and carrying medium, to permanently fix the beads in place without destroying their brilliant effect, enhanced by the underlying color pigment arranged accordingly to a predetermined design representing flowers
95 and other objects.

It is understood that the colors of the fusing and carrying medium are refracted through the glass beads, thus giving the vase a very fine appearance in a plush effect.
100

It is understood that the selection of the fusible and carrying medium and the degree of heat used in firing is of importance as the fusible matter must necessarily fuse at a lower
105 degree than the glass beads C^2, so that only the rear portions of the glass beads which are in contact with the fusible matter melt and fuse with the fusible matter, fused and adhering to the body A of the vase or like
110 article.

It is important in the use of the glass bead covering for the predetermined pattern for the

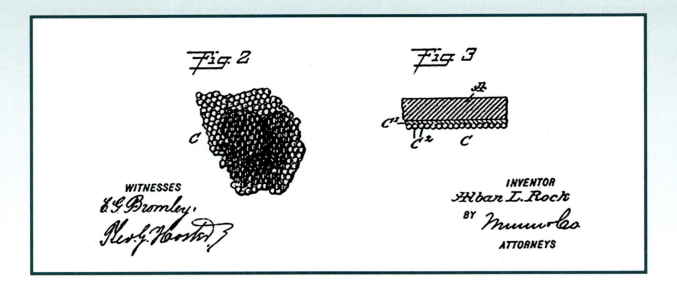

Mark #95, RS NIPPON,
found on coralene pieces.

Mark #241, RS JAPAN,
found on coralene pieces.

Mark #242, US Patent 912171,
found on coralene pieces. Top row translates
"applied for," bottom row "16137."

Mark #243, US Patent 912171,
found on coralene pieces.

Mark #244, Kinran US Patent
912171, found on coralene pieces.

Mark #245, Patent applied for no. 38257,
found on coralene pieces. Left vertical column
translates "38257," center column "specialty
sale," right column "Patent applied for."

Mark #246, Kinran patent no.
16137, found on coralene pieces.

The coralene technique was
originally put on glass items.
Close-up of coralene beads on glass.

Close-up of coralene beads on porcelain.

Covered urn, 15" tall, mark #242, $3,600.00 – 4,000.00.

Bolted ewer, 11" tall, mark #242,
$2,100.00 – 2,400.00.

Vase, 4½" tall, mark #243, $850.00 – 950.00.

Ewer, 10½" tall, mark #244,
$1,000.00 – 1,300.00.

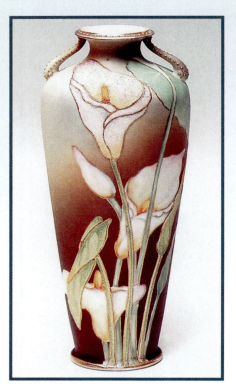

Vase, 13" tall, mark #244,
$1,400.00 – 1,900.00.

Vase, 11" tall, mark #244,
$1,300.00 – 1,700.00.

Vase, 9" tall, mark #244, $900.00 – 1,050.00.

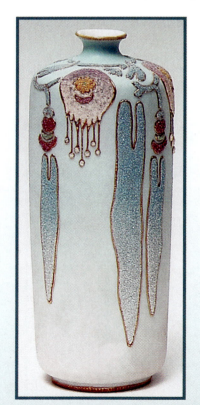

Vase, 8¾" tall, mark #244,
$850.00 – 1,000.00.

Vase, 10" tall, mark #242,
$1,300.00 – 1,700.00.

Vase, 10" tall, mark #245,
$1,400.00 – 1,800.00.

⧗ *Coralene — Bleeding Heart* ⧗

Bleeding heart coralene pattern has a background of pale yellow color fading to pale green. This design features soft pink and purple bleeding hearts and vines. Bleeding hearts are unique drooping heart-shaped flowers, hence the name given to them. They bloom in the spring, grow to be between two to four feet tall and are an old fashioned flower. This design is known only to exist on vases and carries patent mark #242 or #245.

Vase, 7" tall, mark #245, $950.00 – 1,100.00.

Vase, 13½" tall, mark #242,
$1,700.00 – 2,100.00.

ᔶ *Coralene — Cobalt Lilies* ᔶ

Cobalt lilies coralene features stunning multicolored lilies over a mottled green background with cobalt trim. This is a very desirable pattern with collectors. This design is known to exist on urns, ewers, and vases and they carry the patent mark #242.

Vase, 10³/₄" tall, mark #242,
$1,300.00 – 1,600.00.

Tankard, 13¹/₄" tall, mark #242,
$1,900.00 – 2,300.00.

ᔶ *Coralene — Cypress Village* ᔶ

Cypress village coralene features a village by a lake decorated with coralene beading. Cypress village is one of the more coveted coralene decors. This decoration is only known to exist on vases and carries the patent mark #242.

Vase, 6¹/₄" tall, mark #242,
$950.00 – 1,100.00.

Vase, 8³/₄" tall, mark #242,
$1,000.00 – 1,150.00.

...

ᔟ *Coralene — Golden Mum* ᔠ

Golden mum coralene has a background fading from soft gold to pastel blue. These pieces are decorated with bi-colored golden mums. This design is known to exist on various vase molds and cracker jars. These items carry the patent marks #242 or #245.

Cracker jar, 6¾" tall, has original paper label
"Nagoya Sample," mark #242, $1,800.00 – 2,200.00.

Vase 6½" tall, mark #245, $800.00 – 900.00.
Vase, 12½" tall, mark #242, $1,300.00 – 1,600.00.

ᔟ *Coralene — Lavender Hollyhocks* ᔠ

Lavender hollyhocks coralene has a lavender background and features lavender and white hollyhocks on stout stems having pale green leaves. This decoration is only known to exist on vases and carries patent mark #242.

Vase, 6¾" tall, mark #242, $850.00 – 950.00.

✑ *Coralene — Pastel Poppy* ✑

Pastel poppy coralene pattern is done in soft pastels of pink, green, and lavender. This decoration can be found with and without cobalt trim. It is only known to exist on various molds of vases and carries either patent mark #242 or #245.

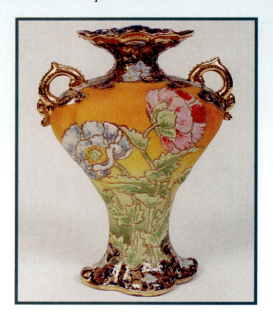

Vase, 8¼" tall, mark #245, $1,200.00 – 1,400.00.

Vase, 8¾" tall, mark #242, $1,300.00 – 1,500.00.

✑ *Coralene — Spring Hollyhocks* ✑

Spring hollyhocks coralene is generally found on larger molds. These pieces feature pink and white hollyhocks on a field of mottled green. This décor has been found on tankards, urns, and larger vases. They carry either patent mark #242 or #245.

Covered urn, 15" tall, mark #242, $3,500.00 – 4,000.00.

☙ *Coralene — Sweet Pea* ❧

Sweet pea coralene pieces feature a bank of sweet peas on a field of golden browns, and this decoration has only been found on vases carrying patent marks #242 or #245.

Vase, 5¹/₂" tall, mark #242, $700.00 – 800.00.

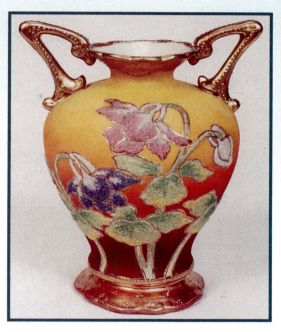

Vase, 6¹/₂" tall, mark #245, $850.00 – 1,000.00.

☙ *Cypress by the Lake* ❧

Cypress by the lake scene features a house and lake scene with a stand of cypress in the foreground. The scene is executed in green and rust tone enamels. This decoration is found on wall plaques, vases, and humidors and they carry the green #47 backstamp.

Humidor, 7" tall, green mark #47, $800.00 – 925.00.

ᔟ *Dancing Peasants* ᔠ

Dancing peasants features a stylized group of peasants standing on a beach on a blue and gray marbleized background. Peasants were one of the lowest class of tillers of the soil in European countries. They often held festivals although they had little in the way of funds. Perhaps this is a depiction of one of those days. Pieces bearing this design are urns, steins, humidors, and various vase molds. These items are marked with the #47 back-stamp.

Urn, 11½" tall, green mark #47, $700.00 – 900.00.

ᔟ *Desert Scenes* ᔠ

There are a number of Nippon pieces decorated with desert scenes. They feature palm trees, Bedouin tents, mosques and other buildings, and Arabs on camels. Some of the Middle Eastern men are found wrapped in a long white robe with hood that is called a jalabijya. Most of these scenes are realistic but a few are painted in cartoon fashion.

Matchbox holder, 3¼" tall, green mark #47,
$250.00 – 300.00.

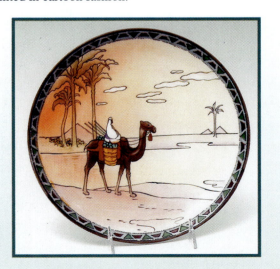

Wall plaque, 10" wide, green mark #47,
$325.00 – 375.00.

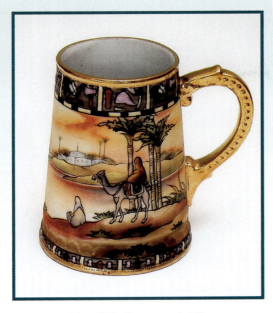

Mug, 5½" tall, green mark #47,
$350.00 – 400.00.

Wall plaque, 10" wide, green mark #47,
$500.00 – 600.00.

Bolted urn, 16" tall, green mark #47, $3,200.00 – 3,600.00.

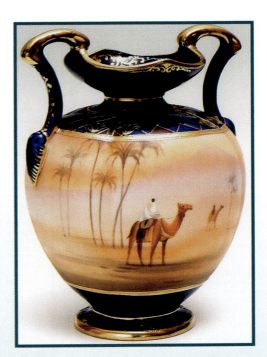

Cobalt scenic vase, 10¾" tall, blue mark #52,
$700.00 – 850.00.

Wall plaque, 10¼" wide, green mark #47,
$400.00 – 475.00.

Wall plaque, 10¼" wide, green mark #47,
$350.00 – 425.00.

Wall plaque, molded in relief, 10½" wide,
green mark #47, $1,100.00 – 1,300.00.

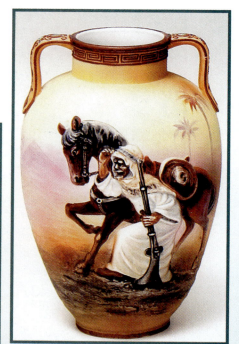

Vase, molded in relief, 10" tall, green mark #47,
$3,000.00 – 4,000.00.

Humidor, molded in relief, 6½" tall, green mark
#47, $2,300.00 – 2,800.00.

⤳ *Desert Scenes — Man on a Camel* ⤳

Man on a camel is an extremely popular décor featuring an Arab on the back of a camel returning to his tent. It was produced on a large number of molds including vases, urns, wall plaques (both round and rectangular), candlesticks, jugs, smoking pieces, and chocolate and tea sets. These pieces are generally marked with the green #47 backstamp.

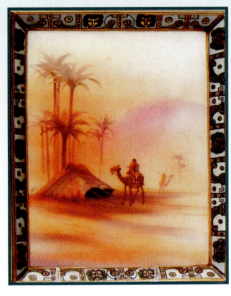

Wall plaque, 10¼" long, green mark #47, $3,000.00 – 3,600.00.

Urn, 15¼" tall, green mark #47, $2,500.00 – 3,000.00.

⤳ *Desert Scenes — Moriage Palm Tree and Camel Rider* ⤳

Moriage palm tree and camel rider scene is a highly detailed moriage decorated design. These vases, jugs, wall plaques, tankards, and mugs carry the green #47 backstamp.

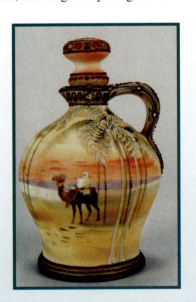

Wine jug, 9¼" tall, green mark #47, $1,200.00 – 1,400.00.

Wall plaque, 10" wide, green mark #47, $600.00 – 700.00.

Vase, 9¼" tall, green mark #47, $700.00 – 850.00.

⌒ *Desk Items* ⌒

Today we don't need many of the desk items required in the late 1800s and early 1900s. Rolling ink blotters and inkwells were necessities back then. They were often part of a desk set. They were found in schools, offices, and homes and were made of all kinds of materials and into all kinds of shapes. The development of the ballpoint pen in 1930 made inkwells and blotters almost extinct. Some desk items collectors may encounter are blotter corners, calendar holders, letter holders, stamp boxes, inkwells, rolling ink blotters, and complete desk sets which include a tray.

Letter holder, 4½" tall, 7¼" long, blue mark #4, $300.00 – 375.00.

Desk calender, 3" tall, green mark #47, $300.00 – 400.00.

Stamp box, 2¾" long, green mark #47, $85.00 – 125.00.

Letter holder, 6" long, green mark #47, $225.00 – 275.00.

❧ *Dolls* ❧

Nippon doll — the term itself conjures up visions of the Orient and young girls in colorful kimonos, yet these dolls were made to appeal to Western tastes. During the early 1900s Japan had a large, willing labor force and they were anxious to jump on any opportunity to expand into as many markets as possible. World War I and the effect it would have on European doll makers opened the door for them to begin manufacturing vast amounts of dolls and playthings needed by the doll and toy importers. Since the 1880s the Japanese had been major producers and exporters of porcelain products such as vases, tea sets, and other utilitarian wares. Their products were known for their hand-painted decoration and, of course, their low price. Because the Japanese already had experience in creating porcelain products and because dolls play an important role in Japanese society, it was a natural step that the Japanese would begin producing all-bisque, bisque head, and china dolls as well as children's porcelain products such as tea sets and feeding dishes.

Some of the first dolls made during the Nippon era (1891 – 1921) were all-bisque dolls. In fact, there's evidence that some Nippon-marked dolls may have been made as early as 1891. However, the vast majority were produced from 1915 through 1921. These dolls were easy for the Japanese to produce since little doll-making skill was required — only the mold, the bisque slip, and elastic to string the arms was needed. And because all-bisque dolls remained popular throughout the Nippon era there are literally hundreds of different shapes and designs of Nippon-marked all-bisque dolls. The Japanese copied all of the popular German dolls — Kewpie, Baby Bud, Chubby, Happifats, Wide-Awake, and the Kewpie soldier. Additionally, they came out with many new designs. Morimura Brothers produced a number of original designs including Queue San Baby and Dolly, both of which were patented in the United States. Dolls with molded clothes, figurals (including bathtub babies), dolls with jointed arms and legs, and unusual dolls such as piano babies are just a few of the different types of Nippon all-bisque dolls that were made.

Around 1915, the Japanese also started producing small bisque head dolls with cloth or composition bodies. Those dolls with the cloth bodies usually have a bisque shoulderplate and bisque arms and legs and most are made of 'stone' bisque. This bisque is heavier and less translucent than the bisque used on most other Nippon dolls and the color is often not fired on, causing some dolls to lose their facial and hair coloring. Usually the limbs are not well executed either in terms of the modeling or the painting and the arms and legs are often left 'in the white' with no flesh coloring added. Sometimes simple shoes are painted on. These dolls are usually found with red or white muslin bodies but occasionally it's possible to find one with an "ABC" cloth body. They came in a variety of sizes and, since they are fairly easy to find, obviously sold in large quantities. However, today they are not as popular with collectors as some of the other Nippon dolls.

More popular today are those small Nippon dolls with bisque heads and bodies made of composition or papier-mache. These Nippon bisque-head dolls are generally small in size with most being less than 10 inches tall. It is likely that the same companies making the all-bisque dolls made many of these dolls. In fact, it's possible to find bisque head dolls that match all-bisque dolls. Many of these dolls are marked with a mold number or letter in addition to the word "NIPPON." These small bisque heads are socket heads that are strung onto what is usually a crudely made five-piece composition or papier-mache body. The dolls were modeled in a variety of character faces including those with painted googly eyes.

Germany was making dolls of this type prior to World War I. Gebruder Heubach and Armand Marseille were two of the Germans firms producing these small bisque head dolls, and it is evident that the Japanese copied many of their designs including the Heubach googly dolls and the Armand Marseille mold number 322. Like the all-bisque dolls, these small bisque-head dolls were probably easier to produce since they did not require the same technical doll making expertise as the larger bisque-head dolls.

Producing the larger bisque-head dolls was another matter entirely. At first the Japanese had a difficult time making the bisque-head dolls wanted by consumers and many of their first products were unusable. Because of this, the major doll and toy importers such as George Borgfeldt, Louis Wolf & Company, and Haber Brothers, sent representatives to Japan to provide advice, assistance, and samples of what products were desired. The Japanese were quick learners and soon were able to master the techniques necessary to compete with the German doll makers. The Japanese copied many of the most popular German dolls. The Kestner Hilda, mold no. 245 (introduced in 1914), the Heubach pouty mold no. 6969 (circa 1912), and the Hertel Schwab mold no. 151 are just three examples. If you look through any of the doll books you'll notice a distinct similarity between the Nippon dolls and dolls produced by companies such as Armand Marseille, Hertel Schwab, Franz Schmidt, and Kestner.

The Japanese produced many different character and dolly-faced dolls with a variety of bisque finishes including some rare 'oily' bisque finishes. They also made both open and closed mouth dolls, dolls with wobble tongues, dolls with glass or painted eyes, dolls with pierced nostrils, and dolls with a crying mechanism in their heads. If the Germans made a certain type of doll then it's likely the Japanese made a similar type. The Nippon character dolls have wonderful expressions ranging from flirty to serious, impish to sweet. The most sought after characters are the pouty and the googly molds and these dolls are a rare find today.

Morimura Brothers was one of the largest manufacturers of Nippon-era bisque head dolls and they are also one of the best known because the majority of their bisque head dolls are marked with their distinctive "spider" symbol and the letters M B. They were one of the first companies in Japan to realize the potential of the doll and toy market in the United States and, at the start of World War I began experimenting with the manufacture of bisque head dolls. Their most productive five years were from 1917 through 1921 when they manufactured and advertised a wide variety of bisque head dolls. The most famous and popular is the character baby named "Baby Ella" which was one of the first dolls produced by Morimura Brothers and was still in production in 1921. Morimura Brothers also produced a solid dome head doll named "My Darling," and a variety of dolls on kidaline (imitation kid), ball-jointed, and baby bodies.

The Japanese also produced china glazed dolls. The Nippon-marked china glazed dolls fall into two categories: china heads that were used on cloth bodies and half-dolls which are some-times referred to as "pincushion dolls." Nippon china head dolls have blond hair molded in what is called a low-brow hairstyle - wavy hair parted in the middle that comes down onto the forehead. To date, no Nippon china head dolls have surfaced that have any other color of hair. They are usually incised "NIPPON" on the back outside of the shoulderplate but one example has been found where "NIPPON" was inside the shoulderplate. By the early 1900s the popularity of china head dolls was declining and that likely explains why Nippon china-head dolls today are hard to find.

While Nippon china head dolls are hard to find because of declining popularity, Nippon china glazed half-dolls are hard to find because by 1921 half-dolls had not yet reached their full popularity. Called pincushion dolls by many collectors, they were not used solely for pincushions. They could be found on a variety of items including powder boxes, clothes brushes, even small lamps. They enjoyed their greatest popularity from the 1920s through the 1930s — well after the Nippon era. It may also be hard to find Nippon-marked half-dolls because of the way they were marked — in black lettering over the glaze on the back of the flange (the lower area of the half-doll where the sew holes are). This mark is easy to remove and may be impossible to see if the doll has its original pincushion with it. The Japanese did copy German designs for their china half-dolls, and some designs were popular for years, so it's possible to find the same style half-doll marked Germany, Nippon, and Japan.

Close-up of original sticker.

13" tall, bisque head, composition body, sleep eyes, mohair rug, all original mint condition, mark #358, $400.00 – 500.00.

18" tall, bisque head, composition body, unusual jointed wrists, sleep eyes, wabble tongue, original wig, mark #357, $600.00 – 700.00.

Rare and unusual pair of Happifats, 3¹/₂" tall, extremely rare mold, mark #55 original stickers, $500.00 – 600.00 for the pair.

Left: 5¹/₄", incised Nippon, mark #55, $150.00 – 175.00.
Right: 4³/₄", rare mold, incised Nippon mark #55, $200.00 – 225.00.

Left: 5³/₄" tall, original "Sonny" sticker, mark #55, stamped "Nippon" on bottom of feet, very rare.
Right: 6³/₄" tall (when legs are extended), mark #55, very rare. $250.00 – 275.00 each.

Left: 5¹/₄" tall, incised mark #55, $95.00 – 125.00.
Right: 4" tall, incised mark #55, $75.00 – 100.00.
Note: Both dolls came from England.

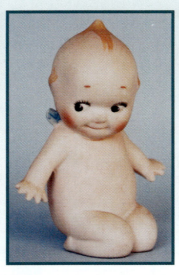

Left: 5½" tall, rare with molded gun in hand, incised mark #55, $175.00 – 225.00.
Right: Figural soldier, incised mark #55, $175.00 – 225.00.

Figural kneeling kewpie, extremely rare, incised mark #55, $350.00 – 400.00.

5½" tall, bisque head, composition body, original crocheted clothing, incised mark #55, $200.00 for pair with original clothing.

22" tall, bisque head, composition body, original mohair wig, brown sleep eyes, mark #350, $600.00 – 700.00.

Morimura Bros. "Baby Ella," 17" tall, bisque head, composition body, original wig, mint condition, mark #355, $400.00 – 500.00.

12" tall, bisque head, composition body, sleep eyes, painted hair, mark #152, $225.00 – 275.00.

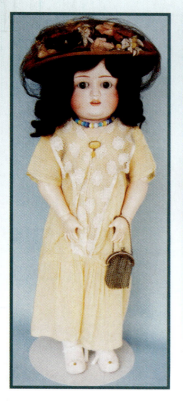

Box label, note the original price of $3.98 is written in pencil.

14" tall, bisque head, composition body, sleep eyes,
original wig, with original box, mark #213,
$500.00 – 550.00 with box.

24" tall, bisque head, composition
body, sleep eyes, original wig,
mark #124, $450.00 – 500.00.

ᔕ *Dragon Decoration* ᔕ

The mythological dragon lives in heaven in the spring, in the water in autumn, it travels in the clouds in summer and in the winter it lives dormant in the earth. It always dwells alone and is thought to be the most powerful animal in existence, a creature of a very superior order of being!

The majority of the Nippon dragon pieces are done in the traditional gray moriage style and most bear the green M in wreath backstamp. Many have either jeweled or glass eyes.

This pattern can be found on all types of items: vases, humidors, tankards, mugs, loving cups, dresser pieces, demitasse sets, tea sets, condensed milk containers, chocolate sets, urns, ashtrays, creamer and sugar sets, cracker jars, and ferners.

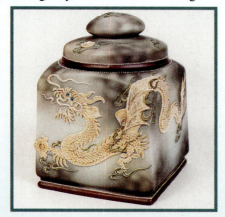

Humidor, 6¾" tall, green mark #47, $750.00 – 850.00.

Pair of vases, 6½" tall, green mark #47, $375.00 – 450.00.

Moriage vases, $250.00 – 300.00 each.
Left: 4³/₄" tall, blue mark #52.
Right: 5" tall, green mark #47.

Moriage ashtray, 5¹/₄" wide, green mark #47,
$275.00 – 350.00.

Vase, 10" tall, green mark #47,
$650.00 – 750.00.

Moriage dresser set, tray: 11¹/₄" long, green mark #47, $1,300.00 – 1,500.00.

⁓ *Dresser Items* ⁓

Dresser items are found in abundance bearing a Nippon back-stamp. Some of the pieces collectors can find are hatpin holders, hanging hatpin holders, perfume and cologne bottles, pin boxes, salve boxes, talcum powder flasks, vanity organizers, hairpin holders, dresser sets including matching trays, hair receivers, powder boxes, ring holders, trinket boxes, stickpin holders, man-icure sets, and even toothbrush holders. Most are hand painted although decals can be found on the portrait pieces. And most are naturally more feminine in decoration featuring a myriad of flowers. Some have scenic designs while others may have a bird decoration. There seems to be something for everyone, from lav-ishly decorated pieces to the very simple designs.

Hair receiver and powder box, 3¹/₂" tall, green mark #47,
$160.00 – 210.00.

Vanity organizer, 4¹/₂" tall, magenta mark #4,
$150.00 – 200.00.

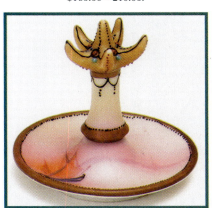

Ring tree, 2³/₄" tall, green mark #47,
$65.00 – 95.00.

Open hanging hatpin holder, 7" long,
green mark #52, $425.00 – 500.00.

Stickpin holder, 1¹/₂" tall, green mark #52,
$150.00 – 200.00.

Hanging hatpin holder, 7" long, blue mark #52, $425.00 – 500.00.
Talcum flask, 5" tall, mark #103, $150.00 – 175.00.

Hair pin holder, 3¼" tall,
blue mark #52,
$135.00 – 165.00.

Hatpin holder, 4¼" tall, blue mark #47,
$125.00 – 160.00.

Dresser set, mark #228, $1,500.00 – 1,700.00.

Blue mark #52.
Ring tree, $100.00 – 135.00. Powder box, $90.00 – 120.00.
Trinket box, $100.00 – 135.00. Trinket box, $110.00 – 140.00.

ᔟ *Dutch Scenes* ᔟ

Dutch scenes are featured on a number of Nippon items. Many have a windmill in the decoration or Dutch people or still life scenes reminiscent of Dutch painters of the seventeenth century. Some are painted in a cartoon-like style. Gouda styled pieces are imitations of a Dutch technique rather than a scene. The people featured wear traditional folk clothing. Women wear skirts with aprons, flowered blouses, wooden shoes or clogs (also called klompens), and a lace or cotton hat called a hul. The men and boys wear large baggy trousers, Dutch hats, and wooden shoes. Wooden shoes are still worn in the Netherlands by rural people. They are favored by farmers working in the fields because they are warmer and dryer then rubber boots.

Small dish, 7" wide, mark #104, $265.00 – 325.00.

Wall plaque, 10" wide, blue mark #52,
$375.00 – 425.00.

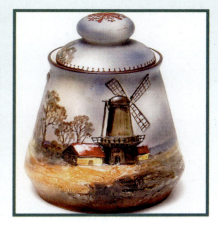

Humidor, molded in relief, 6¼" tall,
green mark #47, $1,600.00 – 1,800.00.

Wall plaque, 10" wide, green mark #47,
$350.00 – 400.00.

Wall plaque, 9" wide, green mark #47,
$150.00 – 200.00.

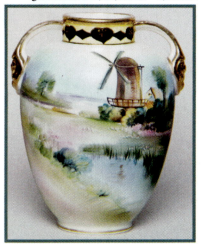

Vase, 6¾" tall, green mark #47,
$250.00 – 325.00.

Vase, 18¼" tall,
green mark #47,
$1,800.00 – 2,100.00.

Pitcher, 4½" tall, green mark #47,
$450.00 – 550.00.

☙ *Dutch Scenes — Dog Walk* ❧

Dutch dog walk is a scene done in a stylized décor. These pieces feature a Dutch woman and boy walking a dog. This decoration is found on numerous items including vases, jugs, humidors, candlesticks, bowls, steins, wall plaques, and dresser, smoke, and tea sets. These items have the blue or green #47 backstamp.

Stein, 7" tall, green mark #47,
$700.00 – 800.00.

Humidor, 7" tall, green mark #47,
$1,100.00 – 1,400.00.

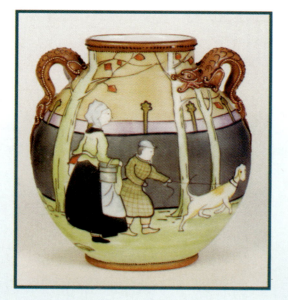

Vase, 5¾" tall, blue mark #47, $550.00 – 650.00.

Wall plaque, 8½" wide, blue mark #47, $350.00 – 450.00.

⤠ *Dutch Scenes — Girl with Umbrella* ⤠

Dutch girl with umbrella is painted in blue and white. The girl is wearing traditional Dutch clothing including an apron and Dutch shoes. She is carrying a huge umbrella over her head. A white and blue stone fence and a body of water and boat are painted in the background.

Years ago, salesmen in the United States working for the Noritake Company, took painted pictures of the various designs found on wares to stores and wholesalers. Many of these sample pages also listed what items could be purchased with the specific scene. This page below shows the Dutch girl with umbrella.

Trivet, 5³/₄" wide, green mark #47, $200.00 – 250.00.

Salesmsn's sample page.

Vase, 7¹/₄" tall, mark #47, $550.00 – 650.00.

⤠ *Dutch Scenes — Heidi Herding Ducks* ⤠

Heidi herding ducks is a stylized Dutch scene of a girl herding ducks. This scene is found on vases, smoke sets, wall plaques, and humidors and carries the blue or green #47 backstamp.

Smoke set, green mark #47, $1,000.00 – 1,200.00.

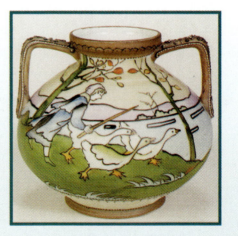

Vase, 4¹/₂" tall, green mark #47, $600.00 – 725.00.

Vase, 5½" tall, blue mark #47, $600.00 – 725.00.

Humidor, 8", tall, green mark #47,
$1,100.00 – 1,300.00.

Dutch Scenes — Man's Best Friend

Man's best friend is a décor of an old Dutch man sitting next to a green building. A body of water lies in the distance. In this scene we also find two other Dutch men at the wharf, a sail ship out in the water, and a little white dog facing the old man. Pieces found with this decoration are vases, humidors, and wall plaques and they carry the green #47 backstamp.

Wall plaque, 10" wide, green mark #47, $450.00 – 500.00.

Humidor, 7" tall, green mark #47, $1,100.00 – 1,300.00.

✒ *Dutch Scenes — Midnight Windmill* ✑

Midnight windmill scene depicts a Dutch windmill and one or two people on a moonlit night. This decor carries the green #47 or blue #52 backstamp and can be found on humidors, chocolate and tea sets, vases, urns, cake plates, wall plaques, etc.

Vase, 14¼" tall, green mark #47, $1,100.00 – 1,300.00.

Vase, 15" tall, green mark #47, $1,200.00 – 1,400.00.

Cake plate, 10¾" wide, green mark #47, $450.00 – 550.00.

✒ *Egyptian Scenes* ✑

Egyptian scenes are found on a variety of Nippon pieces. Several different techniques were employed with these designs; some are hand painted, and some have decals, and others are molded in relief or found in figural form. One can find pyramids, palm trees, stylized gods and goddesses, scarabs, hieroglyphics, lotus flowers, various Middle East scenes, etc.

In 1922, Howard Carter and Lord Carnarvon found the mummy of King Tut in the Valley of the Kings after a five-year search. King Tutankhamen reined from 1333 – 1323 BC and although he died at the age of eighteen, he is the most famous of all the Egyptian kings. For years, people believed that there was a curse attached to his tomb because so many of the workers died mysteriously. It was later discovered that the bacteria that had been sealed in the tomb had killed the workers when it got into their lungs.

Prior to the finding of King Tut's tomb there was almost a frenzy in the United States about all things Egyptian and these items were no doubt produced as a result of that mania. New and wonderful pieces are being discovered all the time and lucky is the collector who finds one of these gems.

Bowls, 6½" wide each, green mark #47, $200.00 – 275.00 each.

Chocolate set, pot, 8³/₄" tall, set comes with six cups and
saucers, green mark #52, $450.00 – 550.00.

Ferner, 7" tall, green mark #47, $800.00 – 950.00.

Vase, 8" tall, green mark #47,
$450.00 – 550.00.

Whiskey jug, 6" tall, green mark #47,
$850.00 – 1,000.00.

Humidor, 5¹/₂" tall, green mark #47,
$850.00 – 1,000.00.

⤳ *Egyptian Scenes — Cleopatra's Barge* ⤳

Cleopatra's barge scene appears on plaques, both round and rectangular, vases, urns, smoking sets, and jugs. This scene features an Egyptian barge that one might think of as being like the one Cleopatra once used, hence the name ascribed to this design. Cleopatra fell in love with Marc Antony and they ruled Egypt and Rome together. It is said that she once came sailing up the river Cydnus on a barge that had outspread sails of purple and oars of silver that beat time to the music of flutes and fifes and harps. The barge supposedly had a gilded stem and Cleopatra sat under a canopy of gold cloth dressed as Venus. She was the daughter of an Egyptian pharaoh and by the description given of her arrival, she certainly arrived in style. Pieces are decorated with various trimwork and carry the green #47 or the blue #52 backstamp

Vase, 12" tall, green mark #47,
$900.00 – 1,000.00.

Wall plaque, 10¼" wide, green mark #47,
$400.00 – 475.00.

Vase, 17¾" tall, green mark #47,
$1,800.00 – 2,100.00.

⤳ *Egyptian Scenes — Kneeling Pharaohs* ⤳

This brightly colored decoration features hieroglyphics, scarabs, and kneeling pharaohs. Pharaohs in ancient Egypt were considered to be all-powerful rulers with divine connections. The Egyptian type designs featured on these wares look as though they may have been ones found on the walls of the old kings' tombs. This décor is known to exist on candlesticks, vases, bowls, desk items, and jugs and carries the green #47 backstamp.

Rolling blotter, 4¼" wide, green mark #47, $350.00 – 425.00.
Inkwell, 4" wide, green mark #47, $450.00 – 525.00.

Whiskey jug, 6¼" tall, green mark #47,
$1,100.00 – 1,300.00.

Bowl, 10" wide including handles, green mark #47, $350.00 – 425.00.

≈ *Egyptian Scenes — Molded Egyptian* ≈

Molded Egyptian is a rare molded-in-relief decoration found on various desk set pieces, humidors, cigarette boxes, and candlesticks. The inkwells and humidors feature a scarab on top of the finial and the candlesticks are molded in the shape of columns.

Hieroglyphics are featured on the pieces but they are not actual Egyptian ones. These pieces are marked with the green #47 backstamp

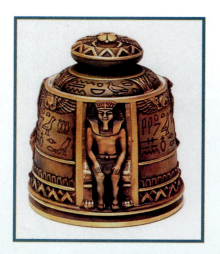

Humidor, molded in relief, 6¼" tall,
green mark #47, $3,000.00 – 3,500.00.

Humidor, molded in relief, 6¼" tall,
blue mark #52, $3,000.00 – 3,500.00.
Letter holder, 5½" long, green mark #47,
$2,400.00 – 2,700.00.

Candlesticks, molded in relief, 8¾" tall, green
mark #47, $1,900.00 – 2,300.00 each.

☙ *Enameling and Jeweling on Nippon* ❧

Enameling was one type of paint used to good effect on Nippon. Heavy enameling on china provides texture and definition to the design. The build-up of glossy enamel on Nippon pieces gives a three-dimensional look that enhances its visual interest.

Enamel is a painting material composed of colored glass. There are four types of enamel that are made commercially — the opaque, the transparent or translucent, the opalescent, and the overglazes or overpainting enamels. Opaque enamels are solid colors which cover completely. The transparent and overglaze types allow light or other colors to show through. "Flux" is a clear, colorless enamel that is the basis for all colored enamels. The primary ingredient is silica or sand. Potash or soda, plus lime, is added to make the clear form, then iron or lead oxide colors it.

Heavy enameling has been used on Nippon to produce both geometric and scenic designs. It is glassy to the eye and slick to the touch. If you feel the design with your fingers, it is definitely raised. Do not confuse it with either moriage or relief molded decorating techniques. Moriage work consists of separate pieces of clay that have been applied to the main body. Relief molded

(also referred to as blown-out by some collectors) work is actually pushed out from the inside, and is accomplished in the mold, not with paint.

Nippon with heavy enamel work often resembles pottery. The most common examples are in bright, primary colors. Art Nouveau and Art Deco designs that imitate the work of the Gouda Pottery Company of Holland were also made.

Enamel paint was also piled onto a piece to depict scenes. This is easy to confuse with moriage. Look carefully! Moriage is pebbly looking and rough to the touch. Enamel is usually brightly colored.

Blobs of enamel were used as "jewels" in many designs. These large jewels are often an integral part of the design.

Small dots of enamel were used as "beaded" decoration. Gold was the predominant color, but many other colors were also used. Collectors prize pieces that have been lavishly covered with enamel beads. Turquoise beads on a gold background are particularly desirable.

Bowl set, comes with master bowl and six smaller ones, master bowl: 10" wide, blue mark #52, $1,400.00 – 1,600.00.

Tea strainer, 6" long, unmarked, $200.00 – 275.00.

Dresser set, tray: 11" long, green mark #52, $800.00 – 925.00.

Close-up of jeweling.

Vase, 15½" tall, green mark #47,
$1,800.00 – 2,000.00.

ᴥ *Enameling and Jeweling — Jeweled Butterfly* ᴥ

Jeweled butterflies are found on a green background with light to dark pink plush roses. The different colors of enamel placed on the butterfly wings make them appear as though they have jewels. It is a spectacular decoration and a very desirable design to collect.

Cake plate, 10½" wide, blue mark #52, $650.00 – 750.00.

Close-up of butterfly.

ᴥ *Enameling and Jeweling — Pink Enamel Swirl* ᴥ

Pink enamel swirl pattern depicts a gentle floral motif over a field of pink and yellow mottled swirls. This decoration can be found on vases, chocolate and tea sets, and cracker jars. Pieces are marked with the green #52 backstamp.

Vase, 10" tall, green mark #52, $550.00 – 625.00.

Vase, 11" tall, green mark #52, $600.00 – 675.00.

ᴥ *Enchanted Forest* ᴥ

The enchanted forest scene depicts a stylized scene of a house, trees, and stream. It has a surreal look and is known to exist on a number of vases, humidors, wine jugs, and ewers. These items carry the green #47 backstamp.

Humidor, 7" tall, green mark #47, $1,100.00 – 1,300.00.

Wine jug, 11" tall, green mark #47, $1,300.00 – 1,500.00.

⇜ *Farm Scenes* ⇝

Farm related scenes are found on a variety of Nippon pieces from wall plaques to humidors, bowls, vases, urns, etc. One can find hay wagons, gleaners in the field, horses in and out of barns, chickens and sheep and even oxen working in the field. *The Angelus* scene depicts two people in a field giving noontime thanks for their crops, *The Sower* shows a man throwing seed in the furrows in the ground. *The Gleaners* features women in the field picking the meager remains of a harvest after it has been reaped. Most of these scenes are hand painted although a few are decals. Several other Nippon techniques were utilized including the molded in relief work.

Wall plaque, 9" wide, green mark #47, $800.00 – 900.00.

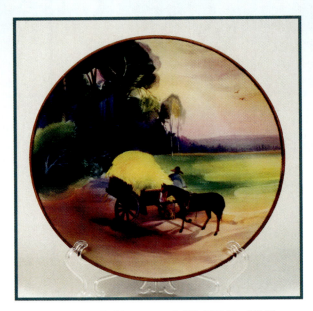

Wall plaque, 11" wide, green mark #47, $550.00 – 650.00.

Wall plaque, 10¼" wide, green mark #47, $500.00 – 600.00.

Wall plaque, 8¾" wide, green mark #47, $175.00 – 225.00.

Farm Scenes — Stylized Barnyard

Stylized barnyard features a barnyard scene done in several variations. There are people in some; chickens in others, and the barns vary in style and coloring. This decoration has been found on several different items including mugs, wall plaques, steins, humidors, tankards, cigarette boxes, and vases. These items carry the green #47 backstamp.

Vase, 7½" tall, green mark #47,
$350.00 – 425.00.

Wall plaque, 10¼" wide, green mark #47,
$400.00 – 500.00.

Tankard set with six mugs, tankard: 10¾" tall,
mug: 4½", green mark #47, $1,800.00 – 2,200.00 set.

Faux Cloisonné

Faux cloisonné décor features an Art Deco Oriental motif and many of the items have a Greek key border. This decoration is found on various vase molds, ferners, humidors, and steins. They have vivid colors and look a bit like Gouda wares. They carry the green #47 backstamp.

Compote, 6" tall, green mark #47,
$425.00 – 500.00.

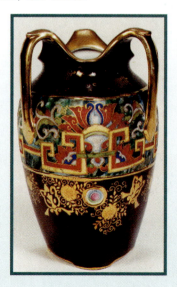

Vase, 7½" tall, green mark #47,
$375.00 – 450.00.

Stein, 7¼" tall, green mark #47, $650.00 – 750.00.

ᔗ *Fisherman* ᔗ

The fisherman scene is an extremely rare molded décor only known to exist on vases, wine jugs, humidors, rectangular plaques, and tankard sets. The fisherman is sitting on shore next to his row boat and appears to be lighting his pipe. The items have a pale yellow background and each carries a green #47 backstamp.

Humidor, 7¼" tall, green mark #47, $8,000.00 – 10,000.00.

ᔗ *Floral Decoration* ᔗ

Floral decoration on Nippon wares is a favorite with collectors. Flowers can be found on all types of items. Some of the most popular flowers are bleeding heart, chrysanthemum, daffodil, hollyhock, iris, lily, lily of the valley, lotus, orchid, pansy, petunia, poinsettia, poppy, rose, snap dragon, sunflower, sweet pea, water lily, and wisteria. All kinds of techniques have been used to create the flowers, some are hand painted, others utilize decals, tapestry decoration, coralene, moriage, and molded in relief. Floral decoration can also be found in conjunction with scenes.

Vase, 12" tall, green mark #52,
$900.00 – 1,000.00.

Vase, 14" tall, green mark #47,
$1,300.00 – 1,600.00.

Vase, 7" tall, mark #47, $275.00 – 350.00.

Vase, 12" tall, green mark #47,
$325.00 – 400.00.

Wall plaque, 10" wide, green mark #47,
$350.00 – 450.00.

Wall plaque, 10" wide, green mark #47, $350.00 – 450.00.

⟿ *Floral — Swirl Pattern* ⟿

Floral swirl pattern features lovely roses or mums on a background of mottled yellow and magenta swirls in combination with heavy gold overlay. This pattern is found on vases, urns, and chocolate and tea sets and the items are generally backstamped with the blue or green #52 mark.

Chocolate set, six cups and saucers, green mark #52, $2,600.00 – 3,000.00.

Bowl set, master bowl: 10¼" wide, comes with six smaller bowls, unmarked, $650.00 – 750.00.

Close-up.

Covered urn, 13½" tall, unmarked, $1,300.00 – 2,000.00.

ᔓ *Floral — Gold and Roses* ᔒ

Gold and roses is a pattern featuring a shiny gold background with light pink to dark pink roses in an allover design. Numerous molds have been found with this design, chocolate sets, mustard pots, pitchers, etc. It is a very desirable design with collectors and the price usually reflects this fact.

Pitcher, 8½" tall, mark scratched off, $575.00 – 700.00.

Mustard jar, 4½" tall, blue mark #52, $150.00 – 200.00.

Chocolate set, pot: 10¾" tall, five cups and saucers, unmarked, $3,000.00 – 3,500.00.

❧ *Floral — Jeweled Orchid Pattern* ❧

Jeweled orchid pattern is possibly one of the best painted and most sought after of the floral decors. This pattern has been found on urns, chocolate and tea sets, and vases and these pieces carry the green #47 backstamp.

Urn, bolted,
15½" tall,
green mark #47,
$4,000.00 – 4,500.00.

❧ *Floral — Painted Wisteria* ❧

This design features beautiful trailing wisteria flowers with dramatic gold decoration. This design is also found on tapestry pieces, however the pieces shown here have the violet wisteria flowers hand painted on them. It is found on urns, wall plaques, and a number of vase molds and wine jugs and is a favorite with collectors.

Wall plaque, 9¾" wide,
blue mark #52, $600.00 – 700.00.

Vase, 18" tall, blue mark
#52, $4,000.00 – 4,500.00.

Vase, 15¼" tall, blue mark
#52, $3,000.00 – 3,500.00.

Urn, bolted, 15¼" tall, blue mark
#52, $3,000.00 – 3,500.00.

⤳ *Floral — Palette Roses Design* ⤳

Palette roses design features a medallion of roses on a field of matte green and gold overlay. The décor is reminiscent of those having a definite Victorian influence. The decoration is known to exist on chocolate and tea sets, crackers jars, urns, vases, and serving trays. Pieces in this pattern bear the blue #52 backstamp.

⤳ *Floral — Texas Rose Pattern* ⤳

Texas roses just have to be bigger than others. This pattern features big plushy cream and rust tone roses lavishly adorning humidors, various molds of vases, urns, and chocolate and tea sets. The wares are backstamped with mark #52.

Basket vase, 8½" tall, blue mark #52,
$800.00 – 900.00.

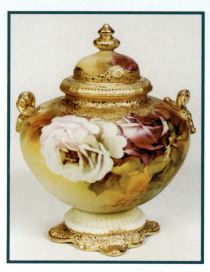

Urn, 7¾" tall, green mark #52,
$1,250.00 – 1,450.00.

⤳ *Fruit* ⤳

Pictures of fruit are found on many pieces of Nippon, especially wall plaques, punch sets, and utilitarian items. Among those found are the apple, avocado, cherry, grapes, melon, orange, peach, pear, pineapple, plum, raspberry, tomato (yes, it's a fruit by definition), and the watermelon. Some of these scenes are painted in the still life style reminiscenet of seventeenth century Dutch paintings.

Wall plaque, 12½" wide, blue mark #52,
$500.00 – 600.00.

Wall plaque, still life scene, 11" wide, green mark #47, $425.00 – 500.00.

Wall plaque, still life scene, 12" wide,
green mark #47, $575.00 – 675.00.

☙ *Galle Styled Pieces* ❧

Orange Galle pieces show a river scene done in rich rust tones with moriage trees and heavy enameled bead and trim work. Collectors assigned this name to these pieces many years ago. It is thought that this pattern resembled Emille Galle's cameo glass. Whether this was an attempt by the Noritake Company to copy these wares is not known, but the similarity is definitely there.

The technique for engraving layered or cameo glass was Galle's specialty. His pieces were constructed of several layers of glass, each of a different color. The engraver pared away, thinning each layer to create a blended intermediate range of colors. Galle's wares were symbolist or naturalistic in theme and shape.

Emille Galle (1846 – 1904) was the premier glass artist of his generation. His work is immediately recognizable by collectors. He mastered all kinds of techniques for making and decorating glass. His love and knowledge of botany had a big effect on his work. He had an intense interest in nature and an intimate knowledge of plant and insect life. Galle also had a passion for Japanese art using deliberate asymmetry and silhouettes. He used the technique of pitting of tree trunks to make them look more realistic.

This design is known to exist on vases, covered jars, jugs, wall plaques, steins, smoke sets, humidors, chocolate sets, and cracker jars. Pieces carry the blue #52 or green #47 backstamp.

Tray, 11" long, blue mark #52, $750.00 – 900.00.

Humidor, 5½" tall, green mark #47, $2,200.00 – 2,500.00.

Covered urn, 5½" tall, green mark #47, $1,000.00 – 1,200.00.

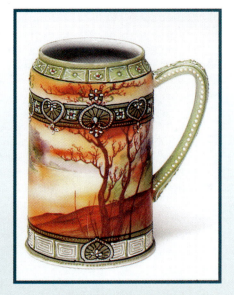

Stein, 8" tall, blue mark #52, $1,000.00 – 1,200.00.

Wine jug, 11" tall, blue mark #52, $2,000.00 – 2,500.00.

Vase, 13" tall, blue mark #52, $1,500.00 – 2,000.00.

⌒ *Gleaners* ⌒

Jean Francois Millet painted *The Gleaners* in 1857. Millet (1814 – 1875) was a master painter in France and also painted *The Angelus* and *The Sower*, which are featured on Nippon wares. The Gleaners is a decal found on pieces of Nippon and portrays three peasant women collecting the scanty remains of the harvest after it has been reaped. The gleaners are reduced to laboring over the slim pickings, which have been left. The painting has a cool, golden light, which gives dignity to the figures.

Vase, 12" tall, green mark #47, $2,400.00 – 2,900.00.

⌒ *Gold Etched* ⌒

Vase, 6" tall, mark #75, artist signed A. Richter,
$300.00 – 375.00.
Bowl, 7" wide, mark #77, $225.00 – 275.00 .

Years ago, many Nippon pieces were imported into the United States as "in the white" blanks. One of the companies who decorated these blanks was the Pickard Company. These pieces will bear a dual backstamp, both Nippon and Pickard. Collectors can refer to backstamp marks number 75, 76, and 77 to view these. Research indicates that number 75 was used in the 1919 through 1921 period, number 76 was used from 1912 – 1918, and mark number 77 could have been used as early as 1898 through 1912 depending on the color of the backstamp. Collectors should refer to the comprehensive book written by Alan B. Reed entitled *Collector's Encyclopedia of Pickard China*, published by Collector Books in 1995 for further information.

Mr. Reed states that the Pickard Company had an acid etching room at their Chicago location. Gold etching is described as the "eating away" of the glaze using hydrofluoric acid. Selected areas of the china were protected from the acid. The depth of the etching was due to how strong the acid was and the length of time the item was immersed in the acid. Once the item was removed from the acid bath it was rinsed in kerosene followed by hot baths of soap and a final rinse. The item was then painted with two coats of gold and had two firings.

The Pickard Company had been using china blanks imported from France and other European manufacturers but in 1916 they notified their dealers that they could no longer purchase European stock due to the war. The Pickard Company did not manufacture porcelain initially but were actually known as one of the finest decorating companies of that time. They were, however, able to get chinaware blanks from the Noritake Company in Japan during the war and most of the items with the double Nippon/Pickard backstamps were manufactured and decorated from this point on. There was little usage of Japanese china until World War I.

The Pickard decorating studio, now the Pickard China Co., had many artists on their staff, several from Chicago's famous Art Institute. The Nippon/Pickard vase features butterflies and is

artist signed A. Richter. Anton Richter was one of the Pickard Company's best and prolific artists. He studied in Bohemia, Dresden, and Paris and worked at the Pickard Company from 1905 through 1922. According to the backstamp found on the vase we are able to date it from the 1919 to 1921 time period.

An old Thayer and Chandler catalog, circa 1918, featured a number of Nippon blanks that had been "acid etched" for encrusted gold decoration. The company suggested that ceramists use Hubbard Roman Gold all over the china to achieve the gold etched effect.

⌘ *Gold Overlay* ⌘

When gold decoration is raised up on an item collectors refer to this as gold overlay. It may be a case of heavy gold decoration or it could be that the item had heavy clay decoration placed on it and then painted gold to give the appearance of raised gold.

Gold always had to be fired at a lower temperature so it had to be applied last after all the other decoration had been completed.

Gold melts at a much lower temperature than other colors and it would have melted into the other decoration. If the potter overfired the piece, the gold would become discolored; hence pieces decorated in this manner had to be treated with extreme care.

Vase, 12¼" tall, blue mark #52,
$1,400.00 – 1,700.00.

Vase, 9½" tall, green mark #74,
$650.00 – 800.00.

Close-up of gold overlay.

Vase, 5" tall, blue mark #52,
$550.00 – 675.00.

Urn, 13" tall, blue mark #52,
$2,700.00 – 3,100.00.

✎ *Gouda Imitations* ✎

The Japanese copied the designs of the pottery wares manufactured in South Holland. One of the most famous companies in The Netherlands producing these pieces was located in the city of Gouda. Although all authentic Gouda pottery is not necessarily made in Gouda, the term Gouda is still used to describe these wares. There were many factories in the Netherlands producing the Gouda style.

As with many other popular designs of the Art Nouveau time period this style was also imitated. Every piece I have encountered has been backstamped with the M in wreath mark, which indicates that the Noritake Company manufactured them. The company began using this backstamp in 1911 and was registered by Noritake for export to the United States. The M in the mark stands for the family crest of the Morimura family.

These pieces are painted in very vivid colors and are unlike any of the other Nippon wares. All kinds of items can be found in the Nippon Gouda style from vases to humidors, candlesticks, chambersticks, and various smoking items. These pieces carry the green #47 backstamp.

Match holder/ashtray, 5½" wide, 3" tall, green mark #47, $300.00 – 375.00.

Bouillon cup and underplate, 6" wide, green mark #47, $275.00 – 335.00.

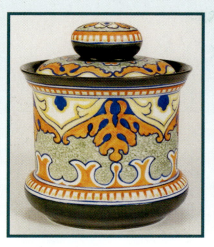

Humidor, 5" tall, green mark #47,
$550.00 – 625.00.

Bowl, 6³/4" wide, green mark #47,
$130.00 – 170.00.

⌒ *Halloween* ⌒

There are two so-called Halloween scenes. One is the traditional Halloween scene and the other is the tapestry Halloween. The traditional Halloween scene features a stylized village painted in primary colors. It is hand painted using a matte glaze finish. It can be found on ewers, plaques, humidors, and a wide number of vase molds. These pieces carry the blue #52 backstamp.

Halloween tapestry is one of the rarest of the tapestry decors. This scene is painted in bright pastel tones depicting the same stylized village. This decoration is known to exist on humidors, ewers, and vases and they carry the blue #52 backstamp.

Humidor, tapestry, 6" tall, blue mark #52,
$3,000.00 – 3,600.00.

Vase, 7³/4" tall, blue mark #52, $800.00 – 900.00.

Wall plaque, 9¹/2" wide, blue mark #52,
traditional Halloween scene, $475.00 – 600.00.

ᔟ *Hidden Door* ᔠ

The hidden door scene features a mountain village painted in primary colors. This scene is of interest due to the "hidden door" painted onto the side of a mountain. It is known to exist on wall plaques, jugs, humidors, vases, and cigarette boxes. These pieces carry the green #47 backstamp.

Wall plaque, 10¾" wide, green mark #47, $525.00 – 625.00.

Humidor, 6½" tall, green mark #47, $900.00 – 1,000.00.

ᔟ *Haunted Lagoon* ᔠ

The haunted lagoon scene depicts a pond or swamp scene with enameled green and blue trees in the foreground. These pieces are backstamped with the #47 mark and this décor is found on vases and plaques.

Vase, 7½" tall, green mark #47, $725.00 – 825.00.

⇜ *Howo Bird* ⇝

Blue Howo bird decoration was first introduced on Nippon pieces in 1914. Old ads tell us that it was originally called Howo Chinaware. In 1919, the name was changed to Blue and White Howo Bird China Dinnerware. The pattern consists of howo birds and scroll decoration in two-color Oriental blue.

The howo bird seems to be a combination of the pheasant and peacock. Legend says that the howo bird has the head of a fowl, the crest of a swallow, the neck of a snake, and the tail of a fish.

The blue and white pattern was sold by a number of companies and also given as a premium by a few. Some of the known com-

panies are Butler Bros., F.W. Woolworth's Five and Tens, A.A. Vantine, Montgomery Ward, and Charles Williams Stores.

The Howo bird is the Japanese bird of paradise and this pattern has somehow acquired two other names over the years, the Phoenix Bird and the Flying Turkey.

The traditional howo bird decoration found on other Nippon pieces is a stylized design. It is found primarily on desk sets and smoke set pieces. These pieces carry the green #47 backstamp.

Smoke set, green mark #47, $850.00 – 950.00.

Cigarette box, green mark #47, $300.00 – 375.00.
Ashtray, green mark #47, $300.00 – 375.00.

Close-up of design.

Plate, 6" wide, mark #55, $20.00 – 25.00.

⤳ *Hunt Scenes* ⤳

English hunt scenes are featured on a number of Nippon pieces. British gentry and country folk have long favored riding with hounds. Some of the scenes are more realistic than others, almost like fine paintings and are evidently adaptations of designs used on Royal Doulton wares. The more complex the painting, the more likely that the design is a decal.

Years ago, fox hunting was an obvious example of the life of the titled rich. It was available only to those who had the wealth and land to pursue it. Hunting prints were popular items during the Nippon era and this no doubt led to some of these scenes being portrayed on pieces of Nippon porcelain.

The hunt scene or English riding scene is found on many different types of articles from wall plaques to vases. There are more than ten different scenes depicted from a stylized version to those that are very realistic. Sometimes the riders are jumping, other times they are milling about.

The so-called white hunt scene is known to exist on vases, jugs, tankard sets, humidors, and plaques. These pieces are marked with the green or blue #47 backstamp.

The green hunt scene is stylized and has light moriage treatment over a field of green. This decoration is found on wall plaques, jugs, tea and chocolate sets, humidors, and dresser sets. Many pieces are marked with the blue #52 backstamp indicating that they were produced earlier than others.

The tapestry hunt scene is also stylized and is only known to exist on ewers and vases. It has a section of coarse tapestry-like material around the middle of the items. These pieces carry the blue #52 backstamp, which indicates that they were made at an earlier time than some of the others.

Green hunt scene, ferner, 4" tall, blue mark #52, $600.00 – 700.00.

Green hunt scene, blue mark #52, $1,000.00 – 1,200.00/set.
Hair receiver, 4½" wide.
Powder box, 4½" wide.
Hatpin holder, 5" tall.

Wall plaque, 9¼" wide, blue mark #52,
$800.00 – 900.00.

Tapestry hunt scene, vase, 7½" tall, blue mark #52,
$1,600.00 – 1,900.00.

Tapestry hunt scene, ewer, 7" tall, blue mark #52,
$1,700.00 – 2,000.00.

Stein, 7¼" tall, green mark #47,
$900.00 – 1,050.00.

Humidor, 8¼" tall, blue mark #52,
$1,700.00 – 2,000.00.

White enameled portrait, wine jug, 11" tall,
blue mark #52, $1,750.00 – 2,000.00.

White hunt scene, pair of vases, 6¼" tall, green mark #47,
$750.00 – 850.00 each.

Wall plaque, 11¼" wide, green mark #47, $800.00 – 1,000.00.

Wall plaque, 8¾" wide, green mark #47,
$425.00 – 525.00 each.

Green hunt scene, wall plaque, 10" wide, green mark #47, $600.00 – 700.00.

Wall plaque, 8¾" wide, green mark #47,
$325.00 – 400.00.

Green hunt scene, stein, 7" tall,
green mark #47, $800.00 – 900.00.

Incised Decoration

Incised decoration is found on very few Nippon items. While the piece was still in a state of soft clay the subject outline was etched into the body thus creating the design. Pointed tools were used to carve out the design.

Vase, 12" tall, mark #91, $350.00 – 425.00.

Insects and Bugs

Insect and bug designs are found on surprisingly very few pieces of Nippon. Insects are the most successful group of animals in the world today. Of the world's species, they collectively outweigh every other form of life on the planet, and in fact, some termite colonies and locust colonies can contain up to a billion individuals. The few featured on Nippon wares were generally hand painted, although a few are in relief molded, some on coralene pieces, moriage, cloisonné on porcelain, and even gold etched wares. Nine different little creatures are featured: the butterfly, dragonfly, hornet, honeybee, praying mantis, scarab or beetle, grasshopper, housefly, and there's even evidence of a spider via his spider web.

Moriage ewer, 9½" tall, blue mark #52, $1,800.00 – 2,200.00.

Moriage vase, 10½" tall, blue mark #52, $1,200.00 – 1,400.00.

Moriage vase, 7" tall, blue mark #52, $825.00 – 950.00.

Wall plaque, 8¾" wide, green mark #47, $300.00 – 350.00.

⌾ *Island Waves* ⌾

Island waves design is a scene featuring waves rushing to shore on a beautifully painted pastel décor. This particular decoration is found on humidors, chocolate and tea sets, and vases. These pieces are backstamped with the green mark #47.

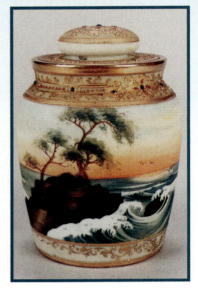

Humidor, 7" tall, green mark #47,
$850.00 – 950.00.

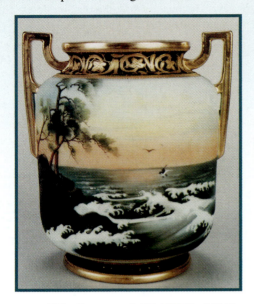

Vase, 8¹/₂" tall, green mark #47, $775.00 – 900.00.

⌾ *Kitchenalia* ⌾

Kitchenalia is a term that's been coined to mean all kinds of items used in the kitchen, including kitchen equipment and appliances. It covers a broad spectrum of pieces and most of the items are for utilitarian purposes. Some of these pieces are mustard jars, syrup containers, reamers, coasters, condiment sets, sherbet dishes, gravy boats, toast racks, tea strainers, toothpick holders, small bowls, cracker jars, and many, many other items. Most of these wares are hand painted. Some are plain in decoration while others may be well executed with allover handwork.

Reamer (juicer), 4³/₄" wide, green mark #47,
$175.00 – 225.00.

Sherbet cup and saucer, cup is 2¹/₂" tall,
blue mark #52, $85.00 – 125.00.

Bowl, 9" wide, green mark #47, $160.00 – 225.00.

Tea strainer, 5½" wide, green mark #47,
$150.00 – 200.00.

Syrup with underplate, 4¾" tall, mark #81,
$200.00 – 275.00.

Butter pat, 3¾" wide, $15.00 – 20.00.

Open salt, 3¾" long, green mark #47, $15.00 – 20.00.

Open salts and pepper shakers, 2¼" tall each.
Left: green mark #47. Middle: green mark #47. Right: mark #54.
#200.00 – 250.00 each set.

Knife rest, 3½" long, mark #84, $100.00 – 135.00.

Sugar shakers, blue mark #52, $150.00 – 200.00 each.
Left: 5¼" tall. Right: 5" tall.

Trivet, 6½" wide, green mark #47, $150.00 – 200.00.
Ramiken, 5" wide, blue mark #52, $50.00 – 65.00.

Egg warmer, 5½" wide, green mark #47,
$300.00 – 350.00.

Toothpick holder, 2¼" tall, green mark #47, $75.00 – 115.00.

Condensed milk container, 5" tall, green mark #47, $250.00 – 300.00.

Toast rack, 5" long, mark #84, $150.00 – 200.00.

Snack set (also called refreshment set, dessert set, sandwich set, toast set), blue mark #96, $700.00 – 900.00 set.

Mustard pot and underplate, pot: 3¼" tall, magenta #47 backstamp, $60.00 – 80.00.

Sugar bowl and creamer, sugar bowl: 6½" wide, unmarked, $160.00 – 200.00.

Gravy boat with underplate, underplate: 7" long, green mark #52, $175.00 – 225.00.

ᔒ *Knights at War* ᔒ

Knights at war scene features a highly stylized décor of two knights going to battle. The knights' suits of armor were made of metal plate and protected their bodies against weapons. Their lances were long poles with pointed metal heads. This scene is known to exist only on vases and humidors and carries the green #47 backstamp.

Humidor, 7¹/₂" tall, green mark #47,
$2,400.00 – 2,800.00.

ᔒ *Lamplighter* ᔒ

The lamplighter is featured on a molded in relief humidor and is a very desirable item as well as being an illusive one. It has a brown background with a medallion in the middle, which features a lamplighter who is smoking a pipe and carrying a pole with a pot of lamp lighting fluid. This design has a shiny appearance as opposed to the matte finish found on most of the blown-out wares.

Humidor, molded in relief, 7¹/₄" tall,
green mark #47, $2,500.00 – 3,000.00.

ᔒ *Lighting* ᔒ

Lighting includes many different items from lamps to candlesticks to chambersticks. Some of the lamps found are original from the factory while others will be a vase that has been converted to a lamp. Some of the candle lamps have been electrified. There are also nightlights, which are in the shape of a rabbit, owl, or lady. A chamber stick is shorter than a candlestick and has a handle.

Candlestick lamp, 11" tall, green mark #47, $2,000.00 – 2,500.00.

Another view of candlestick lamp.

Chamberstick, 7" wide including handle, blue mark #52, $225.00 – 275.00.

Candlesticks, 8" tall, green mark #47, $500.00 – 600.00 pair.

Candlesticks, 7" tall, green mark #47, $350.00 – 400.00 pair.

Lamp, 13½" tall, blue mark #67, $2,000.00 – 2,500.00.

Chamberstick, 6" wide, blue mark #52, $225.00 – 275.00.

Candlestick lamp, 12" tall, green mark #47, $1,900.00 – 2,400.00.

Candlestick lamp, 11¾" tall green, mark #47,
$1,900.00 – 2,400.00.

Another view of candlestick lamp.

Lamp, base: 14" tall, green mark #47,
$900.00 – 1,000.00.

ᴥ *Macabre Designs* ᴥ

Macabre designs have not been found on very many pieces of Nippon and the few that exist were placed on smoking items, humidors, and ashtrays. On one piece the devil is featured. His pointed ears, evil smile, and horns are intended to produce an effect of horror. The head of a skeleton is featured on the others and has a gruesome, ghastly grin. These pieces have death as their design and although not attractive to look at, are very much in demand by collectors and they carry hefty price tags when and if one manages to locate one.

Humidor, 6" tall, green mark #47,
$1,400.00 – 1,800.00.

Ashtray, 5½" wide, green mark #47,
$900.00 – 1,100.00.

Humidor, moriage decoration,
5½" tall, green mark #47,
$1,800.00. – 2,200.00.

Ashtray, 5½" wide, green mark #47,
$900.00 – 1,1,00.00.

❧ *Man in a Boat* ❧

Man in a boat scene is known to exist on a variety of items including wall plaques, cake plates, chocolate sets, and a number of vase molds. These pieces generally have highly decorative trim and they depict a man preparing to go out on the water in his rowboat. A cottage or two and trees provide the background for this design. These items usually carry the green #47 backstamp.

Cake plate, 10¾" wide, green mark #47,
$425.00 – 525.00.

Wall plaque, 10¼" wide, green mark #47,
$300.00 – 350.00.

Vase, 16¾" tall, green mark #47,
$2,500.00 – 3,000.00.

❧ *Man on a Cart* ❧

Man on a cart scene has the feeling of an Old World painting. These pieces depict a man driving a cart near what appears to be a beach. Pieces are known to exist on two molds of vases and wall plaques and are marked with the green #47 backstamp.

Wall plaque, 11" wide, green mark #47, $700.00 – 800.00.

Vase, 15¼" tall, green mark #47, $2,800.00 – 3,300.00.

☙ *Man on a Horse* ☞

Man on a horse features a man watering his horse highlighted by trees in raised gold. A lavender tinted sky is in the background. These pieces are occasionally decorated with cobalt trim work. This décor can be found on urns, plaques, and vases and carries the green #47 backstamp.

Vase, 12³/₄" tall, green mark #47, $1,200.00 – 1,500.00.

☙ *Mexican Cowboy* ☞

Mexican cowboy is painted in silhouette form. He has a lasso in the air while riding his horse. The scene appears to take place at sunset because of the orange background coloring. His large sombrero completes his outfit.

Ashtray, 6¹/₂" wide, blue mark #38, $275.00 – 350.00.

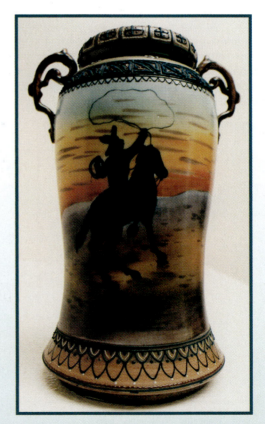

Vase, 12¹/₄" tall, blue mark #38, $750.00 – 850.00.

☙ *Mirror Image* ❧

Mirror image items are generally backstamped with marks that were placed on pieces shipped to Great Britain and not to the United States. And they will usually be a pair of vases although we have found mirror image humidors and plaques, which were sent to the United States. Mirror image merely means that the design was painted in the reverse and when the two items are placed next to each other they will "mirror" each other. Although, no two hand painted items will ever be exact, the artist does attempt to follow the design he is given and try to make the pieces look alike. A pair of mirror image vases must have been more in fashion in England than they were in the United States at this particular time in history.

Bolted urns, 6" tall, mark #230, $225.00 – 275.00 each.

Humidors, 7¼" tall each, green mark #47, $1,100.00 – 1,300.00 each.

☙ *Miscellaneous Items* ❧

Miscellaneous items are a group of pieces not listed in any of the other categories featured in this book. These include such items as ferners, shaving mugs, hanging toothbrush holders, potpourri jars, cinnamon stick holders, etc. The Japanese not only used a variety of techniques when decorating wares, they also produced a multitude of items, ranging from small toothpick holders to giant vases and urns. Whatever the West wanted they were able to supply. Most of these odds and ends are hand painted and can add a nice touch to any collection.

Compote, 8½" tall, blue maple leaf,
$1,200.00 – 1,400.00.

Covered jars, 3½" tall.
Left: Two-piece moriage, unmarked, $200.00 – 225.00.
Right: Two-piece, blue mark #52, $100.00 – 125.00.

Shaving mugs, 3³/₄" tall, green mark #47, $200.00 – 250.00 each.

Covered jar, 6¹/₂" tall, two-piece,
blue mark #52, $175.00 – 225.00.

Hanging toothbrush holder, 4¹/₈" tall,
green mark #47, $350.00 – 425.00.

Ferner, 6" tall, 10¹/₂" wide including handles,
green mark #47, $800.00 – 1,000.00.

Spittoon, 3" wide, blue mark #52, $200.00 – 275.00.

Potpourri jar, 6¹/₂" tall,
green mark #47, $235.00 – 300.00.

Covered jars, $175.00 – 200.00 each.
Left: 6¹/₂" tall, three-piece with inner lid,
blue mark #52, Moriage trim.
Right: 7¹/₂" tall, two-piece, green mark #47.

Basket, 6" long, blue mark #52,
$225.00 – 275.00.

Ferner, 4¼" tall, green mark #47,
$135.00 – 180.00.

Loving cup, 5¾" tall, green mark #47,
$400.00 – 500.00.

Hanging ferner, 4½" tall, green mark #47,
$400.00 – 500.00.

Loving cup, 4" tall, green mark #47,
$200.00 – 225.00.

⧉ *Monastic Series* ⧉

Six scenes are known to exist in the so-called monastic or monk series. Three of the featured monks are what we might call monastic tipplers, and the other three are smelling flowers, playing the violin, or reading a newspaper. The bibulous monks are all drinking wine. One has a wine glass in his hand, another a wine bottle in one hand and a basket with grapes in the other, and the third has a blue and white covered stein. There are five known backgrounds, green with moriage trim, mustard color background with moriage trim, enameled grape background, white enameled background, and the so-called moriage portrait monk décor. This décor features portrait monks surrounded by heavy brown moriage accented with white. They carry the green #52 backstamp.

The majority of the monastic decorated pieces are backstamped with the maple leaf mark and the remainder has the M in wreath mark. This decoration is most commonly found on humidors, steins, mugs, jugs, and vases on rare occasion. The word "monk" comes from the Greek "monos" which means solitary man. Most lived and worked in a monastery, and this word comes from the Greek meaning living alone. Monasticism is a mode of life practiced by persons who have abandoned the world for religious reasons to devote their lives either separately or in a community, to spiritual perfection.

Humidor, 8" tall, green mark #47, mustard
background with moriage trim,
$2,600.00 – 3,200.00.

Humidor, 8" tall, green mark #47,
mustard background with moriage trim,
$2,600.00 – 3,200.00.

Stein, 7" tall, green mark #47,
enameled grape portraits,
$900.00 – 1,100.00.

Stein, 7" tall, green mark #47,
enameled grape portraits,
$900.00 – 1,100.00.

Humidor, 8" tall, blue mark #52,
green with moriage trim,
$2,800.00 – 3,200.00.

Wine jugs, 9½" tall, green mark #47, enameled grape
portraits, $2,100.00 – 2,500.00.

Mugs, 5½" tall, green mark #52, moriage portrait monks, $700.00 – 900.00.

Wine jugs, 9¹/₂" tall, green mark #52, moriage portrait monks,
$2,300.00 – 2,700.00.

Wine jugs, 9¹/₂" tall, blue mark #52, white enameled portraits,
$2,000.00 – 2,400.00.

⚞ *Moriage Decoration* ⚟

Moriage decoration has the appearance of dried cake frosting. It was applied to the piece via the use of the icchin, which consisted of a piece of paper infused with persimmon tannin and rolled into a funnel shape. A tip was put on the end and used much like one would utilize a cake decorator today. Clay slip (liquefied clay) was put inside and the artist would decorate the item. Sometimes the moriage was painted gold and then called gold overlay, sometimes it was made into beading.

We find moriage items decorated in a myriad of colors; however, white moriage trim is found more than any of the other colors. Dragons, lacy designs, and the wheat pattern are very popular with collectors. The body of the article to be decorated had to be in a state of firm moist clay or the decoration might have fallen off or cracked when it dried.

Collectors will find that a number of moriage wares are not backstamped, which may mean that they possibly pre-date the Nippon period, post date it, or perhaps were never marked; or a paper label could have been originally affixed which has washed off over the years. Collectors must exercise judgment when selecting unmarked pieces. The quality of the porcelain and its decoration should be weighed heavily before purchase.

Moriage decoration is found in a "raised" appearance, usually the result of the slip trailing of liquefied clay on the item to make the design. Collectors should be careful not to confuse this type of work with pieces that are molded in relief (blown-out) and have a raised appearance due to the particular mold used.

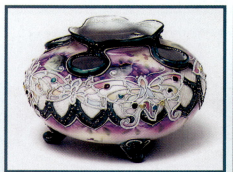

Vase, 4" tall, unmarked,
$500.00 – 600.00.

Humidor, 5³/₄" tall, blue mark #47,
$1,500.00 – 2,000.00.

Unmarked vases.
Left: 4¹/₂" tall, $350.00 – 400.00.
Right: 6" tall, $400.00 – 450.00.

Vase, 7" tall, unmarked,
$600.00 – 700.00.

Vase, 6" tall, green mark #52,
$500.00 – 600.00.

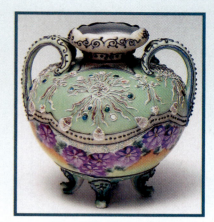

Vase, 8¼" tall, unmarked,
$800.00 – 900.00.

Vase, 6¼" tall, unmarked,
$450.00 – 500.00.

Vase, 7¾" tall, blue mark #52,
$600.00 – 700.00.

Mug, 5½" tall, unmarked,
$350.00 – 400.00.

Wall plaque, 10" wide, blue mark #52,
$400.00 – 500.00.

Wall plaque, 7¾" wide, blue mark #47,
$225.00 – 260.00.

Wall plaque, 9½" wide, green mark #52,
$500.00 – 600.00.

Wall plaque, 8¹⁄₂" wide, blue mark #52,
$400.00 – 500.00.

Vase, 9¹⁄₂" tall, green mark #47,
$400.00 – 500.00.

Vase, 9¹⁄₄" tall, mark #359,
$400.00 – 500.00.

Humidor, 8¹⁄₂" tall, unmarked,
$900.00 – 1,000.00.

Tankard set with 6 mugs, green mark #47,
tankard: 10³⁄₄" tall, mug: 4³⁄₄" tall,
$1,700.00 – 2,000.00.

Vase, 13¹⁄₂" tall, blue mark #52,
$2,200.00 – 2,600.00.

Vase, 11³⁄₄" tall, unmarked,
$450.00 – 600.00.

Vase, 9" tall, magenta mark #4,
$700.00 – 850.00.

Urn, 11½" tall, unmarked,
$1,500.00 – 2,000.00.

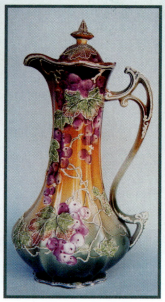

Chocolate pot, 12½" tall,
unmarked, $700.00 – 800.00.

Wine jug, 8" tall, blue mark #52,
$850.00 – 950.00.

Ewer, 11" tall, blue mark #52,
$700.00 – 800.00.

Vase, 9" tall, blue mark #52,
$800.00 – 1,000.00.

Vase, 9" tall, blue mark #52,
$600.00 – 800.00.

Vase, 9¾" tall, unmarked,
$700.00 – 900.00.

Vase, 8" tall, blue mark #52,
$700.00 – 900.00.

Moriage — Burnished Copper Design

Moriage burnished copper is a highly detailed decoration of jeweled moriage with gold and copper tone overlay. This décor is known to exist on chocolate and tea sets, vases, and cracker jars and these items carry the green #47 backstamp and blue mark #52.

Chocolate set, blue mark #52, $2,500.00 – 3,000.00.

Moriage — Cockatoo in Pines

The cockatoo in pines pattern features a beautifully painted white cockatoo preparing to fly while perched in a pine tree. This bird proudly displays his erectile crest. This design is known to exist on vases and plaques and carries the blue #52 backstamp.

Vase, 9¾" tall, blue mark #52, $1,200.00 – 1,500.00.

Wall plaque, 13¼" wide, blue mark #52, $2,800.00 – 3,300.00.

⤙ *Moriage — Enchanted Forest* ⤚

The moriage enchanted forest pattern is one of the most intricate of all the moriage decors. It features a forest of moriage trees all done in high relief. At present, this decoration has only been found on vases and they carry the blue #52 backstamp.

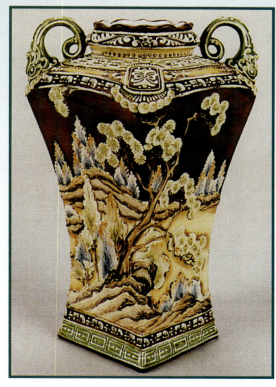

Vase, 9¹/₂" tall, blue mark #52, $875.00 – 1,000.00.

⤙ *Moriage — Flower Basket* ⤚

The moriage flower basket design features a moriage flower basket filled with roses as the centerpiece. The basketweave decoration enhances the beauty of the multiple pastel colored roses. It is known to exist on both ten and eleven inch wall plaques and chocolate and tea sets. These pieces carry the green and blue #47 backstamp.

Chocolate set, six cups and saucers, green market #47,
$2,500.00 – 3,000.00.

Wall plaque, 11" wide, blue mark #47, $500.00 – 600.00.

ᔒ *Moriage — Flying Swans* ᔒ

The traditional moriage flying swan pattern has finely decorated flying swans on a gray background. This décor generally carries the blue #52 backstamp. It is known to exist on a wide range of items including humidors, vases, urns, and wall plaques.

Vase, 3" tall, blue mark #52, $950.00 – 1,100.00

Vase, 14" tall, blue mark #52,
$1,700.00 – 2,000.00.

Wall plaque, 12¼" wide,
blue mark #52, $1,500.00 – 2,000.00.

Vase, 9½" tall, blue mark #52,
$1,100.00 – 1,300.00.

ᔒ *Moriage — Grapes with Swan Pattern* ᔒ

Moriage grapes with swans pattern features muted earth tones with two swans on a lake framed by moriage grapes and leaves as the main attraction on these pieces. This design is known to exist on vases, ewers, and plaques and carry the blue #52 backstamp.

Vase, 9½" tall, blue mark #52, $600.00 – 700.00.

ᔒ *Moriage — Jeweled Owl* ᔒ

The moriage jeweled owl pattern consists of an intricate decoration of an owl and tree branch executed in moriage. This nocturnal bird of prey has a hawk-like beak and claws; it has a large head with large front facing eyes. It has soft feathers and a short neck. This decoration is found on numerous vase molds, wall plaques, and humidors. This design can also be found on items using a tapestry technique. Pieces are generally marked with the green #47 or blue #52 backstamp.

Wall plaque, 9½" wide,
blue mark #52, $750.00 – 900.00.

Tapestry and moriage humidor, 6½" tall,
green mark #47, $4,000.00 – 5,000.00.

Humidor, 7½" tall, blue mark #52,
$1,500.00 – 1,800.00.

ᔒ *Moriage — Lotus and Cranes* ᔒ

Moriage lotus and cranes pattern features a large moriage crane stalking among the moriage lotus leaves on this unusual décor. The crane is a long necked, long legged wading bird that lives in the marshes and plains. The large lotus flower and leaves accompanying it in this pattern make it an outstanding combination. This decoration is only known to have been used on vases. Generally, these are unmarked as are a lot of the moriage pieces but some do have a blue #52 backstamp.

Vase, 10¼" tall, blue mark #52, $1,000.00 – 1,250.00.

☞ *Moriage — Plum Blossoms* ☜

The moriage plum blossoms pattern is found on a variety of Nippon pieces. These items have a yellow to light green background and moriage brown tree branches adorned with white and pink blossoms. Some of the pieces collectors will find bearing this design are vases, ewers, jugs, mustache cups, spittoons, handled baskets, etc.

It is believed that the source of inspiration for this particular design came from the painted gold leaf screens by the Japanese artist, Ogata Korin (1658 – 1716). These screens are considered the best of all his works and one of the greatest masterpieces in the history of Japanese art. They are in the collection of the MOA Museum of Art located in the hot spring resort town of Atami, Japan.

Korin's works show the influence of two earlier artists, Sotatsu and Koetsu. Korin was born in Kyoto, descended from a sumari and is best known for his paintings on screens and lacquer work. The screens displayed at the MOA Museum are entitled *Red and White Plum Blossoms* and were painted circa 1700. The screens depict white plum tree trunks with young branches extending forward. Plum buds are scattered among the fully opened flowers on the screens.

When I was at the museum recently I was able to view these wonderful works of art. A sign near the screens indicated that the technique used on the screens was known as "Korin Plum Flowers." The tarashikomi technique is one in which colors are blended by dripping one over another that is still wet. It was used to depict the tree trunks. On Nippon wares the plum blossoms and tree trunks are decorated with the moriage (clay slip) technique to give a raised look to the pieces.

Korin was a prolific artist and some of his works can be found in the states at the Smithsonian as well as museums in Japan. The *Red and White Plum Blossoms* screens on display at the MOA Museum are considered a national treasure in Japan.

Wine jug, 8" tall, green mark #52, $1,300.00 – 1,500.00.
Vase, 2" tall, blue mark #52, $300.00 – 400.00.
Shaving mug, 3¼" tall, blue mark #52, $450.00 – 550.00.
Spittoon, base: 1½" tall, 7" across, blue mark #52, spittoon: 3" tall,
green mark #52, $1,000.00 – 1,300.00.

☞ *Moriage — Seagulls in the Waves* ☜

Seagulls in the waves pattern features seagulls frolicking in the waves. Seagulls are white aquatic birds that have pointed wings and short legs and are found near coastal areas. This design can be found on humidors, vases, plaques, and urns. These pieces are generally backstamped with the blue or green #52 mark.

Vase, 7" tall, green mark #52,
$800.00 – 925.00.

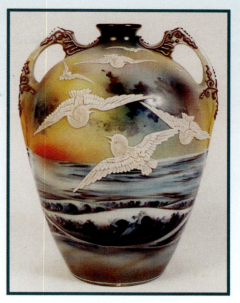

Vase, 10" tall, green mark #52,
$1,650.00 – 1,850.00.

⚹ *Moriage — Swans at Sunset* ⚹

Swans at sunset features moriage swans flying through a brightly colored marsh at sunset. This pattern was produced on vases, plaques, tankards, and mugs. These pieces generally carry the blue or green #52 backstamp.

Vase, 8" tall, blue mark #52,
$1,150.00 – 1,350.00.

Vase, 11½" tall, green mark #52,
$1,800.00 – 2,100.00.

⤳ *Moriage — Wheat* ⤳

The moriage wheat pattern found on Nippon wares has a light blue background with chaffs of wheat as the decoration. Laven- der violets are in the background. This particular design can be found on a variety of items and is a very desirable pattern.

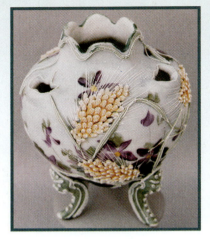

Vase, 5½" tall, unmarked, $525.00 – 625.00.

Vase, 6½" tall, blue mark #52, $600.00 – 725.00.

Humidor, 7½" tall, unmarked, $850.00 – 950.00.

Dresser set, tray: 11¼" long, unmarked, $950.00 – 1,100.00.

Close-up of pattern.

⤳ *Moriage — Winter Cottage* ⤳

The moriage winter cottage décor features a winter scene with cot- tage, all done in white moriage. The trees, as well as the ground, are covered with snow. This particular pattern is only known to exist on vases, chocolate sets, and tea sets. The vases are always molded in relief. These pieces carry the #47 backstamp.

Vase, molded in relief, 9½" tall, green mark #47, $1,900.00 – 2,200.00.

Chocolate pot, 9¼" tall, green mark #47, $1,500.00 – 2,000.00.

⌒ *Moriage — Wren* ⌒

The moriage wren pattern is a colorful combination of painted and moriage decorated wrens. Bands of spider-like enamel moriage treatment also decorate these pieces. This decoration is known to exist on various vase molds, humidors, and urns and they carry the blue #52 or green #47 backstamps.

Vase, 8½" tall, blue mark #52,
$1,500.00 – 1,800.00.

Vase, 11½" tall, blue mark #52, $1,700.00 – 2,000.00.

⌒ *Motoring Scenes* ⌒

Motoring scenes on Nippon items are few and far between and lucky is the collector who finds one. They are found on all kinds of items such as humidors, spittoons, ashtrays, inkwells, desk sets, dresser trays, cups and saucers, nut dishes, and even children's tea sets. Most bear the M in wreath mark or the rising sun backstamp, which indicates that the Noritake Company in Japan manufactured them after 1910.

It's difficult to imagine life without automobiles but it really hasn't been that long since cars have been in use. Henry Ford built his first car in 1893, and by 1900 there were 8,000 autos in the United States. In 1903, Britain set the speed limit at twenty miles per hour in an attempt to control accidents!

Most of the women featured on the "motoring" pieces wear special headwear as this was needed in an open car. They wore automobile veils over their hats, which secured them more confidently than pins. Both men and women wore silk or linen dusters to keep their clothes clean and to keep the wind out. One scene even features geisha girls out and about in their automobile.

Humidor, 6¾" tall, green mark #47,
$2,600.00 – 3,000.00.

Ashtray, 5¾" wide, green mark #47, $275.00 – 350.00.

Close-up of motoring scene.

⚭ *Mountainside Brambles* ⚭

Mountainside brambles décor resembles the side of a mountain and has fall colored brambles as accent. The brambles are thorny shrubs that have no flowers or fruit and can dig into clothing and flesh if touched. Pieces in this pattern are marked with the #47 backstamp.

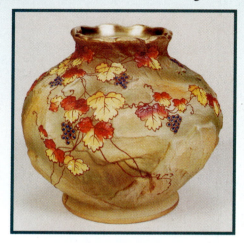

Vase, 6¾" tall, green mark #47,
$1,050.00 – 1,200.00.

Vase, 8¾" tall, blue mark #47,
$1,200.00 – 1,400.00.

⚭ *Nautical Scenes* ⚭

Nautical scenes can be found on a variety of Nippon pieces. The majority are found on wall plaques, vases, urns, and utilitarian items. Sailing vessels are featured on both calm and rough seas. There are even battleships of the World War I era most likely carrying big guns and heavy armor. The numerous styles of sailboats have cloth or canvas sails, which catch the wind and propel them forward. Boats are even shown docked at the wharf. Travel on water at this particular time in history was very important and this no doubt prompted the designers to display these boats and ships on Nippon wares.

Tankard with six mugs, tankard: 8¾" tall, mug, 4"
tall, green mark #47, $900.00 – 1,100.00.

Bowl, 6½" wide, green mark #47,
$160.00 – 210.00.

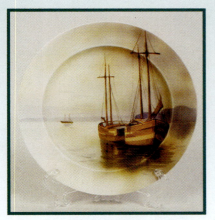

Plate, 12" diameter, unmarked,
$300.00 – 400.00.

Wall plaque, 10³/4" wide, green mark #47,
$450.00 – 500.00.

Wall plaque, 10" wide, green mark #47,
$300.00 – 350.00.

Wall plaque, 11" wide, green mark #47,
$400.00 – 450.00.

Wall plaque, 10" wide, green mark #47,
$350.00 – 400.00.

Wall plaque, 8¹/2" wide, mark #17,
$275.00 – 375.00.

Child's play set, teapot: 3¹/2" tall, comes with six cups and saucers,
blue mark #84, $350.00 – 425.00.

☙ *Nautical Scenes — Clipper Ship* ❧

The so-called clipper ship scene is beautifully painted with clipper ships at sea. Clipper ships are powered by the wind and were first used in the United States after the War of 1812. The United States ships ranged in size from 150 feet to 250 feet. They were the fastest of the sailing ships.

This decoration has been found on vases, urns, plaques (both round and rectangular), humidors, chocolate sets, and tea sets. These items carry the green #47 backstamp.

Vase, 12" tall, green mark #47, $850.00 – 975.00.

Vase, 10" tall, green mark #47, $700.00 – 850.00.

Wall plaque, 10" wide, green mark #47, $450.00 – 550.00.

Wall plaque, 10¼" wide, green mark #47, $3,000.00 – 3,400.00.

☙ *New England Winter* ❧

New England winter décor depicts a barn in a snowy countryside and has been found on urns, vases, wall plaques, and dresser items. It is a relatively rare scene and on occasion this décor will have silver overlay trees. The pieces are marked with the green or blue #47 backstamp or RC when silver overlay is used.

Dresser set, tray: 10" long, hatpin: 5" tall, items have a mixture of blue and green mark #47, $1,200.00 – 1,400.00.

Vase, 7" tall, blue mark #47, $600.00 – 700.00.

Vase, 8¹/₂" tall, blue mark #47, $800.00 – 950.00.

Urn, 13¹/₄" tall, blue mark #47,
$1,500.00 – 1,800.00.

☙ *Novelties and Figural Items* ☙

Novelty pieces cover a broad collecting field and among the most popular are the figural items. My interpretation of figural is is an item that either has a relief figure attached for ornamentation or the piece is in the shape of a figure.

Some of the favorites are the night lights that were molded in the shapes of an owl, rabbit, or Dutch girl. There are also ashtrays displaying the kingfisher, seal, penguin, and various dogs. There are molded faces of cartoon-like characters, also miniature Dutch shoes, figural incense burners, and bookends. In this field, new things keep appearing each day.

Napkin rings, green mark #47.
Left: 4" tall, $600.00 – 675.00.
Right: 4¹/₄" tall, $650.00 – 750.00.

Figural ashtray, 4³/₄" wide, green mark #47,
$550.00 – 650.00.

Figural trinket box, 5" long, green mark #47,
$450.00 – 575.00.

Novelty items, 3½" wide each, mark #84, $350.00 – 425.00 each.

Figural Dutch shoes, 3¾" long, blue mark #52, $100.00 – 150.00 each.

Novelty faces, 4" wide each, blue mark #84, $200.00 – 300.00 each.

Novelty faces, 4" wide each, blue mark #84, $200.00 – 300.00 each.

Figural birds, tallest is 4", green mark #47, $400.00 – 500.00 each.

ᔉ *Oil Spot Pattern* ᔉ

The oil spot pattern is found on candlesticks, steins, vases, humidors, and various smoking pieces and these are backstamped with the #47 mark. The prominent feature of these pieces is a dark gray background that appears to be stained with oil.

Vase, 8" tall, green mark #47, $400.00 – 500.00.

✑ *Oriental Designs* ✑

Oriental designs are not found on many Nippon backstamped pieces. Nippon pieces that were exported during the years of 1891 through 1921 were designed for the Western market and not for those in Japan. However, we do find Japanese figures and landscapes on a few items. We may find a torii or a pagoda, garden scenes, and Geisha girls. This decoration is usually found on vases and utilitarian wares. Some are decorated in a Satsuma fashion. There are even collectors who seek out the so-called Geisha Girl pattern which features the kimono-clad ladies and children in scenes of everyday Japanese life of this era. The Geisha Girl pattern is found either totally hand painted, hand painted over a stenciled design, or even with the use of a decal or a coralene technique.

Vase, 13½" tall, green mark #47, $350.00 – 425.00.

Vase, 14" tall, green mark #47, $350.00 – 425.00.

Coralene vase, 6" tall, mark #246, $1,000.00 – 1,200.00.

✑ *Pattern Stamped Decoration* ✑

Pattern stamped decoration is accomplished by using a special stamp or roller that has a design cut into it. This is pressed onto the soft body of a clay piece and the design emerges in low relief. This type of work results in an impressed motif of a repeated pattern.

Vases, 5¾" tall, green mark #47.
Left: $500.00 – 650.00. Right: $450.00 – 600.00.

Close-up of pattern stamped vase.

⤳ *Playing Card Décor* ⤳

Playing card décor is generally found on humidors, smoke set items, mugs, and plaques. In this decoration, playing cards can be found along with pipes, cigarettes, dice, beer steins, dominoes, matches, cigars, and even the devil. It is always found on masculine type items. Playing cards probably had their origin in the East and were most likely introduced to Europe by the Crusaders. These pieces generally carry the #47 backstamp.

Humidor, 5¹/₂" tall, green mark #47,
$750.00 – 875.00.

Humidor, 5¹/₂" tall, blue mark #52,
$925.00 – 1,050.00.

Humidor, 5¹/₂" tall, unmarked,
$925.00 – 1,050.00.

Humidor, 5¹/₂" tall, green mark #47,
$700.00 – 800.00.

Wall plaque, 12" wide, green mark #47,
$700.00 – 850.00.

Humidor, 7¹/₂" tall, blue mark #47,
$925.00 – 1,050.00.

Smoke set, green mark #47, $800.00 – 950.00.

Ashtrays, green mark #47.
Left: 5¹/₂" wide, three names, Bessie, Tessie, and Essie, $350.00 – 450.00.
Right: 5¹/₂" wide, $135.00 – 160.00.

⤜ *Portraits* ⤛

Portrait items are one of the most desirable Nippon pieces that one can purchase. The prices are skyrocketing for all, but especially those surrounded with coralene decoration or having a cobalt background. Almost every portrait featured on a Nippon piece is a decal. Decals are also referred to as transfer prints, and the use of decals was very popular during the Victorian and Edwardian periods. The decalcomanias used on Nippon wares were obtained in Europe because it was felt that the Japanese artist would have a predilection to give Japanese features to the faces.

Decalcomanias were also called penny transfers and today they are found on all sorts of items. Sheets of decals were often made up of repeating separable transfers. The lithography used was very suggestive of the chromolithography technique and of other complex lithography of the period.

Popular portraits featured are Madame Lebrun, Queen Louise, Madame Recamier, Marie Antoinette, Marie de Medici, Empress Josephine de Beauharnais, Countess Anna Potocka, lady with doves, lady with peacock, and the Cardinal.

The majority, however, are presently unidentifiable and at times one must consider that they are just pretty women with no nobility attachment and may just be the artist's wife or friend. When identifying the women, the clothing and hairstyle are quite helpful. The headgear on some indicates that a few may be Russian women. French women always bared their bosom as opposed to the English who wore buttons up to or covering the neck. The German ladies were usually more buxom than the French.

A study of backstamps found on Nippon portrait pieces indicates that the majority was manufactured between the years of 1891 and 1911. They also tell us that the Morimura Bros. or the Noritake Company in Nagoya, Japan, made most of these pieces.

The archives of the Strong Museum Library in Rochester, New York, contain pages of old sales catalogs featuring portrait decals from the German firm of C.S. Pocher, circa 1900 – 1915. Many of the decals look exactly like those used on some Nippon pieces.

Vase, 14¼" tall, green mark #47, $2,700.00 – 3,100.00.

Moriage vase, 9½" tall, unmarked,
$1,500.00 – 2,000.00.

Plate, 10" wide, green mark #52,
$1,500.00 – 1,800.00.

✍ *Portraits — Aqua Jeweled Queen Louise* ✍

The aqua jeweled Queen Louise pieces are the crown jewel of portrait wares. This décor features a medallion of Queen Louise over a glossy aqua glaze accented with heavy gold and enameled jewelling. These items carry the blue #52 backstamp and this décor is only found on vases and urns.

Queen Louise is also featured on a number of other Nippon pieces with other backgrounds. Queen Louise (1776 – 1810) was Queen of Prussia and this particular decal shows her on the palace steps at Charlottenburg. She was married to Frederick William III and was known for her great beauty. She had long,

jet black hair, had a whiteness of complexion, and wore clingy Grecian-styled clothing. She wore a scarf around her throat because she wanted to conceal the fact that she had a goiter.

This particular decal is an adaptation of the original painting by Gustav Richter. Gustav was born thirteen years after Louise's death. He painted her portrait in Berlin in 1879, sixty-nine years after her death. The original panting is displayed at the Wallraf Richartz Museum in Cologne. There are two decals featured on Nippon wares of Queen Louise, one is a full body picture, the other is just of her head.

Vase, 11³/4" tall, blue mark #52,
$3,600.00 – 4,400.00.

Vase, 9¹/4" tall, blue mark #52,
$3,200.00 – 4,000.00.

Painting by Gustov Richter.

✍ *Portraits — Countess Anna Potocka* ✍

Countess Anna Potocka was painted by Madame Lebrun and is shown with an elaborate coiffure complete with a blue ribbon that trails off to the left. The countess has been described as a Polish lady who was married to her third husband when Vigee Lebrun painted her portrait. According to records, she confided to Vigee that she was going to take her first husband back although he was a drunkard. Very few people realize that at times the Catholic Church did not frown on divorce but allowed it. That is why she had been married three times and was still in favor with the Catholic Church.

However, a twist to this story was discovered recently when an old copy of the Aldine published in New York in 1873 was found. This article shows a picture of a lady who collectors have been referring to as Countess Potocka with a much different story and a different name. It identifies her as Sophie Potozki. Perhaps our Countess is Sophie or then again maybe she is Anna. Either way, she is quite beautiful and highly desirable to find on a Nippon piece.

Vase, 8¹/2" tall, unmarked, $1,800.00 – 2,200.00.

ᛜ *Portraits — Empress Josephine* ᛜ

Empress Josephine de Beauharnais was born in 1763 on the island of Martinique and was one of the reigning queens of Parisian Society. She met General Bonaparte when she was a widowed socialite living in Paris. They married but she didn't produce an heir for Napoleon and they were subsequently divorced in 1809.

Josephine was known for her elaborate dresses that were festooned with trinkets and jewels. She led an extremely luxurious life. The pose shown on Nippon pieces appears to be a version of one painted by J. Champagne.

Plate, 10" wide, green mark #52,
$1,500.00 – 1,800.00.

ᛜ *Portraits — Enameled Grapes* ᛜ

Enameled grapes portraits feature various male characters standing behind a stone wall. A number are decorated with monks from the monastic series. Most of the men are featured drinking wine or smoking. Enameled grape vines and grapes accent the pieces. These items are generally jugs or steins and are backstamped with the #47 mark.

Wine jug, 9½" tall, green mark #47,
$2,100.00 – 2,600.00.

⇜ *Portraits — Gold Scroll Décor* ⇝

Gold scroll decorated portraits are one of the most commonly found portrait decors. A portrait medallion surrounded by gold scrollwork on a cream background typifies this decoration. These pieces are generally backstamped with the blue #52 mark but are occasionally found unmarked. This decoration is most commonly found on vases, plates, and occasionally on tea set pieces.

Vase, 11" tall, blue mark #52, $1,600.00 – 2,000.00.

⇜ *Portraits — Golden Ivy Décor* ⇝

Golden ivy portrait décor consists of medallions of Victorian women found on a field of white with gold and pink ivy overlay. Known to exist on various vase molds and ewers, pieces are generally unmarked.

Ewer, 9" tall, unmarked, $1,500.00 – 2,000.00.

⇜ *Portraits — Jeweled Cobalt Décor* ⇝

Jeweled cobalt portraits consist of various portrait medallions of Victorian women on a cobalt background. These items are heavily adorned with gold and jewelling. This decoration is known to exist on plaques and various molds of vases. These pieces carry the #52 backstamp.

Vase, 7³/4" tall, green mark #52, $2,300.00 – 2,800.00.

Basket vase, 10" tall, green mark #52, $3,000.00 – 3,600.00.

⤳ *Portraits — Jeweled Moriage Décor* ⤳

Jeweled moriage portraits feature medallions of Victorian women over a two-toned field of tan and brown on a green background. They are decorated with white clay moriage and multicolored jewelling. These pieces carry the blue #52 backstamp and this decoration is known to exist on vases and urns.

Vases, left shows backside, 6" tall, blue mark #52,
$1,200.00 – 1,400.00.

Queen Louise portrait vase, 12" tall,
blue mark #52, $4,000.00 – 5,000.00.

Close-up of decal of Queen Louise.

⤳ *Portraits — Lady with Doves* ⤳

Lady with doves is a beautiful decal used not only on Nippon wares but also on R.S. Prussia pieces. The lady is wearing a light blue dress and is shown with doves in the scene. This decal has been found on vases, ewers, and cracker jars and bears the #52 backstamp, which indicates that the Morimura Bros. and the Noritake Company in Nagoya, Japan, manufactured these items between the years of 1891 and 1911.

Vase, 12¼" tall, green mark #52,
$1,900.00 – 2,300.00.

Portraits — Lady with Peacock

The lady with peacock decal is the same one found on R.S. Prussia wares. This lady has a flowing gown and this decoration is indicative of designs found during the Art Nouveau period. This decalcomania is found on Nippon vases and covered urns. They are all backstamped with the #52 mark, which is indicative that the Morimura Bros. and the Noritake Co. between the years of 1891 and 1921 manufactured them all in Japan.

Vase, 12¼" tall, blue mark #52,
$1,900.00 – 2,300.00.

Portraits — Madame Recamier

Madame Recamier (1777 – 1849) was described as a brazen beauty by Napoleon. Madame Recamier's maiden name was Jeanne Julie Adelaide Bernard. She was a native of Lyons and married at the age of 16 to a banker. The Recamier couch, a long reclining one like the one she posed on for her famous portrait is named after her. The particular decal featured on Nippon wares is from the painting by J. Champagne, which he adapted from the original painted by Francois Pascal Simon Gerard. There are two variations of this painting used on Nippon pieces.

Plate, 10" wide, green #52 backstamp, $1,500.00 – 1,800.00.

Portraits — Madame Vigee Lebrun

Madame Vigee Lebrun (1755 – 1842) was a French portrait painter trained by her father. She painted Queen Marie Antoinette and her children and also Countess Anna Potocka. Most of her portraits were of pretty women shown in fine feminine costumes of the period. The two decals featuring Lebrun on Nippon wares are both self-portraits. One shows her wearing a white cap and and a white ruffle around her neck while the other has her wearing a white ribbon in her hair.

Urn, 12" tall, blue mark #52, $2,200.00 – 2,600.00.

Powder box, 4" wide, mark #52,
$700.00 – 850.00.

Ewer, 13¼" tall, green mark #52,
$2,600.00 – 3,000.00.

Vase, 7¼" tall, green mark #52,
$1,200.00 – 1,400.00.

⤳ *Portraits — The Red Cardinal* ⤳

The red Cardinal is one of the scarcer portrait decors and features a Cardinal in red. This particular scene can be found with the Cardinal facing in three different directions. There is a combination of both white and brown clay moriage decorating the pieces. This decal is most commonly found on tankards, mugs, whiskey jugs, humidors, and wall plaques and they carry the #52 backstamp.

Cardinals are the highest dignitaries of the Roman Catholic Church after the Pope. They wear a scarlet colored robe and distinctive red cap, or biretta, that is given to them by the Pope. The College of Cardinals has existed since 1059 and has the duty of electing the Pope.

Wine jugs, 9½" tall, blue mark #52, $2,500.00 – 3,000.00.

Mug, 5¼" tall, green mark #52, $850.00 – 1,000.00.

☙ Portraits — White Enameled Décor ❧

White enameled portraits feature medallions of various scenes including Victorian women, monks, and hunt scenes on a field of white. Known to exist only on jugs and humidors, all pieces are trimmed with fine enamel beading and carry the blue #52 backstamp.

Humidor, features Queen Louise, 7³/₄" tall,
blue mark #52, $2,200.00 – 2,600.00.

☙ Questionable Items ❧

Questionable pieces are a collector's and dealer's nightmare. Is this item real or fake, has the piece been damaged and repaired? Repairs are so good today that few of us can spot them just by looking at the piece. Is the gold just too good? Should I spend that much money on an item? The questions go on and on and it is only through study that you can be confident with your purchases. Try to buy from reputable dealers, get a written guarantee if in doubt, and touch as many items as you can. Read everything you can on the subject, talk with other collectors and dealers. In time many of the questions will go away but remember even seasoned collectors get caught with a fake piece now and then. Buy the best you can afford. Knowledge is power so study, study, and study some more!

Some of the items manufactured today are almost exact duplicates of the real thing. Can you tell which cracker jar is the real one and which is the copy? One comes with a label saying Made in China; the other has a genuine Nippon backstamp. The covers vary a little but not that much that a collector might detect the difference. The genuine one is worth several hundred dollars, the fake costs $15.00 at the wholesalers. The fake piece is heavier in weight than the real one and the gold is a little bit different in color. The cracker jar on the left is the genuine Nippon piece; the one on the right is the fake. Study the reproduction chapter featured at the front of this book and learn to spot these items that are manufactured to deceive.

Cracker jar on the right is fake.

Fake cover is on the right.

Sticker found on fake piece.

ᙅ *Red River* ᙒ

The red river scene depicts a peaceful stream flowing through a forest during fall. The numerous deciduous trees have lost all their leaves and this is a highly detailed scene. This décor has been found on vases, plaques, and humidors and carries the green #47 backstamp.

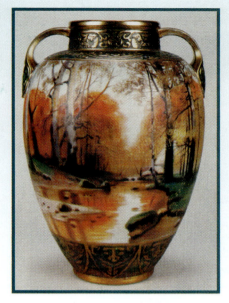

Vase, 15" tall, green mark #47, $2,000.00 – 2,500.00.

ᙅ *Relief Molded Items* ᙒ

Molded in relief Nippon items are also referred to by collectors as "blown-out." This term, however, is a misnomer as the items are not blown-out but the design does protrude out from the background. They are made in *one* piece and are not to be confused with items that have sprigged-on decoration or those with moriage décor. The design was incised in the mold and when the clay slip was poured in, it filled the cut out areas. Thus, the pattern was embossed on the item by the mold in which the item was shaped.

These pieces all appear to have had some type of upward pressure from the underside.

Blown-out items have a three-dimensional appearance which ranges from high relief, where the figures stand out more than half their implied thickness to half relief, right down to low relief, where the figure is just slightly raised.

Vase, 8" tall, blue mark #47, $3,000.00 – 4,000.00.

Wall plaque, 10³/₄" wide, blue mark #47, $2,400.00 – 3,000.00.

Vase, leaves are molded in relief, 10" tall, green mark #47, $600.00 – 700.00.

Vase, 9¾" tall, green mark #47,
$900.00 – 1,200.00.

Vase, 9¾" tall, green mark #47,
$550.00 – 650.00.

Vase, 8¾" tall, blue mark #47,
$1,200.00 – 1,400.00.

Vase, 8½" tall, blue mark #52,
$1,200.00 – 1,400.00.

Vase, 6" tall, green mark #47,
$800.00 – 1,000.00.

Vase, 10" tall, green mark #47,
$5,000.00 – 6,000.00.

Basket, 8" tall, green mark #47,
$400.00 – 500.00.

Vase, 8" tall, green mark #47,
$800.00 – 925.00.

Bowl, 5" wide, green mark #47, $100.00 – 125.00.

Ferner, 4" tall, green mark #47, $2,200.00 – 2,800.00.

☙ *Rookwood Look-alikes* ☙

Rookwood imitations are found in both a satin bisque finish and in a glossy finish. Both bear earth tone irises as their design and are found on vases, plaques, chocolate sets, and tankards. Some are found bearing the artists' initials. One set that shows up from time to time is MK.

Maria Longworth Nichols founded the Rookwood Pottery in 1880. Her father Joseph Longworth purchased an old schoolhouse for her to set up her pottery works. The Rookwood Pottery created distinctive pieces using flora and fauna designs. Each piece was individually decorated and the majority of the artists used sketchbook drawings and photographs for these designs. Most items have simple lines and shapes.

During the late 1800s Japanese designs influenced many of the Rookwood designs. In fact, one of their most famous artists was Kataro Shirayamadani. He was well known for the quality of his underglaze painting.

At this time in history, china painting in America was popular with women and painting societies formed across the country. Wealthy women painted blank china as it was considered an ideal artistic pursuit for women at that time. Due to the quality and high standards at the Rookwood Pottery, the company achieved a greatness that was second to none.

Vase, 4³/4" tall, mark #89, satin bisque finish, $525.00 – 600.00.

Vase, 9¹/2" tall, mark #88, satin bisque finish, $625.00 – 725.00.

Chocolate pot, 10" tall, blue mark #52, glossy finish, $650.00 – 750.00.

Vase, 12" tall, green mark #52, glossy finish, $725.00 – 850.00.

☙ *Royal Kinjo Items* ☙

Royal Kinjo items are backstamped with mark #240. Some collectors refer to the technique used as a salt glaze, orange peel, sharkskin, or sand finish. Although these items are not backstamped with the word Nippon, they are definitely from the so-called Nippon era.

Yasunosuke Doi, who is also the inventor, filed Japanese patent number 17705. It was filed on October 18, 1909, and was allowed on February 26, 1910. The inventor's address was in Nagoya, Japan. Information about how long this patent was in effect is not available because records were destroyed in World War II.

The patent describes the technique used as a process of firing a dew-like surface on the porcelain. The specifications are as follows:

1. Draw an outline of a picture on a white porcelain body.

2. Fire the porcelain.

3. Put color on the picture.

4. Spray the steamed water on the surface of the porcelain, so at this stage there will be tiny water drops or dew on the surface.

5. Sprinkle in the glass powder on top of the porcelain. Fire in the usual manner. The aim for this process is to easily and speedily make the dew-like surface more beautiful.

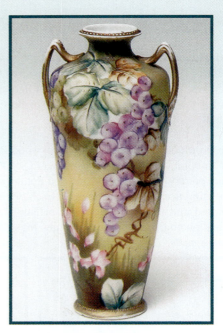

Vase, 10" tall, mark #240,
$600.00 – 800.00.

Vase, 10" tall, mark #240,
$600.00 – 800.00.

Vase, 10¾" tall, mark #240, $600.00 – 800.00.

⌐ *Ruins* ⌐

The ruins scene features an ancient city, perhaps in Greece. The colors make it appear that this is later in the day. White flowers and a green striped background accompany most of the items but the tankard set has a mottled green background. A number of pieces are found in this pattern.

Wall plaque, 10¼" wide, green mark #47, $400.00 – 450.00.

Tankard and eight mugs, mug: 5" tall,
tankard: 11" tall, green mark #47, $3,000.00 – 4,000.00.

Russian Dancers

The Russian dancers features four Russian dressed men dancing outside a city scene. These items have a green background, two of the men are wearing red jackets, one is wearing green, and the other blue. They are all wearing Russian styled hats in different colors. The scene is stylized and almost cartoon like. This design has been found on a number of items including candlesticks and wine jugs.

Wine jug, 9½" tall, green mark #47,
$1,100.00 – 1,300.00.

Scenic Designs

Scenic designs are found on all types of Nippon wares, from wall plaques to vases, urns, utilitarian wares, desk, smoking sets, and dresser items. The scenes can have flowers, birds, animals, people, desert scenes, winter scenes, and many have lots of trees. All types of decorating techniques were utilized in making these designs but the majority found are hand painted. Extra special are those employing tapestry, coralene, moriage, or molded relief in their manufacture.

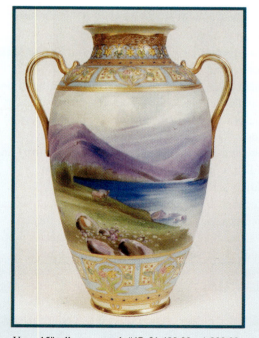

Vase, 15" tall, green mark #47, $1,400.00 – 1,800.00.

Vase, 9½" tall, green mark #47,
$285.00 – 350.00.

Vase, 8¾" tall, green mark #47,
$425.00 – 500.00.

Wall plaque, 9" wide, green mark #47, $325.00 – 375.00.

Wall plaque, 10" wide, green mark #47, $325.00 – 400.00.

Wall plaque, 10" wide, green mark #47, $325.00 – 400.00.

⌐ Sets ⌐

The following is a list of items that may be found in Nippon sets as listed in old catalog ads.

After-dinner coffee set – also called a demitasse set, consists of a tall pot with a long spout, cups, saucers, and sometimes a tray and a creamer and sugar bowl.

Asparagus set (decorated with an asparagus motif) – master dish and smaller serving dishes.

Berry set – several types are found, one is a large bowl with six smaller bowls; the other is a large perforated bowl and underplate with small individual bowls or nappies. The Manning Bowman set has a bowl and metal holder, tray, sugar, and creamer.

Beverage set – a covered beverage container and matching tumblers.

Bread and butter set – large dish (approx. 7¹/₂" wide) and smaller butter pats about 3¹/₂" wide.

Bread and milk set – plate, bowl, and cream pitcher.

Breakfast set – adult size can be made up of an individual size coffee pot, individual chocolate pot, egg cup, pancake server, breakfast plate, cup and saucer, creamer and sugar bowl, salt and pepper; child's size, also called an oatmeal set or a bread and milk set, consists of a bowl, pitcher, and plate.

Bridge set – set of four ashtrays and sometimes a matching tray and cigarette holder.

Butter set – same as a bread and butter set, consists of a larger plate and butter pats; some old ads refer to this as a jelly set.

Cake set – larger serving dish and smaller matching plates.

Celery set – celery tray and individual salts.

Cheese and cracker set – round attached underplate containing a small bowl in the center with a cover. It can also be found with a perforated insert that is placed inside on top of ice chips to keep the cheese cold.

Chip and dip set – similar to cheese and cracker set but does not have a perforated insert.

Chocolate set – tall pot with a short spout at the top, cups, saucers, and sometimes a tray.

Cider set – a pitcher and matching tumblers, also called a lemonade set.

Coaster set – six to eight individual coasters.

Condiment set – mustard jar with spoon, salt and pepper shakers, toothpick holder, and tray.

Console set – also called a mantle set, consists of a bowl and often a pair of candlesticks and vases or an urn or two side urns.

Cordial set — also called a liquor or decanter set, made up of a decanter and pedestal glasses, often has a matching tray.

Corn set – a master dish (decorated with ears of corn) and smaller serving dishes just big enough for an ear of corn.

Creamer and sugar set – sugar bowl and creamer.

Cruet set – also called an oil and vinegar set, has oil and vinegar containers; sometimes has a salt and pepper and matching tray.

Decanter set – also called a liquor or cordial set, made up of a decanter and pedestal glasses, often has a matching tray.

Demitasse set – also called an after-dinner coffee set, consists of a pot, cups, saucers, and sometimes a matching tray and creamer and sugar bowl.

Desk set – tray, letter holder, stamp box, ink blotter, calendar holder, inkwell with insert and blotter corners.

Dessert set – several individual plates that have an indentation for a cup, also called a snack, sandwich, refreshment, or toast set.

Dinner set – can consist of many pieces, dinner plates, breakfast plates, salad plates, cream soup bowls, bouillon cups and saucers, fruit saucers, cups and saucers, after-dinner cups and saucers, oatmeal dishes, small platter, medium platter, large platter, sugar bowl and cream pitcher, pickle dish, sauce or gravy boat, covered casserole or baker, covered serving dish, open vegetable dish, cake plate, salad plate, teapot, covered butter dish, coasters, celery dish and individual salts, and butter pats. There is also a child's play dinner set made up of a serving platter, covered casserole, dinner plates, cups and saucers, covered teapot, and sugar bowl and creamer.

Dresser set – can consist of a brush and comb, tray, hatpin holder, cologne bottle, pin tray, perfume bottle, trinket dish or box, stickpin holder, powder box, hair receiver, ring tree, hairpin holder, and sometimes a pair of candlesticks.

Fish set – large platter and small individual size plates; dishes are found in the shape of a fish or are decorated with fish scenes.

Fruit set – tray, pedestal bowl, and individual pedestal small bowls, similar to a punch set but smaller in size.

Game set – large serving platter and smaller serving plates, decorated with scenes of wild game.

Hostess set – also called a sweetmeat set, consists of a covered lacquer box with several individual dishes that fit inside.

Ice cream set – main serving dish and smaller bowls or plates, generally the tray is oblong and the plates are square.

Jelly set – larger plate and six individual dishes; old ads also call these butter or nut sets.

Lemonade set – pitcher and matching tumblers, also called a cider set.

Liquor set – also called a cordial or decanter set, made up of a decanter and pedestal glasses, often has a matching tray.

Lobster set – two-piece item made up of a bowl and underplate decorated with lobsters.

Luncheon set – similar to a dinner set, with a smaller luncheon plate but no dinner plates, does not contain all of the items in a complete dinner set. An old ad lists the following pieces: teapot, six bread and butter plates, six table plates, a sugar and creamer, berry bowl, six cups and saucers, six sauce dishes, six individual butter plates.

Manicure set – tray, powder box and different size jars that could be used for cold cream, powdered pumice, cuticle-ice, etc.

Mantle set – also called a console set, consists of a bowl, and often a pair of candlesticks and vases, urn, or two side urns.

Mayonnaise set – bowl, underplate, and often a matching ladle, also called a whip cream set.

Milk set – milk pitcher and matching tumblers.

Nut set – medium size bowl and smaller ones to hold nuts; some are even found decorated with a nut motif.

Oatmeal set – also called a child's breakfast set or bread and milk set, consists of a bowl, small pitcher, and plate.

Oil and vinegar set – also called a cruet set, has oil and vinegar containers and sometimes a salt and pepper and matching tray.

Open salt and pepper set – tray, pepper shaker, and open salt dish.

Punch bowl set – punch bowl (often found with a pedestal base) contains a punch bowl and matching cups.

Refreshment set – also called a dessert, snack, sandwich, or toast set, consists of several individual plates that have an indentation for a cup; each plate comes with a matching cup.

Relish set – main serving dish is smaller than a celery dish; set includes individual salts.

Salad set – large bowl and smaller matching bowls, nappies, or plates; some sets even come with porcelain serving utensils, a long-handled fork and spoon.

Salt and pepper set – salt shaker or open salt and pepper shaker.

Sandwich set – also called a refreshment, snack, toast, or dessert set; it's a two-piece item consisting of a cup and matching plate that has an indentation for holding the cup.

Seasoning set – tray, oil and vinegar cruets, salt and pepper shakers, and a mustard jar and spoon.

Sherbet set – tray and a set of metal containers that hold small porcelain bowls for sherbet.

Smoke set (smoker's set) – tray, ashtray, humidor, tobacco jar, match holder, cigarette, cigar holder.

Stacked tea set – teapot, tea tile, creamer, and sugar bowl that stack on one another.

Sweetmeat set – also called a hostess set, consists of a covered lacquer box with several individual dishes that fit inside.

Table set – sugar, creamer, butter dish, spoon holder.

Tankard set – tankard and matching mugs or steins.

Tea set – adult size contains teapot, cups, saucers, sugar bowl, creamer, and sometimes a matching tray. Children's play size and doll size can have same items. Old ads indicate that some children's sets came with only two, three, or four cups and saucers, and some came with six.

Tête-à-tête set – teapot, sugar bowl, creamer, two cups and saucers.

Toast set – also referred to as a dessert, refreshment, sandwich, or snack set. Set consists of several individual plates that have an indentation for a cup; each plate comes with a matching cup.

Vanity set – two perfume bottles and a powder box.

Whip cream set – also referred to as a mayonnaise set, with bowl, underplate, matching ladle.

ᴥ *Silver Overlay* ᴥ

Silver overlay items are unusual to find. Generally a heavy application of silver trim decorates these wares and collectors must exercise care when cleaning these pieces as they can be damaged. Sometimes the items will tarnish but harsh abrasives must not be used to clean them. Like the gold overlay, silver decoration was different in make-up from other glazes and had to be handled differently. Silver melts at a much lower temperature than the other colors used and the manufacturer had to fire the silver separately. The silver can be quite thick or very thin. Silver overlay decoration can also be found on other types of wares such as Haviland and Lenox.

Vase, 7¹/₂" tall, magenta mark #82,
$1,400.00 – 1,800.00.

Vase, 10" tall, mark #79,
$1,400.00 – 1,800.00.

ᴥ *Smoking Items* ᴥ

Smoking items generally have a masculine decoration although some are found in a more feminine manner with floral decor. Smoke sets can contain a number of items including a tray, humidor, cigarette holder, and ashtray. Some humidors have been found that are as tall as 9" while others are much smaller in size. A true humidor will have a hole in the cover in which to place a sponge. Some have handles, some have no handles, and there are even those that have finials, which are a combination match holder/striker. All kinds of designs can be found on humidors. Some of the other smoke items collectors might locate are cigar and cigarette boxes, cigar ashtrays, match holders, hanging match holders, match holders with attached tray, pipe holders, and spittoons.

Humidor, 7³/₄" tall, blue mark #52,
$1,500.00 – 2,000.00.

Ashtray, 4³/₄" wide, green mark #47, $175.00 – 225.00.

Match box holders. 4¼" wide each, mark #55.
Left: $75.00 – 100.00. Middle: also has numbers D13495,
$125.00 – 160.00. Right: $75.00 – 100.00.

Match box holders.
Left: Tray: 5" x 3", green mark #47, $125.00 – 150.00.
Right: 2¾" tall, mark #55, $100.00 – 120.00.

Cigarette holder, 3½" tall, green mark #47, $100.00 – 125.00.
Match holder, 2¼" tall, green mark #47, $100.00 – 125.00.

Smoke set, tray: 7¾" wide, green mark #47,
$600.00 – 700.00.

Ashtray, 5½" wide, green mark #47, $225.00 – 275.00.

Humidor, 8¼" tall, blue mark #52,
$1,000.00 – 1,200.00.

Humidor, 6¹/₂" tall, green mark #47,
$800.00 – 900.00.

Humidor, 5¹/₄" tall, blue mark #52,
$800.00 – 950.00.

Humidor, 5³/₄" tall, green mark #47,
$800.00 – 1,000.00.

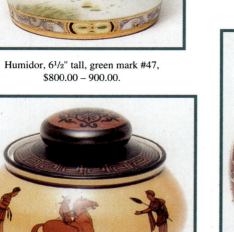

Humidor, 3³/₄" tall, green mark #47,
$300.00 – 350.00.

Humidor, 7¹/₄" tall, blue mark #52,
$800.00 – 1,000.00.

Smoke set, features chess pieces, dominoes, and
checkers, tray: 6³/₄" wide, green mark #47,
$500.00 – 600.00.

Two-piece ashtray, 4¹/₄" wide, green mark #47,
$375.00 – 450.00.

Another view of ashtray.

Hanging double matchbox holder, 5"
long, green mark #47,
$250.00 – 325.00.

Ashtray, 5" wide, green mark #47,
$180.00 – 240.00.

Cigar ashtray, 3³/₄" tall, green mark #47,
$150.00 – 200.00.

⚘ *Souvenirs* ⚘

Various Nippon items were souvenirs of such places as Washington, D.C.; Miami, Florida; Newport, Rhode Island; Saratoga, New York; Lake George, New York; Delaware Water Gap; Mt. Rainier and Lake Washington; Atlantic City; 1000 Islands; Watergap, Pennsylvania; and Prospect Point, Niagara Falls.

Most are small in size. A favorite with collectors are those pieces having a decal of the Capitol Building in Washington, D.C. on them. This particular decal portrays the Capitol at the turn of the century. Numerous items are found with this decoration.

Mount Rainier and Lake Washington, mark #100,
plate: 7¹/₂" wide, bowl: 6" wide, $150.00 – 200.00 each.

Pin tray, 1,000 Islands, 6¹/₄" long, blue mark #52, $125.00 – 160.00.

Toothpick holder, Newport, Rhode Island, 2¹/₂" tall,
green mark #47, $100.00 – 140.00.

Pitcher, Capitol at Washington. 5¹/₄" tall, green
mark #52, $250.00 – 325.00.

Capitol at Washington.
Sugar shaker, 5½" tall, green mark #47, $150.00 – 200.00.
Creamer, 2½" tall, green mark #47, $50.00 – 75.00.
Candy dish, 7½" wide, mark #80, $150.00 – 200.00.
Toothpick holder, 2¼" tall, green mark #47, $50.00 – 75.00.
Hatpin holder, 2¼" tall, green mark #47, $150.00 – 200.00.

Capitol at Washington.
Bowl, 5½" wide, mark #38, $100.00 – 140.00.
Sugar bowl, 3¾" tall, mark #38, $100.00 – 140.00.

❦ Sower Scene ❦

The Sower scene is an adaptation of the original painted by Jean Francois Millet circa 1850. Some collectors refer to it as Johnny Appleseed. The molded in relief design has a hazy atmosphere and depicts a man with a grain bag filled with seed on his left arm. He is wearing a shirt and breeches and is throwing grain in the furrows as he walks alone. The Nippon version is slightly different than the original painted by Millet. Millet (1814 – 1875) was a French master painter. He had a deeply rooted respect for the rural laborers. Millet had a romanticized feeling for the soil and the sad solemnities of the peasant's toil. All his work depicts the noble toil of the peasants. *The Gleaners* and *The Angelus* are two other works of Millet's that are featured on Nippon wares.

❦ Sponge Tapestry ❦

Most collectors are at loss in trying to describe this type of ware and have ascribed the name sponge tapestry to this technique. All the pieces found to date have a front panel that has a pitted appearance looking almost like a sponge. These items are unlike tapestry pieces because of their irregular texture. The area is decorated with flowers or a scene and is usually surrounded with heavy gold trim.

Wall plaque, molded in relief, 12" wide, green mark #47, $3,000.00 – 3,500.00.

Vase, 8¼" tall, blue mark #52, $600.00 – 750.00.

Close-up of sponge tapestry.

⌒ *Sports* ⌒

Sports are featured on very few Nippon pieces. To date, collectors have found baseball scenes, football, hockey, badminton, horse racing, golf, and hunting. Some of the scenes are quite whimsical and include cartoon-looking figures playing baseball, dogs playing hockey, and two little girls playing badminton. A shuttlecock is displayed still in the air and on the ground their dog has chewed up another one. People are featured in clothing of the time period. Boys and men are wearing knickers, women wear long pantaloons when they play golf as well as beret type hats.

Smoking pieces and children's items seem to be the most popular for this type of décor. These items provide a historical view to the pastime activities of this time period.

Wall plaque, 9" wide, green mark #47,
$325.00 – 400.00.

Ashtray, 4½" wide, mark #47, $475.00 – 575.00.

Wall plaque, 10" wide, green mark #47,
$625.00 – 725.00.

Smoke set, tray: 6¾" wide, green mark #47,
$1,300.00 – 1,600.00.

Back side of humidor.

Child's feeding dishes, mark #84.
Mug: 2½" tall, $75.00 – 100.00.
Feeding dish: 7" across, $85.00 – 110.00.
Bowl: 5½" across, $75.00 – 100.00.

Close-up of child's oatmeal bowl,
displaying children playing badminton.

ᴥ *Sprigged-on Decoration* ᴥ

Sprigged-on decoration is achieved by applying small molded pieces to the surface of a clay item using liquid clay called slip. Two or more pieces are necessary for this type of work and it differs from relief molded items where the decoration is molded right on the item.

The decoration is made in a small press mold. After it is removed from the mold, the back is moistened with clay slip and it is attached to the piece. Both the item and decoration needed to have the same degree of shrinkage or the decoration may crack off during the firing or even before.

Sardine container, tray: 6¼" long, green mark #47, $300.00 – 400.00.
Finial is sprigged-on decoration.

ᴥ *Still Life Scenes* ᴥ

Still life scenes found on Nippon wares are reminiscent of Dutch seventeenth century still life scenes. They depict flowers, fruit, banquet pieces, lavish arrangements of expensive foodstuffs, and serving pieces. Also found are a variety of vegetables, wine bottles, dead game, fish, lobsters, crabs, dead birds, and even nuts.

These scenes are usually found on wall plaques, both round and rectangular. Wall plaques are differentiated from plates by the holes found on their backside. String or wire was placed in the holes in order to hang the plaque on the wall.

Charger, 14¼" wide, green mark #47,
$800.00 – 1,000.00.

Wall plaque, 12" wide, green mark #47,
$600.00 – 700.00.

Wall plaque, 12" wide, green mark #47,
$500.00 – 600.00.

Wall plaque, 12" wide, green mark #47,
$600.00 – 700.00.

Wall plaque, 12¼" wide, green mark #47,
$600.00 – 700.00.

Platter, 16" wide, green mark #47,
$900.00 – 1,200.00.

Wall plaque, 11" wide, green mark #47,
$450.00 – 550.00.

Wall plaque, 12¼" wide, green mark #47,
$600.00 – 700.00.

⬲ *Stone Bridge* ⬳

The so-called stone bridge design features a curved bridge over a small stream of water. The scene has painted woods in the background and the orange background gives one the sense that it may be sunset. All types of items are found with this pattern and some even have a cobalt blue trim.

Basket vase, 9¾" tall, blue mark #47, $600.00 – 700.00.

Ferner, 10¾" wide, green mark #47,
$900.00 – 1,000.00.

Wall plaque, 9½" wide, green mark #47,
$450.00 – 550.00.

∽ *Tapestry Decoration* ∽

The tapestry technique found on Nippon items is similar to that of the Royal Bayreuth pieces. A cloth was first dipped in porcelain slip. The artisan then spread this cloth out on his hands to pat out the excess clay. The material was tightly stretched over the damp piece of porcelain and during the bisque firing the material was consumed in the kiln. The heat in the kiln destroyed the threads of material leaving a texture on some items that resembled cheesecloth or linen. Some pieces have a fine-grained appearance; others have a slight pebbly look resembling needlepoint. Many tapestry items appear as though they had originally been covered with netting, cheesecloth, linen, or muslin. Whatever weave the fabric had now became the background texture on the porcelain item. Sometimes the item will look as though a coarsely woven cloth had been used while another will look as though a linen material was utilized. The piece was then painted and fired again. Some Nippon tapestry decorated articles can be found that also have a slip-trailing décor (moriage) applied over the top of the painted fabric look.

The tapestry technique is found mostly on vases but it has also appeared on humidors, covered urns, wall plaques, ewers, and pitchers. Most of the pieces bear the maple leaf mark that indicates they were manufactured between 1891 and 1911. A few have been found bearing marks #4, #47, and #91.

Vase, 5½" tall, blue mark #52,
$1,400.00 – 1,700.00.

Vase, 9½" tall, blue mark #52,
$1,900.00 – 2,300.00.

Ewer, 7" tall, blue mark #52,
$1,500.00 – 1,900.00.

Ewer, 7½" tall, blue mark #52,
$1,800.00 – 2,200.00.

Vase, 7¾" tall, blue mark #52, $1,800.00 –
2,200.00.

Ewer, 10½" tall, blue mark #52,
$2,000.00 – 2,400.00.

⚘ *Tapestry — Allover Roses* ⚘

The rose tapestry pattern found on Nippon vases features a design of allover roses in a tapestry technique. The large, plush roses are found in a myriad of colors: yellow, white, and light to dark pink. This design also has jewelling as part of its decoration and is found on a coarser type of background. A band of tapestry decoration is placed on the middle of the vases and does not cover the entire item as it does on other tapestry pieces.

Vase, 6" tall, blue mark #52, $1,400.00 – 1,600.00.

Close-up of tapestry technique.

⚘ *Tapestry — Blue Gallé* ⚘

Blue Gallé tapestry is unlike the traditional orange Galle décor. This variation is painted in soft pastel shades of blue and lavender. The pieces exhibit extensive collar enameling and lavender trees decorated with enamel moriage. It is thought that this pattern resembled Emille Galle's (1846 – 1904) cameo glass. He was the premier glass artist of his generation and he used a technique for engraving layered or cameo glass, each of a different color. The engraver pared away, thinning each layer to create a blended intermediate range of colors. Galle's wares were symbolist or naturalistic in theme and shape. He had an intense interest in nature and an intimate knowledge of plant and insect life.

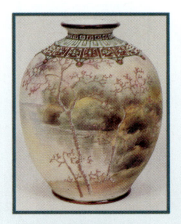

Vase, 6" tall, blue mark #52,
$2,600.00 – 3,000.00.

Vase, 8" tall, blue mark #52, $3,000.00 – 3,400.00.

⤙ *Tapestry — Castle on the Lake* ⤚

Castle on the lake tapestry is a pattern that is reminiscent of an old English castle beside a lake. Enameled jewelling and gold decoration add to the beauty of these items. This décor is only found on the coarser type tapestry. These items bear the blue #52 backstamp and the pattern is found on vases and ewers.

Ewer, 7" tall, blue mark #52,
$1,600.00 – 2,000.00.

Vase, 6" tall, blue mark #52,
$1,200.00 – 1,400.00.

⤙ *Tapestry — Day on the Pond* ⤚

Day on the pond tapestry is generally regarded as one of the best tapestry patterns. It features a man and woman preparing for a day of boating and is painted in soft pastel tones of blues, greens, and yellows. The majority of the pieces feature heavy gold work in relief around the tops and some on the bottoms. These items carry the blue #52 backstamp and this desirable scene is found on vases, humidors, and ewers.

Ewer, 11" tall, blue mark #52, $2,500.00 – 3,000.00.

Vase, 8¼" tall, blue mark #52, $1,900.00 – 2,200.00.

⤙ *Tapestry — Deco Pendant* ⤚

Deco pendant tapestry décor is only known to exist on vases. The deco styled ornamental pendants seem to be suspended on the items. Enameled jewels also appear in this pattern. Art Deco styles began as early as the 1900s and ended around 1930. Art Deco took its name from the Paris Exposition Internationale des Arts Decoratifs that was held in 1925. Deco items have geometric styles and many have zigzagging lines. Art Nouveau has been characterized as having curves and Art Deco as having angles. These pieces carry the blue #52 backstamp.

Vase, 9½" tall, blue mark #52, $1,900.00 – 2,300.00.

Vase, 5½" tall, blue mark #52, $1,400.00 – 1,700.00.

⤙ *Tapestry — Florabunda* ⤚

Floribunda tapestry features large, plush pink and yellow roses. There are an abundance of roses on these pieces and this is one of the more commonly seen tapestry decors. Pieces are occasionally found unmarked but generally they are backstamped with the blue #52 mark. This decoration is known to exist on vases, ewers, and wall plaques.

Vase, 8½" tall, blue mark #52, $1,900.00 – 2,300.00.

Vase, 8½" tall, blue mark #52, $1,800.00 – 2,200.00.

☙ *Tapestry — Grapes* ☙

Grape tapestry decoration has only been found on ewers and vases. It features clusters of grapes hanging on the vine and is painted in soft pastel tones of green and purple. The collars of the items are done in heavy gold in relief. These items bear the blue #52 backstamp.

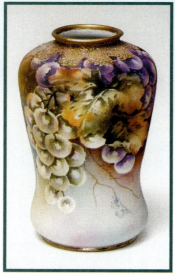

Vase, 8" tall, blue mark #52, $1,900.00 – 2,300.00.

Vase, 5¹/₂" tall, blue mark #52, $1,500.00 – 1,800.00.

☙ *Tapestry — Peach* ☙

Tapestry items featuring lush ripening peaches have only been found on covered urns and vases. Shaded leaves on a light green background surround the colorfully painted peaches. These items carry the blue #52 backstamp.

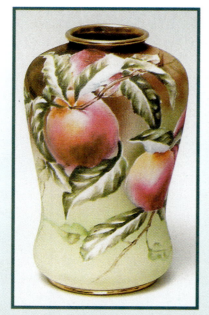

Vase, 8" tall, blue mark #52, $1,900.00 – 2,300.00.

Covered urn, 10¹/₂" tall, blue mark #52, $2,800.00 – 3,200.00.

✑ *Tapestry — Pink Lily* ✑

Pink lily tapestry is only known to exist on vases. This beautiful pattern depicts newly blooming lilies on a green background. To date, all the pieces found bear the blue #52 backstamp.

Basket vase, 8½" tall, blue mark #52,
$2,600.00 – 3,000.00.

Vase, 9" tall, blue mark #52,
$1,800.00 – 2,200.00.

✑ *Tapestry — Swan* ✑

Swan tapestry features two swans on a pond and is painted in pale yellow and green tones. These stately birds have long necks, white plumage, and one can imagine that they have graceful movements when swimming. This scene is one of the less common ones featured on tapestry. It carries the blue #52 backstamp and is found on vases, ewers, and humidors.

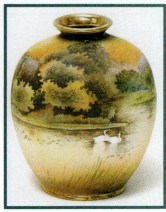

Basket vase, 9" tall, blue mark #52,
$2,600.00 – 3,000.00.

Vase, 6¼" tall, blue mark #52,
$1,900.00 – 2,300.00.

✑ *Tapestry — Wisteria* ✑

Wisteria tapestry features pale purple flowers in large drooping clusters on a soft green background. This décor has only been found on vases and bears the blue #52 backstamp.

Basket vase, 8½" tall, blue mark #52,
$2,600.00 – 3,000.00.

Vase, 9" tall, blue mark #52,
$1,900.00 – 2,300.00.

⤳ *Urns* ⤳

Urns can be found that have covers and many are bolted at the base. Urns can be as large as 28 inches in size. Hand-painted ones are the most commonly found while there are those decorated with coralene beading, moriage slipwork, and decal por-traits. Some are painted with scenes, others have flowers or birds, etc. The very large urns are difficult to find and are generally expensive in price.

16" tall, green mark #47,
$4,000.00 – 4,500.00.

14½" tall, blue mark #47,
$2,000.00 – 2,500.00.

17½" tall, green mark #47,
$2,400.00 – 3,000.00.

Vase, 17½" tall, blue mark
#52, $2,000.00 – 2,300.00.

16" tall, green mark #47,
$2,500.00 – 3,000.00.

16½" tall, blue mark #52,
$1,500.00 – 2,000.00.

10¼" tall, blue mark #230,
$600.00 – 800.00.

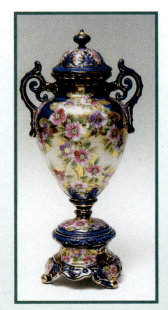

18½" tall, unmarked,
$2,000.00 – 2,500.00.

16½" tall, green mark #47,
$2,200.00 – 2,600.00.

8¾" tall, green mark #52,
$400.00 – 500.00.

16¾" tall, blue mark #47,
$2,500.00 – 3,000.00.

Covered urn, 9¼" tall, mark #229,
$600.00 – 725.00.

17¼" tall, green mark #47,
$1,500.00 – 1,800.00.

⁀ *Vases and Ewers* ⁀

Vases can be found in all sizes, from the tiniest of just a couple inches to those that are as big as 25 inches tall. They can be found decorated with animals, birds, flowers, scenes, fruit, portraits, geometrics, etc. Some have handles, others are found without any handles. Others have basket type handles and then there are ones that have handles in the shapes of seahorses. They can be found hand painted, having decals as their decoration, also decorated in a moriage, coralene, or molded in relief fashion. Some have large amounts of beading or enameling, others have silver or gold overlay. Ewers have handles and a flaring spout for pouring.

The Japanese were both innovative and imitative with their designs. They copied the works of many countries including The Netherlands and England. Some of the handwork is exquisite and some it is borderline acceptable. Beauty is in the eye of the beholder but collectors should strive to buy vases of the best quality that they can afford. Size does not always increase the price. A wonderful small well-decorated vase is always worth more than a poorly decorated large one.

Vase, 8¹/₂" tall, blue mark #52, $375.00 – 450.00.

Vase, 9¹/₂" tall, green mark #47, $275.00 – 300.00.

Vase, 6" tall, blue mark #52, $150.00 – 175.00.

Vase, heavy gold, 8" tall, mark #157, $200.00 – 250.00.

Vase, 7³/₄" tall, blue mark #52, handle is figural lizard, $325.00 – 350.00.

Vase, 6¹/₂" tall, green mark #47, $200.00 – 250.00.

Vase, 9" tall, blue mark #52, $400.00 – 475.00.

Vase, 7½" tall, blue mark #52,
$400.00 – 500.00.

Vase, 10¾" tall, blue mark #52,
$450.00 – 550.00.

Vase, 12½" tall, blue mark #52, $900.00 – 1,050.00.

Vase, 12" tall, blue mark #52,
$900.00 – 1,050.00.

Vase, 12" tall, blue mark #52,
$900.00 – 1,050.00.

Vase, 7¾" tall, green mark #47,
$400.00 – 500.00.

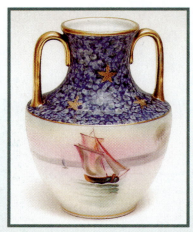

Vase, 6½" tall,
green mark #47,
$150.00 – 200.00.

Vase, 11¼" tall, blue mark #52,
$700.00 – 800.00.

Ewer, 7½" tall, green mark #47,
$300.00 – 350.00.

Vase, 11¼" tall, green mark #47,
$300.00 – 400.00.

Vase, 14½" tall, green mark
#47, $700.00 – 900.00.

Vase, 11½" tall, blue mark #47,
$600.00 – 700.00.

Vase, 12½" tall, green mark #47,
$300.00 – 350.00.

Vase, 11" tall, green mark #47,
$800.00 – 1,000.00.

Vase, 10¾" tall, blue mark #52,
$600.00 – 700.00.

Vase, 11" tall, green mark #47,
$650.00 – 750.00.

Vase, 14" tall, green mark #47,
$2,500.00 – 3,000.00.

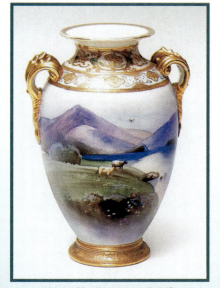

Vase, 10" tall, green mark #47,
$400.00 – 500.00.

Vase, 7¾" tall, blue mark #52,
$300.00 – 400.00.

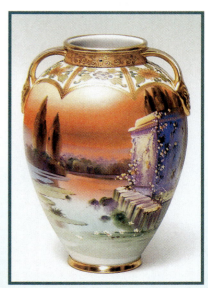

Vase, 10" tall, green mark #47,
$650.00 – 750.00.

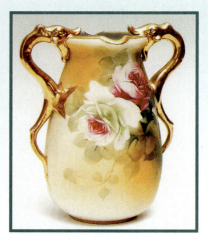

Vase with serpent handles, 7¹/₂" tall, blue
mark #47, $450.00 – 550.00.

Vase, 8¹/₄" tall, green mark #47,
$400.00 – 500.00.

Vase, 8¹/₄" tall, green mark #47,
$400.00 – 475.00.

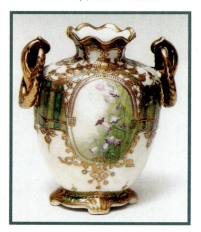

Vase, 8¹/₂" tall, blue mark #47,
$500.00 – 600.00.

Vase, 9¹/₄" tall, blue mark #52,
$250.00 – 300.00.

Vase, 10¹/₄" tall, blue mark #52,
$700.00 – 800.00.

Vase, 10¹/₂" tall, green mark #52,
$650.00 – 750.00.

Vase, 11" tall, green mark #47,
$450.00 – 550.00.

Vase, 11¹/₂" tall, blue mark #52,
$300.00 – 350.00.

Vase, 24" tall, blue mark #52, $8,500.00 – 9,500.00.

Vase, 11¾" tall, green mark #52, $275.00 – 350.00.

Vase, 10½" tall, blue mark #52, $450.00 – 550.00.

Vase with elephant handles, 16¼" tall, blue mark #52, $1,900.00 – 2,200.00.

Vase, 12½" tall, green mark #47, $300.00 – 400.00.

Vase, 9¾" tall, green mark #47, $325.00 – 375.00.

Vase, 12¼" tall, blue mark #52, $400.00 – 600.00.

Vase, 14½" tall, green mark #47, $1,000.00 – 1,200.00.

Vase, 10" tall, green mark #47,
$300.00 – 350.00.

Vase, 13³/₄" tall, green mark #47,
$800.00 – 1,000.00.

Vase, 14" tall, green mark #47,
$1,500.00 – 1,800.00.

Vase, 15" tall, blue mark #52,
$1,900.00 – 2,200.00.

Vase, 9³/₄" tall, green mark #47,
$300.00 – 400.00.

Vase, 15¹/₂" tall, blue mark #52,
$2,000.00 – 2,500.00.

Vase, 15¹/₂" tall, blue mark #52,
$2,400.00 – 2,800.00.

Vase, 18¼" tall, blue mark #52,
$4,000.00 – 5,000.00.

Vase, 8¾" tall, blue mark #47,
$350.00 – 450.00.

Vase, 9" tall, blue mark #47,
$250.00 – 350.00.

Ewer, 11½" tall, Blue mark #52,
$500.00 – 600.00.

❧ *Vegetables* ❧

Vegetables can be found on many Nippon pieces including wall plaques and utilitarian wares that were used everyday. They can be found hand painted or with a decal or in figural form which have been molded in relief. Some of the vegetables featured are asparagus, carrots, celery, corn, cucumbers, lettuce, mushrooms, onions, and radishes. There are sets made specifically for corn and asparagus that are decorated with the vegetable that is to be used in the set.

Tea set, pot: 4" tall, comes with six cups and saucers,
green mark #47, $1,400.00 – 1,800.00.

Sugar and creamer set, molded in relief, sugar bowl is 4½" tall,
green mark #47, $300.00 – 400.00 set.

Chocolate set, five cups and saucers, blue mark #4, $600.00 – 750.00.

Plate, 7½" wide, green mark #47.

Asparagus set, master plate: 11¾" long, green mark #47, $250.00 – 300.00 set.

❧ *Wall Plaques* ❧

Wall plaques can be found in all sizes and can be differentiated from plates by the holes found on the backside. Wire or string was placed in the holes in order to hang the piece on the wall. One can find wall plaques that are hand painted or decorated with decals. They can also be found using the techniques of coralene, molded in relief, moriage, or tapestry.

Rectangular wall plaques generally cost more money than the others and to date collectors have located 14 hand-painted ones and two decorated in a molded in relief design. Most of the rectangular ones appear to be "framed." Scenes known to exist are captive horse, Landseer's Newfoundland, Arabs at sunset, clipper ships, polo player, Cleopatra's barge, man on a camel, sail

ship with grape border, blue heron, cows at water's edge, still life, South Seas scene, country scene surrounded by blue enameling, and Roman chariot. Only a handful of the relief molded pieces are known to exist and are extremely expensive to purchase if one is found. The fisherman is 12" wide and Artemis with horse is 14" wide. There are also three oval shaped, molded in relief wall plaques. They are all 18½" long, bear the green mark #47, and have either a dead rabbit, dead duck, or fish.

Wall plaques are found in both scenic and floral designs as well as still life and portraits. A charger is a wall plaque that is 14" wide or larger.

9" wide, green mark #47,
$250.00 – 300.00.

7¾" wide, green mark #47,
$150.00 – 200.00.

7¾" wide, blue mark #47,
$175.00 – 250.00.

10" wide, blue mark #52,
$375.00 – 450.00.

10" wide, green mark #47,
$300.00 – 350.00.

11" wide, blue mark #52,
$375.00 – 450.00.

12¼" wide, blue mark #52,
$375.00 – 450.00.

10" wide, green mark #47,
$325.00 – 375.00.

7¾" wide, green mark #47,
$125.00 – 160.00.

10" wide, green mark #47,
$375.00 – 450.00.

Charger, 14" wide, mark #254,
$700.00 – 850.00.

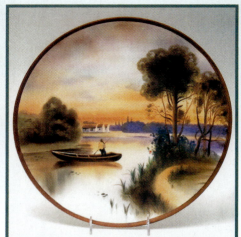

Charger, 14" wide, green mark #47,
$700.00 – 850.00.

Charger, 14¼" wide, green mark #47,
$700.00 – 850.00.

11" wide, green mark #47,
$400.00 – 500.00.

11" wide, green mark #47,
$400.00 – 500.00.

10¾" wide, green mark #47,
$400.00 – 500.00.

10" wide, blue mark #47,
$250.00 – 300.00.

10¼" wide, green mark #47,
$250.00 – 300.00.

10" wide, green mark #47,
$350.00 – 425.00.

10" wide, green mark #47,
$350.00 – 425.00.

10" wide, green mark #47,
$350.00 – 425.00.

11" wide, green mark #47,
$350.00 – 425.00.

10" wide, green mark #47,
$350.00 – 425.00.

10" wide, green mark #47,
$350.00 – 425.00.

9" wide, green mark #47,
$250.00 – 300.00.

10" wide, green mark #47,
$350.00 – 400.00.

10¾" wide, green mark #47,
$500.00 – 600.00.

7¾" wide, green mark #47,
$175.00 – 225.00.

10¼" wide, green mark #47,
$300.00 – 350.00.

10" wide, green mark #47,
$350.00 – 425.00.

7¾" wide, green mark #47,
$700.00 – 800.00.

7½" wide, green mark #47,
$100.00 – 130.00.

7½" wide, mark #7,
$100.00 – 130.00.

10¼" wide, green mark #47, $2,800.00 – 3,400.00.

10¼" wide, green mark #47, $2,800.00 – 3,400.00.

⌒ Wedgwood ⌒

Wedgwood decoration found on Nippon is an imitation of Josiah Wedgwood's popular Jasper ware pieces. Most of the Nippon wares are found having a light blue background with white moriage slip trailed decoration, and some have a green or lavender background. The blue and white colors can also be found in reverse. The lavender orchid Wedgwood pieces, regardless of size, are always breathtaking. Large, lavender orchids in panels circle the vases and are trimmed top, bottom, and sides with a lavender background and white moriage overlay. This design is known to exist on vases, bowls, and compotes and carry the green #47 backstamp.

The Wedgwood look was usually accomplished by means of slip trailing liquid clay on the item just like those decorated in a moriage fashion. Other times it is decorated by means of sprigging on small ornamentation. The Wedgwood look-alike pieces can be found that have an allover covering or just as a border or trim with a scenic or floral décor.

Josiah Wedgwood (1730 – 1795) was an English potter who acquired a reputation for his cream colored earthenware. In 1774 he introduced Jasper ware in pale blue and sage green colors. The most popular pieces were white on a pale blue background. The ornamentation for his pieces were made separately in molds and then applied to the body of the piece.

Ferner, 5½" tall, green mark #47, $800.00 – 950.00.

Vase, 10" tall, green mark #47,
$1,000.00 – 1,200.00.

Mug, 4¾" tall, green mark #47,
$500.00 – 600.00.

Matchbox holder, tray: 6" long,
green mark #47, $450.00 – 5500.00.

Candlesticks, green mark #47,
$450.00 – 550.00 each. Left: 8" tall. Right: 7½" tall.

Compote, 7³/₄" wide, green mark #47, $450.00 – 550.00.

Bowl, 8³/₄" wide including handles,
green mark #47, $225.00 – 275.00.

Compote, 3¹/₂" tall, green mark #47,
$250.00 – 325.00.

Candy bowl, 6³/₄" tall, green mark #47,
$225.00 – 275.00.

Vase, 10" tall, green mark #47,
$1,000.00 – 1,200.00.

Bolted urn, 10" tall, green mark #47,
$1,500.00 – 1,800.00.

Green tea set, green mark #47, $1,100.00 – 1,300.00.

Lavender compote, 5¾" tall, green mark #47,
$900.00 – 1,100.00.

Lavender bowl, 9½" long, green mark #47, $600.00 – 700.00.

Three-piece smoke set, tray: 10½" long, green mark #10, $700.00 – 800.00.

Flower gate vase, 7½" tall, green mark #47, $700.00 – 800.00.

Vase, 8¾" tall, green mark #47,
$1,200.00 – 1,400.00.

Loving cup, 7¾" tall, green mark #47,
$550.00 – 650.00.

❧ *Woodland Scenes* ❧

Woodland scenes consist of both the white woodland and dark woodland patterns. White woodland is decorated in earth tones featuring moriage trees in the foreground. This décor can be found on a wide range of molds including plaques, smoke sets, humidors, and vases. Generally the items are backstamped with the green or blue #47 backstamp.

The dark woodland pattern features a stylized scene featuring trees, cottages, clouds, and heraldry. Larger pieces have more cottages and trees, and the smaller items have less. Four different heraldry shields have been found on these items. There is a cross, an X, a / (called a bend), and a type of stylized flower. Some of the flowers have four petals and four dots while others have three petals and three dots for decoration. Heraldry is like picture writing and through heraldry we can trace the origins of many noble families and distinguish the different branch of and the relations between families.

Most of these pieces are marked with the green or blue #47 backstamp or the blue #52 mark but altogether six backstamps have been found on these items. The others are #4, the cherry blossom; #45 LFH with a crown; #50 MM Nippon; and #119, C.G.N. Nippon. The dark woodland scene has been found on all types of items including after dinner coffee sets, bowls, cake sets, candlesticks, chambersticks, chocolate sets, compotes, condensed milk containers, cracker jars, creamers and sugar bowls, dresser items including trays, hatpin holders, powder boxes, hair receivers, and small compotes, ewers, humidors, ladles, match holder ashtray combinations, matchbox holders with attached ashtrays, mustard pots, nappies, pitchers, relish dishes, salt and pepper sets, steins, tankard and mug sets, smoke sets, tea sets, trays, urns, vases, wall plaques, whiskey jugs, and wine jugs.

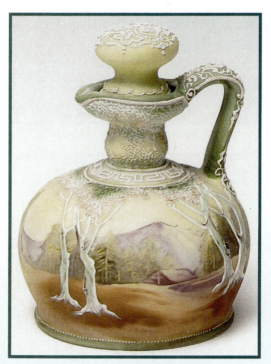

Whiskey jug, 7 1/2" tall, blue mark #47,
$2,600.00 – 3,000.00.

Vase, 6 3/4" tall, blue mark #47,
$1,100.00 – 1,300.00.

Vase, 10" tall, blue mark #47,
$2,000.00 – 2,500.00.

Syrup, 4¹/₂" tall, green mark #47, $500.00 – 600.00.

Vase, 8¹/₂" tall, blue mark #47,
$700.00 – 900.00.

Wine jug, 9¹/₂" tall, blue mark #52,
$1,300.00 – 1,600.00.

⌘ *Xanthic Background Color* ⌘

Xanthic is merely another word for yellow. Collectors will find few Nippon items with this background color. Whether it's due to lack of popularity or difficulty in production is a question to ponder.

Vase, 9" tall, green mark #47, $275.00 – 325.00.

Chocolate set, pot: 9¹/₂" tall, includes two cups and saucers, green mark #47, $275.00 – 350.00.

⌘ *Yultide Decoration* ⌘

Yule occurs in the dead of winter and is a merry season of the year. Holly, laurel, mistletoe, greens, and poinsettia plants decorate homes at this time. The poinsettia plant is a perennial, native to Mexico and was brought to the United States in 1828 by Joel Roberts Poinsett, the first US Ambassador to Mexico. The plant has red, star-shape looking flowers, which are actually leaves, and not flowers.

The so-called Christmas deer is a popular pattern featuring a stag's head surrounded by leaves and trees. It can be found on humidors, tankard sets, jugs, and plaques and is marked with the green or blue #47 backstamp.

Vase, 11" tall, green mark #52, $800.00 – 900.00.

Vase, 14½" tall, blue mark #52, $800.00 – 900.00.

Vase, 11¼" tall, green mark #52, $600.00 – 700.00.

Tankard set, with six mugs, tankard: 11" tall, green mark #47, $4,000.00 – 4,600.00.

Wall plaque, 11" wide, blue mark #47, $700.00 – 800.00.

Wall plaque, 10" wide, blue mark #47, $600.00 – 700.00.

Vase, 10½" tall, green mark #47,
$600.00 – 700.00.

Humidor, 5½" tall, green mark #47, $1,200.00 – 1,500.00.

❧ *Zig Zag and Diaper Pattern* ❧

Zig Zag designs are found on some borders of Nippon pieces. There will be short, sharp turns or angles found in this design. Diaper patterns are geometric designs which can be found on borders or making up the entire pattern. They feature repeated units of design connecting one another often in the shapes of diamonds, squares, flowers, etc.

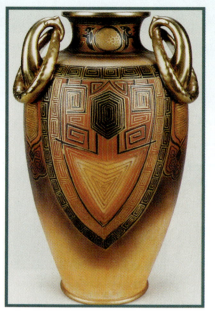

Vase, 15½" tall, mark #239, $1,100.00 – 1,300.00.

Milk pitcher, 4¾" tall, green mark #47, $200.00 – 250.00.

Vase, 18" tall, green mark #47, $1,100.00 – 1,300.00.

Vase, 7" tall, green mark #47, $325.00 – 375.00.

Cracker jar, 8½" tall, blue mark #47, $275.00 – 350.00.

EXAMPLES OF DIAPER (REPETITIVE) PATTERNS
FOUND ON NIPPON PORCELAIN

Basket Weave
Design

Glossary

American Indian design: A popular collectible on Nippon porcelain; these designs include the Indian in a canoe, Indian warrior, Indian hunting wild game, and the Indian maiden.

Apricot (ume): In Japan, stands for strength and nobility, also a symbol of good luck.

Art Deco: A style of decoration which hit its peak in Europe and America around 1925 although items were manufactured with this decor as early as 1910. The style was modernistic; geometric patterns were popular. Motifs used were shapes such as circles, rectangles, cylinders, and cones.

Art Nouveau: The name is derived from the French words meaning "new art." During the period of 1885 – 1925, artists tended to use bolder colors, and realism was rejected. Free-flowing designs were used, breaking away from the imitations of the past.

Artist signed: Items signed by the artist. Most signatures appear to be those of Western artists, probably painted during the heyday of hand painting chinaware at the turn of the century.

Azalea pattern: Pattern found on Nippon items, pink azaleas with green to gray leaves and gold rims. Nippon-marked pieces match the Noritake-marked Azalea pattern items. The Azalea pattern was originally offered by the Larkin Co. to its customers as premiums.

Backstamp: Mark found on Nippon porcelain items identifying the manufacturer, exporter or importer, and country of origin.

Bamboo tree: In Japan, symbolic of strength, faithfulness, and honesty, also a good luck symbol. The bamboo resists the storm, but it yields to it and rises again.

Beading: Generally a series of clay dots applied on Nippon porcelain, very often painted over in gold. Later Nippon pieces merely had dots of enameling.

Biscuit: Clay which has been fired but not glazed.

Bisque: Same as biscuit, term also used by collectors to describe a matte finish on an item.

Blank: Greenware or bisque items devoid of decoration.

Blown-out items: This term is used by collectors and dealers for items that have a molded relief pattern embossed on by the mold in which the article was shaped. It is not actually "blown-out" as the glass items are, but the pattern is raised from the item (see molded relief).

Bottger, Johann F.: A young German alchemist who supposedly discovered the value of kaolin in making porcelain. This discovery helped to revolutionize the china making industry in Europe beginning in the early 1700s.

Carp: Fish that symbolizes strength and perseverance.

Casting: The process of making reproductions by pouring slip into molds.

Cha no yu: Japanese tea ceremony.

Chargers: Archaic term for large platters or plates.

Cheese hard clay: Same as leather hard clay.

Cherry blossoms: National flower of Japan and emblem of the faithful warrior.

Ching-te-Chen: Ancient city in China where nearly a million people lived and worked with almost all devoted to the making of porcelain.

Chrysanthemum: Depicts health and longevity, the crest of the emperor of Japan. The chrysanthemum blooms late in the year and lives longer than other flowers.

Citron: Stands for wealth.

Cloisonné on porcelain: On Nippon porcelain wares it resembles the other cloisonné pieces except that it was produced on a porcelain body instead of metal. The decoration is divided into cells called cloisons. These cloisons were divided by strips of metal wire which kept the colors separated during the firing.

Cobalt oxide: Blue oxide imported to Japan after 1868 for decoration of wares. Gosu, a pebble found in Oriental riverbeds, had previously been used but was scarce and more expensive than the imported oxide. Cobalt oxide is the most powerful of all the coloring oxides for tinting.

Coralene items: Made by firing small colorless beads on the wares. Many are signed Kinran, US Patent, NBR 912171, February 9, 1909, Japan. Tiny glass beads had previously been applied to glass items in the shapes of birds, flowers, leaves, etc. and no doubt this was an attempt to copy it. Japanese coralene was patented by Alban L. Rock, an American living in Yokohama, Japan. The vitreous coating of beads gave the item a plush velvety look. The beads were permanently fired on and gave a luminescence to the design. The most popular design had been one of seaweed and coral, hence the name coralene was given to this type of design.

Crane: A symbol of good luck in Japan, also stands for marital fidelity and is an emblem of longevity.

Daffodil: A sign of spring to the Japanese.

Decalcomania: A process of transferring a wet paper print onto the surface of an item. It was made to resemble hand-painted work.

Deer: Stands for divine messenger.

Diaper pattern: Repetitive pattern of small design used on Nippon porcelain, often geometric or floral.

Dragons (ryu): A symbol of strength, goodness, and good fortune. The Japanese dragon has three claws and was thought to reside in the sky. Clouds, water, and lightning often accompany the dragon. The dragon is often portrayed in high relief using the slip trailing method of decor.

Drain mold: A mold used in making hollow ware. Liquid slip is poured into the mold until the desired thickness of the walls is achieved. The excess clay is poured out. When the item starts to shrink away from the mold, the mold is removed.

Drape mold: Also called flop-over mold. Used to make flat bottomed items. Moist clay is rolled out and draped over the mold. It is then pressed firmly into shape.

Dutch scenes: Popular on Nippon items, includes those of windmills, and men and women dressed in Dutch costumes.

Edo: Or Yedo, the largest city in Japan, later renamed Tokyo, meaning eastern capital.

Embossed design: See molded relief.

Enamel beading: Dots of enameling painted by the artist in gold or other colors and often made to resemble jewels, such as emeralds and rubies. Many times this raised beading will be found in brown or black colors.

Fairings: Items won or bought as souvenirs at fairs.

Feldspar: Most common rock found on earth.

Fern leaves: Symbolic of ample good fortune.

Fettles or mold marks: Ridges formed where sections of molds are joined at the seam. These fettles have to be removed before the item is decorated.

Finial: The top knob on a cover of an item, used to lift off the cover.

Firing: The cooking or baking of clay ware.

Flop-over mold: Same as drape mold.

Flux: An ingredient added to glaze to assist in making the item fire properly. It causes the glaze to melt at a specified temperature.

Glaze: Composed of silica, alumina, and flux, and is applied to porcelain pieces. During the firing process, the glaze joins with the clay item to form a glasslike surface. It seals the pores and makes the item impervious to liquids.

Gold trim: Has to be fired at lower temperatures or the gold would sink into the enameled decoration. If overfired, the gold becomes discolored.

Gouda ceramics: Originally made in Gouda, a province of south Holland. These items were copied on the Nippon wares and were patterned after the Art Nouveau style.

Gosu: Pebble found in Oriental riverbeds, a natural cobalt. It was used to color items until 1868 when oxidized cobalt was introduced into Japan.

Greenware: Clay which has been molded but not fired.

Hard paste porcelain: Paste meaning the body of substance, porcelain being made from clay using kaolin. This produces a hard translucent body when fired.

Ho-o bird: Sort of a bird of paradise who resides on earth and is associated with the empress of Japan. See also Phoenix bird.

Incised backstamp: The backstamp marking scratched into the surface of a clay item.

Incised decoration: A sharp tool or stick was used to produce the design right onto the body of the article while it was still in a state of soft clay.

Iris: The Japanese believe this flower wards off evil; associated with warriors because of its sword-like leaves.

Jasperware: See Wedgwood.

Jigger: A machine resembling a potter's wheel. Soft pliable clay is placed onto a convex revolving mold. As the wheel turns, a template is held against it, trimming off the excess clay on the outside. The revolving mold shapes the inside of the item and the template cuts the outside.

Jolley: A machine like a jigger only in reverse. The revolving mold is concave and the template forms the inside of the item. The template is lowered inside the revolving mold. The mold forms the outside surface while the template cuts the inside.

Jomon: Neolithic hunters and fishermen in Japan dating back to approximately 2500 B.C. Their pottery was hand formed and marked with an overall rope or cord pattern. It was made of unwashed clay, unglazed, and was baked in open fires.

Kaga: Province in Japan.

Kaolin: Highly refractory clay and one of the principal ingredients used in making porcelain. It is a pure white residual clay, a decomposition of granite.

Kao-ling: Chinese word meaning "the high hills," the word kaolin is derived from it.

Kiln: Oven in which pottery is fired.

Leather hard clay: Clay which is dry enough to hold its shape but still damp and moist, no longer in a plastic state, also called cheese hard.

Liquid slip: Clay in a liquid state.

Lobster: Symbol of long life.

Luster decoration: A metallic type of coloring decoration, gives an iridescent effect.

Matte finish: Also "mat" and "matt." A dull glaze having a low reflectance when fired.

McKinley Tariff Act of 1890: Chapter 1244, Section 6 states "That on and after the first day of March, eighteen hundred and ninety-one, all articles of foreign manufacture, such as are usually or ordinarily marked, stamped, branded, or labeled, and all packages containing such or other imported articles, shall, respectively, be plainly marked, stamped, branded, or labeled in legible English words, so as to indicate the country of their origin; and unless so marked, stamped, branded, or labeled, they shall not be admitted to entry."

Meiji period: Period of 1868 – 1912 in Japan when Emperor Mutsuhito reigned. It means "enlightened rule."

Middle East scenes: Designs used on Nippon pieces, featuring pyramids, deserts, palm trees, and riders on camels.

Model: The shape from which the mold is made.

Molded relief items: The pattern is embossed on the item by the mold in which the article is shaped. These items give the appearance that the pattern is caused by some type of upward pressure from the underside. Collectors often refer to these items as "blown-out."

Molds: Contain a cavity in which castings are made. They are generally made from plaster of Paris and are used for shaping clay objects. Both liquid and plastic clay may be used. The mold can also be made of clay or rubber, however, plaster was generally used as it absorbed moisture immediately from the clay. Raised ornamentation may also be formed directly in the mold.

Moriage: Refers to liquid clay (slip) relief decoration. On Nippon items this was usually done by "slip trailing" or hand rolling and shaping the clay on an item.

Morimura Brothers: Importers of Japanese wares in the United States and the sole importers of Noritake wares. The business was opened in New York City in 1876 and closed in 1941.

Mutsuhito: Emperor of Japan from 1868 to 1912. His reign was called the Meiji period which meant enlightened rule.

Nagoya: A large city in Japan, location of Noritake Co.

Narcissus: stands for good fortune.

Ningyo: Japanese name for doll, meaning human being and image.

Nippon: the name the Japanese people called their country. It comes from a Chinese phrase meaning "the source of the sun" and sounds like Neehon in Japanese.

Noritake Co.: This company produced more than 90 percent of the Nippon era wares that now exist. Their main office is located in Nagoya, Japan.

Orchid: means hidden beauty and modesty to the Japanese.

Overglaze decoration: a design is either painted or a decal applied to an item which already has a fired glazed surface. The article is then refired to make the decoration permanent.

Pattern stamping: the design was achieved by using a special stamp or a plaster roll having the design cut into it. The design was pressed into the soft clay body of an item.

Paulownia flower: crest of the empress of Japan.

Peach: stands for marriage.

Peacock: stands for elegance and beauty.

Peony: considered the king of flowers in Japan.

Perry, Matthew, Comm., USN: helped to fashion the Kanagawa treaty in 1854 between the United States and Japan. This treaty opened the small ports of Shimoda and Hakodate to trade. Shipwrecked sailors were also to receive good treatment and an American consul was permitted to reside at Shimoda.

Petuntse: clay found in felspathic rocks such as granite. Its addition to porcelain made the item more durable. Petuntse is also called china stone.

Phoenix bird: sort of bird of paradise which resides on earth and is associated with the empress of Japan. This bird appears to be a cross between a peacock, a pheasant, and a gamecock. There appear to be many designs for this bird as each artist had his own conception of how it should look. It is also a symbol to the Japanese of all that is beautiful.

Pickard Co.: a china decorating studio originally located in Chicago. This firm decorated blank wares imported from a number of countries including Nippon.

Pine tree: to the Japanese this tree is symbolic of friendship and prosperity and depicts the winter season. It is also a sign of good luck and a sign of strength.

Plastic clay: clay in a malleable state, able to be shaped and formed without collapsing.

Plum: stands for womanhood. Plum blossoms reflect bravery.

Porcelain: a mixture composed mainly of kaolin and petuntse which is fired at a high temperature and vitrified.

Porcelain slip: porcelain clay in a liquid form.

Porcellaine: French adaptation of the word "porcelain."

Porcellana: Italian word meaning cowry shell. The Chinese ware which was brought back to Venice in the fifteenth century was thought to resemble the cowry shell and was called porcellana.

Portrait items: items decorated with portraits, many of European beauties. Some appear to be hand painted, most are decal work.

Potter's wheel: rotating device onto which a ball of plastic clay is placed. The wheel is turned and the potter molds the clay with his hands and is capable of producing cylindrical objects.

Pottery: in its broadest sense, includes all forms of wares made from clay.

Press mold: used to make handles, finials, figurines, etc. A two-piece mold into which soft clay is placed. The two pieces are pressed together to form items.

Relief: molded (See molded relief items).

Royal Crockery: name of Nippon pieces marked with RC on backstamp.

Satsuma: a sea-going principality in Japan, an area where many of the old famous kilns are found, and also a type of Japanese ware. Satsuma is a cream-colored glazed pottery which is finely crackled.

Slip: liquid clay.

Slip trailing: a process where liquid clay was applied to porcelain via tubing or a cone-shaped device made of paper with a metal tip. A form of painting but with clay instead of paint. The slip is often applied quite heavily and gives a thick, raised appearance.

Slurry: thick slip.

Solid casting mold: Used for shallow type items such as bowls and plates. In this type of mold, the thickness of the walls is determined by the mold and every piece is formed identically. The mold shapes both the inside and the outside of the piece and the thickness of the walls can be controlled. Solid casting can be done with either liquid or plastic clay.

Sometsuke style decoration: Items decorated with an underglaze of blue and white colors.

Sprigging: The application of small molded relief decoration to the surface of porcelain by use of liquid clay as in Jasperware.

Sprig mold: A one-piece mold used in making ornaments. Clay is fitted or poured into a mold which is incised with a design. Only one side is molded and the exposed side becomes the back of the finished item.

Taisho: Name of the period reigned over by Emperor Yoshihito in Japan from 1912 to 1926. It means "great peace."

Tapestry: A type of decor used on Nippon porcelain. A cloth was dipped into liquid slip and then stretched onto the porcelain item. During the bisque firing, the material burned off and left a textured look on the porcelain piece, resembling needlepoint in many cases. The item was then painted and fired again in the usual manner.

Template: Profile of the pattern being cut.

Throwing: The art of forming a clay object on a potter's wheel.

Tiger (tora): A symbol of longevity.

Transfer print: See Decalcomania.

Translucent: Not transparent, but clear enough to allow rays of light to pass through.

Ultraviolet lamp: Lamp used to detect cracks and hidden repairs in items.

Underglaze decoration: This type of decoration is applied on bisque china (fired once), then the item is glazed and fired again.

Victorian Age design: Decor used on some Nippon pieces, gaudy and extremely bold colors used.

Vitreous: Glass like.

Vitrify: To change into a glasslike substance due to the application of heat.

Wasters: Name given to pieces ruined or marred in the kiln.

Water lilies: Represent autumn in Japan.

Wedgwood: Term used to refer to Nippon pieces which attempt to imitate Josiah Wedgwood's Jasperware. The items usually have a light blue background. The Nippon pieces were generally produced with a slip trailing decor however, rather than the sprigging ornamentation made popular by Wedgwood. White clay slip was trailed onto the background color of the item by use of tubing or a cone-shaped device to form the pattern.

Yamato: District in central Japan.

Yayoi: People of the bronze and iron culture in Japan dating back to 300 – 100 B.C. They were basically an agricultural people. They made pottery using the potter's wheel.

Yedo: Or Edo, the largest city in Japan, renamed Tokyo, meaning eastern capital.

Yoshihito: Emperor of Japan from 1912 to 1926. He took the name of Taisho which meant "great peace."

Bibliography

Duncan, Alastair and Georges deBarthe. *Glass by Gallé*. NY: Harry N. Abrams, Inc., Publishers, 1984.

Garner, Phillippe. *Emile Gallé*. NY: St. Martin's Press, 1976.

Gaston, Mary Frank. *Collector's Encyclopedia of R.S. Prussia, Second Series*. Paducah, KY: Collector Books, 1986.

Hasrick, Royal. *Northern American Indians*. London: Octopus Books, Ltd., 1974.

Hodge, Frederick Webb. *Handbook of American Indians*. NY: Pageant Books, 1959.

LaFarge, Oliver. *A Pictorial History of the American Indian*. NY: Crown Publishers, 1956.

Marple, Leland and Carol. *R.S. Prussia, The Art Nouveau Years*. Atglen, PA: Schiffer Publishing Ltd., 19130.

Moody, C.W. *Gouda Ceramics, The Art Nouveau Era of Holland*. Published by author, 1970.

Morton, W. Scott. *Japan, Its History and Culture*. NY: Thomas Y. Crowell Co., 1970.

Peck, Herbert. *The Books of Rookwood Pottery*. New York: Crown Publishers, Inc., 1968.

Plat, Dorothy. *Pickard, The Story of Pickard China*. Hanover, PA: Everybody's Press Inc., 1970.

Reid, Alan, B. *Collector's Encyclopedia of Pickard China*. Paducah, KY: Collector Books, 1995.

Reynolds, Robert, L. *Commodore Perry in Japan*. NY: American Heritage Publishing Co., Inc., 1963.

Samuels, Peggy and Harold. *Remington the Complete Prints*. NY: Crown Publishers, 1990.

Seward, Jack. *The Japanese*. NY: William Morrow and Co., Inc., 1972.

Tames, Richard. *Josiah Wedgwood*. England: Shire Publications Ltd., Aylesbury, 1972.

Terrell, George, W., Jr. *Collecting R.S. Prussia*. Florence, Alabama: Books America, Inc.

Van Patten, Joan, F. *Collector's Encyclopedia of Nippon Porcelain*. Paducah, KY: Collector Books, 1979.

_____. *Collector's Encyclopedia of Nippon Porcelain, Second Series*. Paducah, KY: Collector Books, 1982.

_____. *Collector's Encyclopedia of Nippon Porcelain, Third Series*. Paducah, KY: Collector Books, 1986.

_____. *Collector's Encyclopedia of Nippon Porcelain, Fourth Series*, Paducah, KY: Collector Books, 1997.

_____. *Collector's Encyclopedia of Nippon Porcelain, Fifth Series*, Paducah, KY: Collector Books, 1998.

_____. *Collector's Encyclopedia of Nippon Porcelain, Sixth Series*, Paducah, KY: Collector Books, 2001.

_____. *Collector's Encyclopedia of Nippon Porcelain, Seventh Series*, Paducah, KY: Collector Books, 2002.

_____. *Collector's Encyclopedia of Noritake*, Paducah, KY: Collector Books, 1984.

Van Patten, Joan, F. and Linda Lau, *Nippon Dolls and Playthings*. Paducah, KY: Collector Books, 2001.

Warmus, William. *Emile Galle, Dreams Into Glass*. Corning, NY: The Corning Museum of Glass, 1988.

Warren, Geoffrey. *All Color Book of Art Nouveau*. London: Octopus Books, Ltd., 1972.

Williams, Barry. *Emerging Japan*. New York, San Francisco, St. Louis: McGraw-Hill Book Co., 1969.

Index

COLLECTOR BOOKS
informing today's collector

BOOKS ON POTTERY, PORCELAIN & FIGURINES

DOLLS, FIGURES & TEDDY BEARS

3981	Evers' Standard **Cut Glass** Value Guide	$12.95
6462	Florence's **Glass Kitchen Shakers**, 1930 – 1950s	$19.95
5042	Florence's **Glassware Pattern Identification** Guide, Vol. I	$18.95
5615	Florence's **Glassware Pattern Identification** Guide, Vol. II	$19.95
6142	Florence's **Glassware Pattern Identification** Guide, Vol. III	$19.95
4719	**Fostoria**, Etched, Carved & Cut Designs, Vol. II, Kerr	$24.95
6226	**Fostoria** Value Guide, Long/Seate	$19.95
5899	**Glass & Ceramic Baskets**, White	$19.95
6460	**Glass Animals**, Second Edition, Spencer	$24.95
6127	The **Glass Candlestick** Book, Volume 1, Akro Agate to Fenton, Felt/Stoer	$24.95
6228	The **Glass Candlestick** Book, Volume 2, Fostoria to Jefferson, Felt/Stoer	$24.95
6461	The **Glass Candlestick** Book, Volume 3, Kanawha to Wright, Felt/Stoer	$29.95
6329	**Glass Tumblers**, 1860s to 1920s, Bredehoft	$29.95
4644	**Imperial Carnival Glass**, Burns	$18.95
5827	**Kitchen Glassware** of the Depression Years, 6th Ed., Florence	$24.95
5600	Much More Early American **Pattern Glass**, Metz	$17.95
6133	**Mt. Washington Art Glass**, Sisk	$49.95
6556	Pocket Guide to **Depression Glass** & More, 14th Ed., Florence	$12.95
6448	Standard Encyclopedia of **Carnival Glass**, 9th Ed., Edwards/Carwile	$29.95
6449	Standard **Carnival Glass** Price Guide, 14th Ed., Edwards/Carwile	$9.95
6035	Standard Encyclopedia of **Opalescent Glass**, 4th Ed., Edwards/Carwile	$24.95
6241	Treasures of **Very Rare Depression Glass**, Florence	$39.95

POTTERY

4929	**American Art Pottery**, Sigafoose	$24.95
1312	**Blue & White Stoneware**, McNerney	$9.95
4851	Collectible **Cups & Saucers**, Harran	$18.95
6326	Collectible **Cups & Saucers**, Book III, Harran	$24.95
6344	Collectible **Vernon Kilns**, 2nd Edition, Nelson	$29.95
6331	Collecting **Head Vases**, Barron	$24.95
1373	Collector's Encyclopedia of **American Dinnerware**, Cunningham	$24.95
4931	Collector's Encyclopedia of **Bauer Pottery**, Chipman	$24.95
5034	Collector's Encyclopedia of **California Pottery**, 2nd Ed., Chipman	$24.95
3723	Collector's Encyclopedia of **Cookie Jars**, Book II, Roerig	$24.95
4939	Collector's Encyclopedia of **Cookie Jars**, Book III, Roerig	$24.95
5748	Collector's Encyclopedia of **Fiesta**, 9th Ed., Huxford	$24.95
3961	Collector's Encyclopedia of **Early Noritake**, Alden	$24.95
3812	Collector's Encyclopedia of **Flow Blue China**, 2nd Ed., Gaston	$24.95
3431	Collector's Encyclopedia of **Homer Laughlin China**, Jasper	$24.95
1276	Collector's Encyclopedia of **Hull Pottery**, Roberts	$19.95
5609	Collector's Encyclopedia of **Limoges Porcelain**, 3rd Ed., Gaston	$29.95
2334	Collector's Encyclopedia of **Majolica Pottery**, Katz-Marks	$19.95
1358	Collector's Encyclopedia of **McCoy Pottery**, Huxford	$19.95
5677	Collector's Encyclopedia of **Niloak**, 2nd Edition, Gifford	$29.95
5564	Collector's Encyclopedia of **Pickard China**, Reed	$29.95
5679	Collector's Encyclopedia of **Red Wing Art Pottery**, Dollen	$24.95
5618	Collector's Encyclopedia of **Rosemeade Pottery**, Dommel	$24.95
5841	Collector's Encyclopedia of **Roseville Pottery**, Revised, Huxford/Nickel	$24.95
5842	Collector's Encyclopedia of **Roseville Pottery**, 2nd Series, Huxford/Nickel	$24.95
5917	Collector's Encyclopedia of **Russel Wright**, 3rd Editon, Kerr	$29.95
5921	Collector's Encyclopedia of **Stangl Artware**, Lamps, and Birds, Runge	$29.95
3314	Collector's Encyclopedia of **Van Briggle Art Pottery**, Sasicki	$24.95
5680	Collector's Guide to **Feather Edge Ware**, McAllister	$19.95
6124	Collector's Guide to **Made in Japan Ceramics**, Book IV, White	$24.95
1425	**Cookie Jars**, Westfall	$9.95
3440	**Cookie Jars**, Book II, Westfall	$19.95
6316	Decorative **American Pottery & Whiteware**, Wilby	$29.95
5909	**Dresden Porcelain** Studios, Harran	$29.95

5918	Florence's Big Book of **Salt & Pepper Shakers**	$24.95
6320	Gaston's **Blue Willow**, 3rd Edition	$19.95
2379	Lehner's Ency. of **U.S. Marks** on Pottery, Porcelain & China	$24.95
4722	**McCoy Pottery**, Collector's Reference & Value Guide, Hanson/Nissen	$19.95
5913	**McCoy Pottery**, Volume III, Hanson & Nissen	$24.95
6333	**McCoy Pottery Wall Pockets** & Decorations, Nissen	$24.95
6135	**North Carolina Art Pottery**, 1900 – 1960, James/Leftwich	$24.95
6335	Pictorial Guide to **Pottery & Porcelain Marks**, Lage	$29.95
5691	**Post86 Fiesta**, Identification & Value Guide, Racheter	$19.95
6037	**Rookwood Pottery**, Nicholson & Thomas	$24.95
6236	**Rookwood Pottery**, 10 Years of Auction Results, 1990 – 2002, Treadway	$39.95
5091	**Salt & Pepper Shakers** II, Guarnaccia	$18.95
3443	**Salt & Pepper Shakers** IV, Guarnaccia	$18.95
3738	**Shawnee Pottery**, Mangus	$24.95
4629	Turn of the Century **American Dinnerware**, 1880s–1920s, Jasper	$24.95
5924	**Zanesville Stoneware** Company, Rans, Ralston & Russell	$24.95

OTHER COLLECTIBLES

5916	Advertising **Paperweights**, Holiner & Kammerman	$24.95
5838	Advertising **Thermometers**, Merritt	$16.95
5898	Antique & Contemporary **Advertising Memorabilia**, Summers	$24.95
5814	Antique **Brass & Copper** Collectibles, Gaston	$24.95
3872	Antique **Tins**, Dodge	$24.95
4845	Antique **Typewriters & Office Collectibles**, Rehr	$19.95
6345	**Business & Tax Guide** for Antiques & Collectibles, Kelly	$14.95
6225	Captain John's **Fishing Tackle** Price Guide, Kolbeck/Lewis	$19.95
3718	Collectible **Aluminum**, Grist	$16.95
6342	Collectible **Soda Pop** Memorabilia, Summers	$24.95
5060	Collectible **Souvenir Spoons**, Bednersh	$19.95
5676	Collectible **Souvenir Spoons**, Book II, Bednersh	$29.95
5666	Collector's Encyclopedia of **Granite Ware**, Book 2, Greguire	$29.95
5836	Collector's Guide to **Antique Radios**, 5th Ed., Bunis	$19.95
3966	Collector's Guide to **Inkwells**, Identification & Values, Badders	$18.95
4947	Collector's Guide to **Inkwells**, Book II, Badders	$19.95
5681	Collector's Guide to **Lunchboxes**, White	$19.95
4864	Collector's Guide to **Wallace Nutting Pictures**, Ivankovich	$18.95
5683	**Fishing Lure** Collectibles, Vol. 1, Murphy/Edmisten	$29.95
6328	**Flea Market Trader**, 14th Ed., Huxford	$12.95
6459	**Garage Sale** & Flea Market Annual, 12th Edition, Huxford	$19.95
4945	**G-Men and FBI Toys** and Collectibles, Whitworth	$18.95
3819	**General Store** Collectibles, Wilson	$24.95
5912	The **Heddon** Legacy, A Century of Classic **Lures**, Roberts & Pavey	$29.95
2216	**Kitchen Antiques**, 1790–1940, McNerney	$14.95
4950	The **Lone Ranger**, Collector's Reference & Value Guide, Felbinger	$18.95
6028	Modern **Fishing Lure** Collectibles, Vol. 1, Lewis	$24.95
6131	Modern **Fishing Lure** Collectibles, Vol. 2, Lewis	$24.95
6322	Pictorial Guide to **Christmas Ornaments** & Collectibles, Johnson	$29.95
2026	**Railroad** Collectibles, 4th Ed., Baker	$14.95
5619	**Roy Rogers and Dale Evans** Toys & Memorabilia, Coyle	$24.95
6570	**Schroeder's Antiques** Price Guide, 23rd Edition	$14.95
5007	**Silverplated Flatware**, Revised 4th Edition, Hagan	$18.95
6239	**Star Wars** Super Collector's Wish Book, 2nd Ed., Carlton	$29.95
6139	Summers' Guide to **Coca-Cola**, 4th Ed.	$24.95
6324	Summers' Pocket Guide to **Coca-Cola**, 4th Ed.	$12.95
3977	Value Guide to **Gas Station Memorabilia**, Summers & Priddy	$24.95
4877	Vintage **Bar Ware**, Visakay	$24.95
6036	Vintage **Quilts**, Aug, Newman & Roy	$24.95
4935	The W.F. Cody **Buffalo Bill** Collector's Guide with Values	$24.9

This is only a partial listing of the books on antiques that are available from Collector Books. All books are well illustrated and contain current values. Most of these books are available from your local book seller, antique dealer, or public library. If you are unable to locate certain titles in your area, you may order by mail from **COLLECTOR BOOKS**, P.O. Box 3009, Paducah, KY 42002-3009. Customers with Visa, Master Card, or Discover may phone in orders from 7:00 a.m. to 5:00 p.m. CT, Monday – Friday, toll free **1-800-626-5420**, or online at **www.collectorbooks.com**. Add $3.00 for postage for the first book ordered and 50¢ for each additional book. Include item number, title, and price when ordering. Allow 14 to 21 days for delivery.

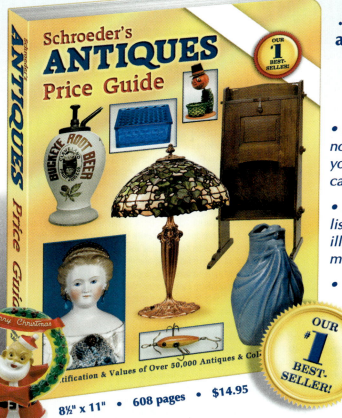